MW01152520

Y. Tony Yang • Dorit R. Reiss

Vaccine Law and Policy

 Springer

Y. Tony Yang
George Washington University
Washington, DC, USA

Dorit R. Reiss
UC Law San Francisco
San Francisco, CA, USA

ISSN 2662-141X   ISSN 2662-1428   (electronic)
Law for Professionals
ISBN 978-3-031-36988-9   ISBN 978-3-031-36989-6   (eBook)
https://doi.org/10.1007/978-3-031-36989-6

© The Editor(s) (if applicable) and The Author(s), under exclusive license to Springer Nature Switzerland AG 2023
This work is subject to copyright. All rights are solely and exclusively licensed by the Publisher, whether the whole or part of the material is concerned, specifically the rights of translation, reprinting, reuse of illustrations, recitation, broadcasting, reproduction on microfilms or in any other physical way, and transmission or information storage and retrieval, electronic adaptation, computer software, or by similar or dissimilar methodology now known or hereafter developed.
The use of general descriptive names, registered names, trademarks, service marks, etc. in this publication does not imply, even in the absence of a specific statement, that such names are exempt from the relevant protective laws and regulations and therefore free for general use.
The publisher, the authors, and the editors are safe to assume that the advice and information in this book are believed to be true and accurate at the date of publication. Neither the publisher nor the authors or the editors give a warranty, expressed or implied, with respect to the material contained herein or for any errors or omissions that may have been made. The publisher remains neutral with regard to jurisdictional claims in published maps and institutional affiliations.

This Springer imprint is published by the registered company Springer Nature Switzerland AG
The registered company address is: Gewerbestrasse 11, 6330 Cham, Switzerland

Acknowledgment

This book, like any other, has greatly benefited from the assistance and encouragement of numerous individuals. We are deeply grateful to our committed student team, consisting of Ani Araklian, Aditi Asthana, Brooke Quesinberry, Vittoria Rainone, Joshua Mannix, and Campbell Dopke, for their invaluable help in bringing this project to fruition. A special note of appreciation goes to Ani for her exceptional organizational skills.

We have learned and gained insights from countless experts in the field, and while it is impossible to acknowledge all of them, we would like to extend our heartfelt gratitude to Arthur Caplan, Michelle Mello, Charlotte Moser, Paul Offit, Wendy Parmet, Ross Silverman, Lindsay Wiley, and Ana Santos Rutschman from the academic community. In the immunization community, we are grateful to the team at Vaccinate Your Family, particularly Amy Pisani and Erica DeWald, for their meticulous information and graphic curation. We also wish to recognize Karen Ernst from Voices for Vaccines and the Immunization Action Coalition for their contributions.

Our institutional colleagues have also provided unwavering support and assistance. We would like to specially acknowledge our co-authors about vaccine law and policy through the years, including Jana Shaw, Robert Olick, Sarah Schaffer DeRoo, Paul Delamater, John Diamond, Rob Schwartz, and Lois Weithorn.

Lastly, our families have been our pillars of support, making this book possible. Y. Tony Yang extends his gratitude to his wife, Katie Yang, and Dorit R. Reiss expresses her appreciation for her husband, Fred Reiss, for their invaluable input and continued support of our vaccine-related endeavors.

Contents

1 Introduction: Vaccines Basics, Balance of Interests, and the
   Legal Framework 1
   1.1 Vaccines Risks and Benefits 1
   1.2 The Balance of Interests in Vaccines 5
   1.3 Book Roadmap 9
   References 11

Part I Vaccine Regulation and Monitoring

2 Regulation and Testing of Vaccines 15
   2.1 Premarket Safety 16
        2.1.1 Clinical Trials 16
        2.1.2 Licensure 17
        2.1.3 Alternative Pathways 19
   2.2 Clinical Recommendations 20
   2.3 Special Considerations 21
   2.4 Conclusion 23
   References 23

3 Postmarket Vaccine Safety 25
   3.1 Postmarket Vaccine Safety 26
        3.1.1 Manufacturing Safety 26
        3.1.2 Surveillance 26
   3.2 Federal Research on Vaccine Safety 30
        3.2.1 CDC, NIH, & FDA 31
        3.2.2 Other Federal Research 31
   3.3 Vaccine Safety Review Challenges 32
   3.4 Safety in Vaccine Distribution 33
   3.5 Conclusion 33
   References 33

4 Vaccines and Intellectual Property 35
   4.1 Vaccines and IP 36
        4.1.1 Positive Examples 36

        4.1.2   Negative Examples   37
   4.2   Patent Waivers and Why They Are the Wrong Tool   38
   4.3   Other Approaches to Vaccine Distribution   39
        4.3.1   Liability Regimes   39
        4.3.2   Public-Private Partnerships   40
        4.3.3   Intellectual Property, Technology, and Know-How
                  Bank   40
   4.4   Conclusion   41
   References   41

5   **Vaccine Injury Compensation in the United States**   43
   5.1   The Case for No-Fault Compensation of Vaccine Injuries   44
   5.2   The Vaccine Injury Compensation Program (VICP)   46
        5.2.1   Background and General Description   46
        5.2.2   The Process   47
        5.2.3   Strengths and Problems of VICP   49
   5.3   The Countermeasures Injury Compensation Program (CICP) . . .   50
   5.4   Conclusion   52
   References   53

6   **Immunization Information Systems**   55
   6.1   Challenges in the Current State   56
        6.1.1   Policy   56
        6.1.2   Data Sharing and Use   58
   6.2   Future State Considerations   59
        6.2.1   Ways to Improve IIS Infrastructure and Facilitate
                  Data Exchange   59
        6.2.2   Ways to Ensure Consistent Implementation and
                  Lower IIS Costs   59
        6.2.3   Ways to Support the Needs of Immunization Data
                  Stakeholders   60
        6.2.4   Sustainable Funding   61
   6.3   Conclusion   61
   References   62

7   **Vaccine Regulation in Global Comparison**   63
   7.1   Bringing a Vaccine to Market   64
   7.2   Post-Market Safety Monitoring   65
   7.3   Compensation Systems   67
   7.4   Conclusion   69
   References   69

Part II   Equity and Vaccines

8   **Funding Vaccinations in the United States**   73
   8.1   Public & Government Programs   74
        8.1.1   Vaccines for Children Program   74

	8.1.2	Medicare	75
	8.1.3	Medicaid and the Children's Health Insurance Program	76
	8.1.4	Section 317	78
	8.1.5	Department of Veterans Affairs	78
8.2	Private Health Insurance		79
8.3	Implications and Shortfalls of Vaccine Financing		80
8.4	Conclusion		80
References			81

9 Vaccine Equity 83
9.1 Inequitable Access to Vaccines 83
9.2 Laws, Policies, and Regulatory Tools to Address Vaccination-Related Disparities 86
    9.2.1 Existing Laws, Policies, and Regulatory Tools 86
    9.2.2 Recommendations 87
9.3 Other Issues 88
    9.3.1 Federalism 88
    9.3.2 Data Gaps 90
9.4 Conclusion 91
References 91

10 Vaccine Access in Global Comparison 93
10.1 Vaccine Development 94
10.2 Procurement 95
10.3 Administration 96
10.4 Vaccine Hesitancy 96
10.5 Leveraging Existing Strengths 97
10.6 Conclusion 99
References 100

Part III   Individual Decision Making and Vaccines

11 Informed Consent 103
11.1 Background 104
11.2 Theoretical Model 104
11.3 United States Legal Framework 106
    11.3.1 Vaccine Information Statement 106
    11.3.2 State Educational Requirements 107
    11.3.3 Liability Protections 108
11.4 Practical Considerations in the United States 109
    11.4.1 General Considerations 109
    11.4.2 Benefits of Accessible Information 110
11.5 Conclusion 112

References 112

12 Adolescent Consent 113
    12.1 Legal Landscape 113
        12.1.1 Doctrine of Parental Consent 114
        12.1.2 Competing Interests 114
        12.1.3 Minor Consent Laws in States and Localities 115
    12.2 Related Issues 116
        12.2.1 Exceptions 116
        12.2.2 Confidentiality 117
    12.3 Reform 117
    12.4 Conclusion 119
    References 119

13 Tort Liability for Failure to Vaccinate 121
    13.1 Framework 122
        13.1.1 Duty 122
        13.1.2 Breach 123
        13.1.3 Causation 125
        13.1.4 Scope of Liability (Also Known as Proximate Cause) . . 125
        13.1.5 Damages 126
    13.2 Arguments 127
    13.3 Counter-arguments 127
    13.4 Suing One's Own Parents 128
    13.5 Conclusion 129
    References 129

Part IV   Vaccine Mandates

14 Introduction to Vaccine Mandates in the United States 133
    14.1 State and Local Authority to Mandate Vaccination 134
    14.2 Federal Authority to Mandate Vaccination 136
    14.3 Private Mandates 137
    14.4 Freedom of Religion 137
    14.5 Conclusion 138
    References 138

15 School Vaccine Mandates and Exemptions 141
    15.1 Mandate Efficacy and Legal Justification 142
    15.2 Exemptions 143
        15.2.1 Medical 144
        15.2.2 Non-medical 144
        15.2.3 Implications for Disease Outbreaks 146
    15.3 Current Landscape 147
    15.4 Conclusion 147

References   148

16 Workplace Vaccine Mandates   149
   16.1   Federal Civil Rights Laws and Employee Vaccination Policies . .   151
         16.1.1   Reasonable Accommodations for Employees with
                 Disabilities   151
         16.1.2   Religious Accommodations Under Title VII   153
         16.1.3   Vaccination and Pregnant Employees   154
         16.1.4   Medical Examinations or Inquiries Under the ADA
                 and the Rehabilitation Act   155
   16.2   Considerations Under the Religious Freedom Restoration Act
        and Other Laws   156
   16.3   Unionized Workers   157
   16.4   EUA Status   157
   16.5   Conclusion   159
   References   159

17 Federal Vaccine Mandates   161
   17.1   Executive Branch Authority to Mandate Vaccination   162
         17.1.1   OSHA's Vaccine Program   163
         17.1.2   The Centers for Medicare and Medicaid Healthcare
                 Workers Requirement   165
         17.1.3   Federal Employees mandate   166
         17.1.4   Federal Contractors Mandate   166
         17.1.5   Head Start Mandate   167
   17.2   Congress's Authority to Mandate Vaccination   167
   17.3   Conclusion   168
   References   168

18 Vaccine Mandates in Global Comparison   169
   18.1   Background   169
   18.2   Global Vaccine Policy   170
   18.3   Approaches   171
   18.4   Efficacy, Challenges, and Opposition   172
   18.5   Conclusion   173
   References   174

19 Vaccine Passports for Travel   175
   19.1   What Are Vaccine Passports and Where Are Vaccine
        Passports Being Used Now?   175
         19.1.1   COVID-19 Vaccine Passports   176
         19.1.2   Where Are COVID-19 Vaccination Passports
                 Required?   176
   19.2   Vaccine Passports and the U.S.   177
   19.3   Key Considerations   178
         19.3.1   Legal Considerations   178
         19.3.2   Ethical Considerations   179
         19.3.3   Practical   180

    19.4   Conclusion.. 181
    References.. 182

Part V   Special Contexts

20   Military Vaccinations..................................... 185
    20.1   The Department of Defense and Vaccines................. 185
    20.2   Issues with Military Vaccine Mandates.................. 186
        20.2.1   Vaccination Opt-Outs......................... 187
        20.2.2   Vaccine Hesitancy............................ 187
    20.3   The Military's COVID-19 Vaccination Mandate............ 188
    20.4   Conclusion.. 190
    References.. 190

21   Vaccine Policy in Emergency Situations..................... 193
    21.1   Function of the PREP Act.............................. 194
        21.1.1   Scope of Immunity from Liability................ 194
        21.1.2   The "Willful Misconduct" Exception.............. 196
        21.1.3   The CICP..................................... 197
    21.2   How the Law Works................................. 198
    21.3   How the Law Affects States........................... 199
    21.4   Conclusion.. 199
    References.. 200

22   Regulating Vaccine Misinformation Online.................. 201
    22.1   Background: Misinformation and Social Media in the U.S..... 202
    22.2   The Role of Government.............................. 203
    22.3   Self-Regulation from Social Media Companies............. 204
    22.4   Challenges of Regulation............................. 205
    22.5   Strategies to Combat Misinformation in the U.S. and Abroad... 205
    22.6   Conclusion.. 207
    References.. 207

Part VI   Policy

23   Vaccine Incentives and Health Insurance Surcharges.......... 211
    23.1   Types of Incentives................................. 212
    23.2   Legal Considerations................................ 213
        23.2.1   HIPAA...................................... 213
        23.2.2   The Affordable Care Act........................ 213
        23.2.3   The Americans with Disabilities Act.............. 214
        23.2.4   Additional Legal Considerations................. 214
    23.3   Policy Considerations............................... 215

23.4   Implications for Employers 216

23.5   Conclusion 217

References 217

24 Vaccine Advocacy, Politics, and Anti-vaccine Movements 219

24.1   History of Opposition and Fear of Vaccines 219

24.2   The Rise of Politically Engaged Anti-vaccine Activists 220

24.3   The Pro-vaccine Apparatus 222

24.4   The Anti-vaccine Movement 223

       24.4.1   Growth of Vaccine Exemptions and
Vaccine-Preventable Diseases 224

       24.4.2   Growth of the Anti-vaccine Movement and the Role
of Social Media 225

24.5   Factors Influencing Anti-vaccine Advocacy 225

24.6   Responding to the Anti-vaccine Movement 226

       24.6.1   Pro Vaccine Advocacy 226

       24.6.2   Broad Support for Vaccines and Immunization
Requirements 227

       24.6.3   Progress of Pro-immunization Advocates 227

24.7   Recommendations for Actions 228

24.8   Conclusion 229

References 230

Introduction: Vaccines Basics, Balance of Interests, and the Legal Framework

1

Abstract

Vaccine law is complex because it covers many issues. Vaccines are developed by scientists but made by corporations, and several areas of law affect their oversight, production, and sales. But vaccines are not just a product, they are a medical product and a tool of public health. Because vaccines affect both the individual receiving them and the society in which they are given, both individual rights and public law become relevant, and the intersection between them is where many disputes arise.

This book maps out the different areas of laws that touch on vaccines and addresses their complexities. In this introduction, we lay out the background, and map out the following chapters. In the background, we first address the science behind vaccines and then discuss the balance of interests in relation to vaccine uptake.

1.1 Vaccines Risks and Benefits

Vaccines are one of several tools that allow mankind to limit—though not conquer—the harms infectious diseases cause. Other tools include anti-biotics and sanitation. The National Academies of Science, Engineering and Medicine stated, in the context of childhood vaccines, that vaccines "have many health benefits and few side effects."[1] Experts point out that vaccines are "safe and effective", but it's important to understand what that means, and qualify it.[2] Nothing is completely safe or completely effective. Vaccines are perceived as safe and effective, because their risks are small and work in most cases. While their benefits are large and may justify their risk, their use is contingent on several factors that must be qualified.

---

[1]CDC (2008).
[2]CDC (2022).

© The Author(s), under exclusive license to Springer Nature Switzerland AG 2023
Y. T. Yang, D. R. Reiss, *Vaccine Law and Policy*, Law for Professionals,
https://doi.org/10.1007/978-3-031-36989-6_1

Let's start with safety. Nothing is absolutely safe, and certainly, nothing can affect the body with zero risks—at the very least, vaccines that trigger an immune response may sometimes trigger a severe allergic reaction. To give a few intuitive examples, walking on the sidewalk is generally safe, but not completely so; you can fall and hurt yourself (even without anyone doing anything to make you fall). Similarly, while eating spinach is generally safe—even recommended—spinach has been linked to several large E Coli outbreaks in the United States (U.S.).[3] When we talk about safety, we almost always mean relatively safe—respective to other behaviors, though we expect that serious harms are relatively uncommon. When it comes to childhood vaccines, the expectation is that serious harms will be very rare, and an order of magnitude—or several—less than the risks the vaccine prevents. This is usually the case—to give one example, the poliovirus causes severe paralysis or death in about 1 in 200 people infected with the disease. The inactivated polio vaccine that is used in the U.S. can cause local reactions, or theoretically a severe allergic reaction, though there are no documented cases of the latter.[4] The oral polio vaccine, used in developing countries, can rarely revert to the wild version of the virus and causes paralysis or death—at a rate of about one case per 2–3 million doses. Obviously, the risks of the vaccines are small—serious harms are rare—and dramatically smaller than the risks of the disease. This is true across the board for routine vaccines.

Independent experts and the World Health Organization (WHO) have shown that vaccines are far safer than therapeutic medicines. Modern research has spurred the development of less reactogenic products, such as acellular pertussis vaccines and rabies vaccines produced in cell culture. Today, vaccines have an excellent safety record and most "vaccine scares" have been shown to be false alarms.[5] This image of safety may be harder to see during an emergency due to the need for fast action. That said, since vaccine side effects usually appear within weeks from the date they are given, it should be possible to know the more common risks of them quickly; and rare risks may appear after a routine vaccine, too.[6]

In both cases, however, the important takeaway is that extensive evidence shows vaccines to be very safe; but that does not mean completely risk-free. Serious harms from vaccines do happen, and that needs to be taken into consideration in relation to the law.

Further, the relative safety discussed above refers to vaccines when used as recommended. Since vaccines are administered by humans, errors can happen. And some errors can lead to harm. In the context of vaccines, for every vaccine there are contraindications—people who should not get vaccinated. For example, live virus vaccines should not be given to people who are immune compromised, and usually those who are pregnant. Live virus vaccines are generally designed so they

---

[3] Charatan (2006).

[4] Weithorn and Reiss (2000), pp. 782–783.

[5] Andre et al. (2008).

[6] Children's Hospital of Philadelphia (2021).

cannot replicate while in the host, so people with working immune systems can clear them quickly and safely. But people with immune systems that are not working well may not be able to do that, and given enough time, even a weakened vaccine can replicate enough to cause harm. This is not a theoretical concern; there are (very rare) cases where some immune compromised children were given, for example, Measles, Mumps, Rubella (MMR), and died from it.[7]

In more extreme cases, sometimes administration is done incorrectly. For example, in Somalia, a nurse wrongly mixed a vaccine with muscle relaxant instead of water and gave it to two very young children who both tragically died.[8]

The risk of errors in administration is another issue to be considered when setting vaccine policy and creating law to support it. One example of a relevant law is compensation for victims of errors. Additionally, mechanisms should be adopted to avoid such errors as much as possible.

Furthermore, vaccines are manufactured by companies run by humans, and errors in manufacturing can also increase the risk of vaccines. In the U.S., an early vaccine tragedy was the Cutter incident, in which several laboratories sent out what was supposed to be an inactivated polio vaccine, but contained the live virus.[9] Over 200 children were paralyzed, many severely, and 11 died. There has not been a similar incident in the U.S. since—in part because of changes in regulation designed to prevent it—but there have been recalls of vaccines when manufacturing problems were found. Other countries have also seen manufacturing crises.

While vaccines are seen as effective, we should be careful about what that means. No vaccine is 100% effective. For example, two doses of MMR are 99% effective at protecting against measles.[10] But that means some vaccinated children will still be vulnerable to the disease, and in a large group that could be a large number (as a reminder, 1% of 10,000 means 100 vaccinated children are vulnerable to measles). Other vaccines are substantially less effective, even if they are effective enough to be very valuable. Pertussis vaccines prevent 85% of cases and reduce severity of illness in people who get vaccinated but still get sick. Two doses of MMR leads to 88% protection against mumps. And in both these cases, protection wanes over time, and boosters may be needed. The influenza vaccine is most likely the least effective in our roster: effectiveness varies by year, but at most, the vaccine is 60–70% effective at preventing infection. However, it does reduce severity even in those who get influenza, for example, reducing child mortality by about two thirds.[11] Even an effective vaccine is not 100% effective, in other words, not everyone who gets the vaccine will be protected.

That does not mean the vaccine is worthless. Even a vaccine with less than 100% efficacy can offer very large benefits by saving lives and preventing harms. For

---

[7]Lievano et al. (2012).

[8]Beat (2019); Stratton et al. (1994).

[9]Carapetis (2006).

[10]Hamborsky (2015).

[11]Flannery (2017).

example, the less-than-effective influenza vaccine prevents thousands of deaths and hospitalizations each year.[12] Even without perfect effectiveness, vaccines have large benefits. For example, in the U.S., a study estimated that vaccines prevented 732,000 early deaths between 1994–2013, millions of hospitalizations, and billions of dollars in costs.[13] Globally, the WHO stated:

> There is arguably no single preventive health intervention more cost-effective than immunization. Time and again, the international community has endorsed the value of vaccines and immunization to prevent and control a large number of infectious diseases and, increasingly, several chronic diseases that are caused by infectious agents.[14]

Further, personal immunity is not the only way vaccines are protective. Vaccines also provide herd immunity, or community immunity. Most vaccines—with the exception of the tetanus vaccine—are targeted to work against communicable diseases. Germs causing communicable disease establish a foothold in a population by jumping from host to host. If enough people in the population are immune—because they received the disease and were likely enough to survive, or because they got vaccinated and became immune without getting sick—the germ does not have enough potential hosts to jump to. Even if it is present in the population, it will die off. For example, every year people come into the U.S. from countries in which diphtheria or measles are still widespread. Some of them likely carry the germs. But most of these arrivals never spark an outbreak because most people in the U.S. are vaccinated against both diseases, and the carriers do not meet anyone that is vulnerable to infection, and the germ dies with them.

This is why high rates of vaccination matter to a country, and why vaccination is not just a personal decision. Low rates of vaccination mean a germ coming in has many potential hosts, and can spread, causing an outbreak with potentially dangerous results. For example, the last polio outbreak in the U.S. was in a Christian science school where many unvaccinated children attended, and it resulted in 9 children being permanently paralyzed.[15]

High rates of vaccination protect a community from an outbreak, and also individually protect those who cannot be vaccinated for medical reasons and those who were vaccinated, but for whom the vaccine was not effective.

---

[12] CDC (2020).

[13] Whitney et al. (2014).

[14] WHO (2018).

[15] Weinstein (1973).

1.2   The Balance of Interests in Vaccines

The science described above should demonstrate why people and governments have a legitimate interest in maintaining high rates of vaccines. But in a democratic country, individual rights matter, and need to be taken into consideration. Several rights are implicated in assessing vaccines, as are several interests.

First, generally speaking, all individuals in society have an interest in assuring that the vaccines that get to the market are safe and effective. Although the benefits may outweigh the risks even in vaccines that do cause occasional harms, assuring that vaccine harms are rare and that we are using the most effective vaccines available is in the interest of society as a whole. Individual manufacturers, of course, may have conflicting interests. Therefore, a regulatory system put in place needs to address the social needs for safety and effectiveness and reduce opportunities for manipulation by companies. Second, there are strong grounds for working towards vaccine equity, though this will be affected by a given society's general approach to equity. A society with historical inequalities will have a harder time achieving vaccine equity, as well. Third, there are strong social grounds for assuring fast and generous compensation to the rare few harmed by vaccines. However, putting this into practice requires addressing challenging questions around showing causation and assessing damages.

Where the most heated legal debates are likely to be is in the area of increasing vaccine uptake. There is, as mentioned, a clear social interest in high vaccine uptake in society, to prevent outbreaks, and provide the benefits of community immunity to society. On the other hand, individuals who do not wish to vaccinate themselves or their children can point to a variety of individual rights arguments. How to balance these competing views raises complex and important ethical, political, and legal questions.

It is important to remember that the balance of interests here is different between vaccine decisions for adults and children. For adults, (Fig. 1.1) the tension is between the individual rights of the adult making the decision and the public health—and the rights of others who may be affected by the choice not to vaccinate. The rights of the individual adult may include the liberty to refuse medical treatment (no democratic country, to our knowledge, have laws permitting adults to be held down and vaccinated by force, though some may have criminal penalties for not vaccinating—although that, too, is rare). The rights in question may, if the reason to refuse the vaccine is religious, also implicate freedom of religion. We address these issues more in depth in Chap. 14, but for now, we will point out that while there are people who have sincere religious objections to vaccines, it is likely that more people use religion to refuse vaccines when they have other concerns regarding vaccines. The approach countries take to religious objections vary, but in the U.S., freedom of religion is a constitutional right—but not an unlimited one, and courts have

Fig. 1.1 The balance of
interests for adults

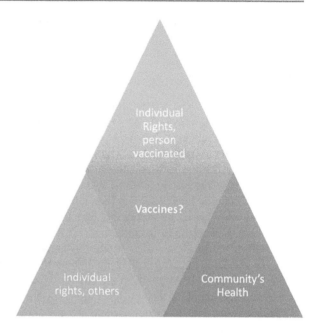

historically upheld vaccine mandates without a religious exemption (though in the
workplace context, the Civil Rights Act of 1964 changes the equation).[16]

On the other side of the equation is the public health. Public health is an old power
of government; as early as 1830, the Supreme Court in Vermont upheld measures to
protect against smallpox (we suspect there are earlier cases, but this is the earliest
vaccine case we found).[17] In 1873, in the Slaughterhouse cases, the U.S. Supreme
Court upheld the power of a legislature to act to protect the public health, in this case
by limiting areas of slaughterhouses.[18] And in a case directly addressing vaccines,
Jacobson v. Massachusetts, the Supreme Court said in words that are still a bedrock
of our public health law:

> The police power of a State embraces such reasonable regulations relating to matters
> completely within its territory, and not affecting the people of other States, established
> directly by legislative enactment, as will protect the public health and safety.
>
> . . .
>
> The liberty secured by the Constitution of the United States does not import an absolute right
> in each person to be at all times, and in all circumstances, wholly freed from restraint, nor is it
> an element in such liberty that one person, or a minority of persons residing in any

---

[16] Reiss (2021)

[17] Hazen v. Strong, 2 Vt. 427 (1830).

[18] Slaughterhouse Cases, 83 U.S. 36 (1872).

community and enjoying the benefits of its local government, should have power to dominate the majority when supported in their action by the authority of the State.[19]

What this means is that the state can act in the public health, and that it can sometimes act in ways that interfere with individual rights, if it is in the public good. Whether that interference is legal, under Jacobson, is assessed by a standard of reasonableness. However, Jacobson is an old case; it is from 1905, though it was cited in many of the cases upholding restrictions set during the COVID-19 pandemic (and many other cases; the pandemic is relatively recent). Since Jacobson, our law has changed, and in some cases—but not others—the standard courts use to assess whether interference with individual rights is permissible is higher.[20] In some cases, courts still use a reasonableness standard; this is referred to as rational review basis, where the state only has to show that its choice was reasonable, and was tied to a legitimate state interest (which public health easily is). This standard was used in most, but not all, cases examining vaccines mandates, and it is relatively deferential: most vaccines mandates would survive it. In some cases, especially when the issue implicates a fundamental right or distinguishes based on a characteristic that was historically subject to discrimination (like race), the law is held to strict scrutiny. Strict scrutiny requires the acting government to show that their measure is adopted to advance a compelling interest. If the measure is a public health measure adopted to prevent death and harms, it can likely withstand that (though courts may sometimes question whether the measure does, in fact, prevent deaths and harms). But this standard also requires the state to use the least restrictive means to protect the state interest, and that is a high bar: opponents will often claim, more or less convincingly, that there are other means to achieve the same goal. Strict scrutiny poses a much higher bar to state action, so naturally, much of the legal fight around public health measures starts with which standard should be applied. So far, as we mentioned, courts usually apply rational basis to vaccines mandates. But as we discuss in more detail in later chapters, this could change.

Finally, often overlooked are the other individual rights, besides not wanting to be vaccinated, that are affected by vaccine policy. For example, people who cannot get vaccinated for medical reasons have to depend on others. A long-term care facility resident or prisoner who is immune compromised for any reason is at high risk for many diseases. Low vaccination rates among the facility or prison's staff increases the risk to that person. What about their right to life? Generally, my right to liberty is affected by the risk of exposure to others with a dangerous disease. Society cannot completely prevent exposure to disease, but we do take measures to reduce risks from some—sometimes going to extremes, like sending people with HIV who did not warn their partner to prison, or confining people with tuberculosis until they undergo treatment. These rights, too, may support measures to increase vaccine rates that impose on other people's rights.

---

[19] Jacobson v. Massachusetts, 197 U.S. 11, 11 (1905).
[20] Wiley and Vladeck (2020), pp. 180–183.

Fig. 1.2 The balance of interest for children

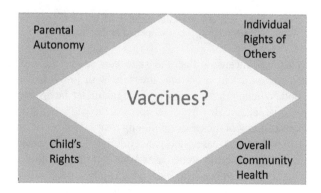

Parental Autonomy

Individual Rights of Others

Vaccines?

Child's Rights

Overall Community Health

For children, the situation is somewhat different (Fig. 1.2). When an adult refuses to vaccinate, measures to push them to vaccinate may implicate their personal autonomy, or their freedom of religion, or other direct rights. But when a parent decides not to vaccinate their child, the right affected is the right of the parent to make medical decisions for the child. We protect parental rights to make decisions for the child; in the U.S., that right is powerfully protected (in one case, the Supreme Court upheld a law denying grandparents visitation rights over parental wishes).[21] But the protection of parental rights has never been absolute, and is at its weakest when a child's health and welfare are at stake.[22] Basically, parents do not have rights to put children at risk. The balance of interests when it comes to measures aimed at increasing childhood vaccination is different because in addition to the public health and other rights, the child has their own rights which support vaccinating. Usually, vaccinating reduces a child's risks, and for modern vaccines, the risk of vaccinating is an order of magnitude smaller than the risk of not vaccinating for all children without medical exemptions (and children with medical reasons not to vaccinate will normally not be caught, for example, in a mandate: they will be medically exempt).

And, here too, the rights of others may support vaccinating. A child with a heart transplant, to give one example, cannot receive live virus vaccines because they are given immune-suppressing medication so that their system does not reject the transplant. With a weakened immune system, live virus vaccines are too dangerous for them. But if that child with a weakened immune system is exposed to measles, then they are also at high risk. That child depends on having a high-vaccine-rate environment to remain safe. When the state allows others not to vaccinate, that child is placed at higher risk. If the child's class has more than 5% unvaccinated children, that class is at real risk of a measles outbreak if any of those children are exposed. That makes that class unsafe for the child with the transplant. What about that child's right to education, and right to life?

---

[21] Buss (2002), p. 637.

[22] Reiss and Weithorn (2015).

1.3   Book Roadmap

In the first part of this book, we set out the framework for regulating vaccines—how do vaccines get to the market, including how do we regulate the intellectual property around them, how do we monitor vaccine safety and compensate the rare cases of vaccines harms, and how do we know who received which vaccines. Chapter 2 looks at the regulatory process, how vaccines get to the market in the U.S. We examine the stages of creating and testing vaccines until they get to the market under regular conditions, and during an emergency. We continue the discussion in Chap. 3 by looking at how vaccines are monitored after they get to the market. In Chap. 2 the Food and Drug Administration (FDA) is the main government agency, while in Chap. 3 the FDA, the Centers for Disease Control and Prevention (CDC) and others all have a role (vaccine companies are also constant players). In Chap. 4 we discuss the framework for protecting intellectual property related to vaccines, the challenges related to it, and some solutions proposed by scholars.

In Chap. 5 we discuss the complex question of compensating those harmed by vaccines, and then in Chap. 6 we discuss the rise of immunization information systems and the challenges around them. Chapter 7 provides a comparative perspective and addresses how different countries regulate and monitor vaccines and compensate those with vaccine harms.

We then look at equity issues around vaccines. Chapters 8 and 9 focus on the U.S. In Chap. 8 we address how the U.S. provides access to vaccines through comprehensive funding schemes. We will demonstrate that for children, the U.S. has a reasonable scheme for funding vaccines, though it can be improved. Furthermore, there are real and large gaps for adults. Chapter 9 examines the role of government in promoting vaccine equity. Chapter 10 then broadens the discussion to vaccine access issues from a comparative perspective.

We then discuss how the law intersects with individual choices to vaccinate or not. We address the importance of informed consent and how the law regulates it in Chap. 11. We then address, in Chap. 12, the question of whether, and under what circumstances, can (and should) adolescents consent to vaccines when their parents disagree. Finally, we address whether the choice not to vaccinate can lead to civil liability in Chap. 13.

The most challenging questions for debates about rights come up in the context of how to increase vaccine rates. If a state wants to bring the power of the state to increase vaccine rates, what can it do? The state has a range of options here. One way to think about this is by ranging the options from most coercive to least (Fig. 1.3).

To our knowledge, no democratic country—and few non-democratic countries—actually used physical coercion of vaccines—holding an adult down and vaccinating them—in the past century (we acknowledge that this might happen, for example, in a prison environment, but we are unaware of any examples). Rarely, children are vaccinated over parental opposition—for example, in the context of a custody dispute. More commonly, vaccines are mandated—required with a condition attached, with or without exemptions. The condition attached can range from criminal law to other requirements, like testing weekly for COVID-19 to remain at

Fig. 1.3 Continuum of legal tools for increasing vaccine rates

your job, if you refuse to vaccinate. We discuss these possibilities in more detail in Chaps. 14–19, which discusses mandates. Because this topic is a focus of controversy, we devote five chapters to it. Chapter 14 sets the ground by providing an introduction to vaccine mandates—as they are in the U.S. and the roles of different levels of government in setting them. Chapter 15 focuses on school immunization mandates, the most common way childhood vaccines rates are increased in the U.S. (and a growing phenomenon abroad, too). We also discuss the potential exemptions—medical, religious and philosophical. Chapter 16 talks about workplace vaccine mandates, both by state actors and by private employers, and the limits to them. Chapter 17 then addresses a new phenomenon, federal vaccine mandates, which appeared for the first time with the COVID-19 pandemic, and the legal challenges they ran into.

Chapter 18 and 19 then move to a more global topic, looking at mandates across nations and for travel.

We then go into more specific contexts that do not fit into the other chapters, talking about vaccines in the U.S. military, vaccines in times of emergency, and vaccine misinformation online. Finally, in Chaps. 23 and 24, we move from law to policy by addressing potential incentives to increase vaccines, vaccine advocacy and politics.

This book attempts to cover a lot of ground. We hope to provide non-lawyer readers with a reasonable introduction to the various topics vaccine law encompasses, at a level that will allow them to think about and assess existing and new proposals. Naturally, our own point of view affects our analysis, and we will try to be very clear on when we are describing the law and when we are giving our own view. That said, our perspective will naturally affect the framing, so we should be upfront about it.

Our view is that vaccines are an important, and a mostly beneficial invention. Furthermore, high vaccine rates are an important goal for most nations. That said, nuance matters. Vaccines are not risk free and needs to be thoroughly regulated to reduce risk and prevent abuse. And whether a vaccine is important depends on context. Vaccines need to be used when appropriate, given a society's situation, prevalent diseases, and the target population. As with many things, the details matter.

With that, we turn over to the essence of vaccines and the law.

References

Andre FE et al (2008) Vaccination greatly reduces disease, disability, death and inequity world-wide. Bull World Health Organ 86(2):140–146. https://doi.org/10.2471/blt.07.040089

Beat P (2019) Samoan nurses jailed over deaths of two babies who were given incorrectly. Mixed Vaccines. https://www.abc.net.au/news/2019-08-02/samoa-nurses-sentenced-manslaughter-infant-vaccination-deaths/11378494

Buss E (2002) "Parental" rights. Va Law Rev 88:635, 637

Carapetis JR (2006) The cutter incident: how America's first polio vaccine led to the growing vaccine crisis. BMJ 332(7543):733. PMCID: PMC1410842

CDC (2008) Vaccines Are Safe. https://www.nationalacademies.org/based-on-science/vaccines-are-safe

CDC (2020) Estimated Influenza Illness, Medical Visits and Hospitalizations Averted by Vaccination in the United States – 2019-2020 Influenza Season. https://www.cdc.gov/flu/about/burden-averted/2019-2020.htm

CDC (2022) Safety of COVID-19 Vaccines. https://www.cdc.gov/coronavirus/2019-ncov/vaccines/safety/safety-of-vaccines.html

Charatan F (2006) FDA warns US consumers not to eat spinach after E coli outbreak. BMJ 333:673. https://doi.org/10.1136/bmj.333.7570.673-c

Children's Hospital of Philadelphia (2021) Long-Term Side Effects of COVID-19 Vaccine? What We Know. https://www.chop.edu/news/long-term-side-effects-covid-19-vaccine

Flannery B (2017) Influenza vaccine effectiveness against pediatric deaths: 2010–2014. Pediatrics 139(5):e20164244. https://doi.org/10.1542/peds.2016-4244

Hamborsky J (2015) Disease control & prevention, epidemiology and prevention of vaccine-preventable diseases 218, 13th edn. Public Health Foundation, Washington DC

Hazen v. Strong, 2 Vt. 427 (1830)

Jacobson v. Massachusetts, 197 U.S. 11, 11 (1905)

Lievano F et al (2012) Measles, mumps, and rubella virus vaccine (M-M-R™II): a review of 32 years of clinical and postmarketing experience. Vaccine 30(48):6918–6926. https://doi.org/10.1016/j.vaccine.2012.08.057

Reiss DR (2021) Vaccines mandates and religion: where are we headed with the current supreme court? J Law Med Ethics 49:552–563. https://doi.org/10.1017/jme.2021.79

Reiss DR, Weithorn LA (2015) Responding to the childhood vaccination crisis: legal frameworks and tools in the context of parental vaccine refusal. Buff Law Rev 63:905–910

Slaughterhouse Cases, 83 U.S. 36 (1872)

Stratton KR et al (1994) Death. In: Adverse events associated with childhood vaccines: evidence bearing on causality, 1st edn. National Academic Press (US), Washington, DC

Weinstein L (1973) Poliomyelitis—a persistent problem. New Engl J Med 288:370. https://doi.org/10.1056/NEJM197302152880714

Weithorn LA, Reiss DR (2000) Providing adolescents with independent and confidential access to childhood vaccines: a proposal to lower the age of consent. Conn Law Rev 52:772–861, 782–783.

Whitney CG et al (2014) Benefits from immunization during the vaccines for children program era – United States, 1994–2013 morbidity & mortality. Wkly Rep 63(16):352–355. https://www.cdc.gov/mmwr/preview/mmwrhtml/mm6316a4.htm

WHO (2018) World Health Organization: 10 Facts on Immunization. https://www.who.int/mongolia/health-topics/vaccines/10-facts-on-immunization

Wiley LF, Vladeck SI (2020) Coronavirus, civil liberties, and the courts: the case against "Suspending" judicial review. Harv Law Rev F 113(179):180–183

Part I

Vaccine Regulation and Monitoring

This part of the book focuses on the regulation and monitoring of vaccines. Topics covered include the processes involved in bringing vaccines to market, monitoring their safety, protecting intellectual property rights, compensating those harmed by vaccines, and tracking vaccine recipients. We examine various aspects of vaccine regulation in the U.S., including the roles of government agencies such as the FDA and CDC, as well as the challenges and solutions related to intellectual property and compensation for vaccine-related harms. Additionally, this part offers a comparative perspective on how different countries regulate and monitor vaccines.

Regulation and Testing of Vaccines

2

Abstract

Federal regulation of vaccine safety began in 1902, with the passage of the Biologics Control Act. Since the act's introduction, several federal agencies have become involved in vaccine safety, including the Centers for Disease Control and Prevention (CDC), the National Institutes of Health (NIH), the Department of Veterans Affairs (VA), and the Food and Drug Administration (FDA). This chapter focuses primarily on the FDA and its Center for Biologics Evaluation and Research (CBER), which is charged with ensuring the safety, purity, and effectiveness of vaccines in the United States (U.S.) (Bodie and Sekar, Congressional Research Service: Vaccine Safety in the United States: Overview and Considerations for COVID-19 Vaccines, 4, 2021.). The FDA's primary statutory authority for regulating vaccines is derived from Section 351 of the Public Health Service Act from 1944 (PHSA) and from the Federal Food, Drug, and Cosmetic Act (FFDCA) (the next chapter will address other ways we monitor and regulate vaccine safety) (Baylor and Marshall, Regulation and Testing of Vaccines, 2013:1431, 2012.). Section 351 of the Provincial Health Services Authority (PHSA) permits the FDA to approve a Biologics License Application (BLA) if: (1) the biologic product is "safe, pure, and potent;" and (2) the facility where the product is manufactured "meets standards designed to assure that the biological product continues to be safe, pure, and potent." (The PHSA's definition of a "biological product" includes vaccines.) The FDA implements its statutory authority to regulate vaccines primarily via Title 21, parts 600 through 680 of the Code of Federal Regulations (CFR). And because vaccines meet the legal definition of a "drug" under the FFDCA, vaccine manufacturers must also comply with regulations for good manufacturing practices found under CFR Title 21, parts 210 and 211. Vaccine safety regulations govern areas like standards for vaccine manufacturing and clinical trial requirements.

This means that vaccines are subject to more oversight than many other kinds of drugs. First, they are subject to two sets of regulatory commands instead of just

© The Author(s), under exclusive license to Springer Nature Switzerland AG 2023
Y. T. Yang, D. R. Reiss, *Vaccine Law and Policy*, Law for Professionals,
https://doi.org/10.1007/978-3-031-36989-6_2

one. Second, in addition to licensing the vaccines, the manufacturing facility needs to be licensed.

2.1   Premarket Safety

To be marketed in the U.S., a new vaccine must usually receive a license from the FDA. A license is typically granted once clinical trials show that the vaccine is safe, pure, and effective. The request for a license is called a BLA, and you will hear the license itself referred to as a BLA at times. In addition to the BLA, there are alternative ways for a vaccine to reach individuals. These include expedited review, the "Animal Rule," and Emergency Use Authorization (EUA).

2.1.1   Clinical Trials

To receive a BLA approval, a vaccine must go through clinical trials. Before beginning clinical trials in humans, a vaccine's sponsor must file an investigational new drug (IND) application requesting FDA authorization to administer the vaccine to humans. The requirements to get to this point include successful testing of the vaccine in animals and subjecting the vaccine to chemical testing to make sure it is not toxic. The IND application also includes information about the proposed clinical trial's design and other pre-testing safety considerations. A vaccine sponsor must also employ an Institutional Review Board (IRB) that will continuously review the clinical trials. They ensure that participants remain aware of the vaccine's investigational status, the risks involved, and are not subjected to unnecessary risk. The FDA has 30 days to review an IND application, after which, if the FDA has not objected, the manufacturer may begin human trials.

There are typically three phases of premarket clinical trials. *Phase 1* trials provide preliminary evaluations of safety and immunogenicity (defined as the ability of a foreign substance to enter a person's body and trigger an immune response), and typically involve a small number of healthy volunteers (approximately 20 to 80). *Phase 2* trials are larger (involving up to several hundred volunteers) and provide further information on safety and immunogenicity. Phase 2 trials assess side effects and conduct dosage-ranging studies (the dosing at which the vaccine may have a protective effect).[1] Some trials engage in "phase 2b studies" that are done after a phase 2 trial but are not considered efficacy studies. These studies are designed to assist in determining whether to move a vaccine into the next phase trial. Finally, *phase 3* trials are large-scale (thousands or tens of thousands of volunteers) and involve extensive testing to provide a more thorough assessment of safety. A phase 3 trial will generally include the vaccine's target audience; if it is a vaccine for infants, it will be tested in infants. If for adults, in adults. If for the elderly, in the

---

[1]Baylor and Marshall (2011), p. S24. https://doi.org/10.1542/peds.2010-1722E.

elderly. Generally, a vaccine moves through each phase of clinical testing upon successful completion of the prior phase.

Most vaccines fail phase 1 trials. Even vaccines that succeed in phase 1 or 2, may not start phase 3 trials—which are very expensive—until the company producing them has good reason to think the vaccine will pass the trials. The COVID-19 vaccines were unusual in that companies started phase 3 trials right after phase 1, in large part because the government, by funding the trials, reduced the financial risk to the companies.

Phase 3 trials are large enough to provide assessments of the vaccine's efficacy, which is determined via the use of "endpoints." Vaccines can use *clinical endpoints*, which directly measure the vaccine's efficacy on patient outcomes; or *surrogate endpoints*, which measure an indicator of a protective immune response (e.g., the presence of antibodies of the targeted disease in the bloodstream showing the vaccine's efficacy). Long-term clinical trials in phase 3—though more expensive and time consuming—can uncover important safety data and detect rare adverse events (Fig. 2.1).

2.1.2 Licensure

After completing clinical trials, a vaccine's sponsor may submit a BLA to CBER's Office of Vaccines Research and Review. A BLA must contain information that shows compliance with the statutory and regulatory requirements for vaccine production, including manufacturing and labeling. CBER will not consider the BLA until CBER determines that it has received all pertinent information and data from the vaccine's sponsor.

Once CBER accepts a BLA, an internal scientific review is conducted. Members of the review committee are selected based on their expertise, and CBER maintains communication with the vaccine's sponsor during the review process. Such communication is necessary because it is possible for the review committee to recommend significant changes to the vaccine.

After CBER and its internal review committee consider the BLA, it is reviewed by CBER's Vaccines and Related Biological Products Advisory Committee (VRBPAC), which meets to discuss the vaccine data publicly (these days, the meetings are broadcast virtually, too). VRBPAC is made up of medical and scientific experts who "review and evaluate data concerning the safety, effectiveness, and appropriate use of vaccines and related biological products." VRBPAC reviews the data regarding a vaccine's safety and efficacy, and considers the vaccine's benefit-to-risk ratio. Regulatory standards allow VRBPAC flexibility in determining whether a certain ratio is scientifically appropriate based on the vaccine product. Ultimately, once CBER determines that the data and information contained in the BLA support the vaccine's safety and efficacy, the vaccine is licensed.

Fig. 2.1 The process of developing, approving, and manufacturing a new vaccine. Source: CDC https://www.cdc.gov/vaccines/parents/infographics/journey-of-child-vaccine-h.pdf

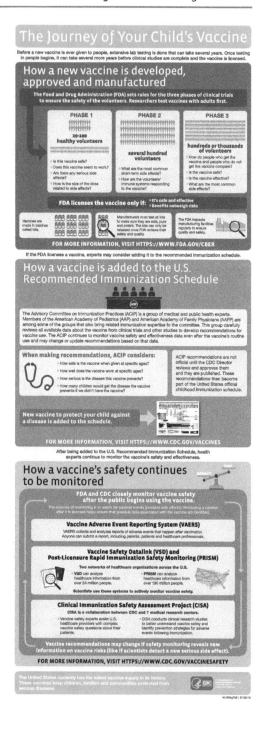

2.1.3 Alternative Pathways

The aforementioned "traditional" licensing process can take several years. But over time, Congress and the FDA have established mechanisms for expediting premarket review of vaccines for severe and life-threatening illnesses. These include: (a) expedited development and review; (b) the "Animal Rule;" and (c) EUA.

2.1.3.1 Expedited Development and Review

The FDA has four programs to expedite the development and review processes for vaccines designed to prevent serious or life-threatening diseases. The first 2 programs are designed to streamline the clinical development process and allow a vaccine to qualify for multiple programs. A *fast-track product designation* applies to a vaccine intended for a serious condition where preliminary data proves that the vaccine meets an "unmet" medical need. A fast-track vaccine qualifies for priority and rolling review (meaning the FDA reviews portions of the BLA before a complete application is submitted). A *Breakthrough designation* applies to a vaccine intended for a serious condition where evidence indicates potentially substantial improvement over currently available treatments. A vaccine with a breakthrough designation receives rolling BLA review, intensive FDA guidance on designing an efficient drug development program, and involvement of experienced regulatory management staff to expedite the development and review of the vaccine. Note that these programs' standards for safety are neither relaxed nor sacrificed.

The *accelerated approval* pathway applies to vaccines for which evidence can "predict" a clinical benefit with reasonable certainty. This can be established through surrogate endpoints that predict effectiveness, or clinical endpoints that can be measured earlier than patient outcomes such as death. A vaccine receiving accelerated approval must provide a meaningful advantage over current treatments, and the vaccine is generally subject to post-market studies ensuring *actual* effectiveness (though all vaccines are subject to post-market monitoring). Finally, CBER may designate a vaccine for *priority review* if the vaccine is intended for a serious condition and would provide a significant improvement in safety or effectiveness. If a BLA is designated for priority review, the CBER has six months to complete its review—as opposed to ten months for a standard BLA submission.

2.1.3.2 Animal Rule

The FDA typically requires that a vaccine be shown effective in human beings prior to licensure. But sometimes the vaccine is designed to treat or prevent serious or life-threatening conditions from exposure to toxic chemicals or biologics, for example via bioterrorism. In these situations, you cannot study effectiveness because the agent causing the harm is not naturally present in the population, and intentional exposure would be unethical. In these unusual cases, the FDA can approve a license if animal studies establish the vaccine's safety and effectiveness. Animal studies can only be used if: (1) there is a well-established connection between the vaccine and its intended target; (2) the vaccine's safety and effectiveness is demonstrated in an animal species providing an adequate prediction for the human body's response;

(3) the evidence shows that the vaccine improved survival or prevention rates; and (4) the data allows for a reasonable expectation of the effective dosage rate in human beings.

The Animal Rule does not apply if other FDA standards provide approval of the vaccine (e.g., the accelerated approval program). Furthermore, post-market studies must be conducted once feasible and the FDA may impose post-marketing restrictions on the vaccine's distribution if necessary. As of early 2021, the FDA has only used the Animal Rule to license *one* vaccine, an anthrax vaccine that was already in use, for other uses after suspected or confirmed exposure to the bacteria.[2]

2.1.3.3 Emergency Use Authorization

The previously mentioned licensing alternatives all end with the same general result, vaccine licensing and approval. Under EUA however, the FDA can enable access to an *unapproved* vaccine. The FDA can only grant an EUA after an emergency has been declared by the Secretary of the Department of Health and Human Services (HHS). Until December 2020, an EUA had never been granted for an unlicensed vaccine (a licensed and used anthrax vaccine was given an EUA for a secondary use in 2005). However, since December of 2020, an EUA has been granted to the Pfizer, Moderna, and Janssen COVID-19 vaccines. EUAs can only be issued if the targeted disease or condition is serious or life-threatening; it is reasonable to believe that the vaccine *may be effective* in treating the disease or condition (as opposed to traditional licensure, which requires substantial evidence showing safety and effectiveness); under best available evidence, the vaccine's benefits outweigh its risks; and there is no adequate alternative to the vaccine.

In reality, when approving the EUA for COVID-19 vaccines, the FDA imposed a higher standard, an EUA-plus standard, requiring data from large, well-controlled human trials on safety and effectiveness. It is likely that the FDA will continue to apply this demanding standard to future vaccines, though the language of the statute does not require it.

If an EUA is granted, the FDA can impose conditions and restrictions. For example, the FDA can require the vaccine manufacturer to distribute certain information to healthcare providers and patients. Under an EUA, the FDA may waive regulations normally required to produce vaccines—referred to as "good manufacturing practices"—and prescription dispensing requirements. Lastly, the FDA may establish conditions on vaccine advertisements and other promotional matters.

2.2   Clinical Recommendations

After the FDA licenses a vaccine, the Advisory Committee on Immunization Practices (ACIP) under the CDC typically makes a clinical recommendation. A clinical recommendation usually concerns the age and population groups

[2]FDA, CDER Drug and biologic animal rule approvals (Feb. 15, 2022), https://www.fda.gov/drugs/nda-and-bla-approvals/animal-rule-approvals.

recommended to receive the vaccine and the number of doses or interval between doses of the vaccine. ACIP typically makes one of two clinical recommendations, full recommendation or clinical decision making. A full recommendation (also known as "Category A") means that a vaccine is recommended for *all* people in a defined group, except for individuals with specific conditions that would make the vaccine too risky. Clinical decision making ("Category B") means ACIP recommends the vaccine for certain subpopulations, such as those with increased exposure to a targeted disease. ACIP's recommendations are made after considering the disease, the vaccine's efficacy and safety, the cost-effectiveness of the vaccine program, and the strength of the supporting evidence behind the vaccine.

The CDC reviews ACIP's recommendations and usually adopts them as the CDC's official recommendations. ACIP's recommendations are important because they determine which vaccines are offered through various CDC programs. Once clinical recommendations are made, the CDC provides resources and training for healthcare providers who may administer the vaccine. We will learn more about ACIP in Chap. 3, when we discuss safety monitoring.

2.3   Special Considerations

As time progresses, manufacturers look for novel approaches to vaccine development. These novel approaches—specifically combination vaccines and vaccines designed to combat emerging infectious diseases and biothreat agents—can produce more effective vaccines, but present challenges for regulators and manufacturers.[3]

A *combination vaccine* consists of "two or more live organisms . . . combined either by the manufacture or mixed immediately before administration." Combination vaccines are either intended to prevent multiple diseases, or one disease caused by different strains of the same organism. Examples of combination vaccines include DTaP (diphtheria, tetanus, and pertussis) and the combination of hepatitis A and B vaccines. Two CFR provisions apply to combination vaccine development and licensure. Title 21, part 300.50 requires a combination drug to "demonstrate that each component makes a contribution to the claimed treatment effects, and that the dosage is such that it is safe and effective." Part 601.25(d) requires each component to contribute to the drug's effects while the combination does not decrease the purity and safety of each individual component. This is referred to as a non-inferiority requirement: the combination vaccine has to be at least as effective and at least as safe as each component separately.

The compatibility of the individual components is a major issue in preclinical development. A vaccine manufacturer must prove that combining the components does not adversely affect each individual component's safety and purity. Challenges in clinical testing of combination vaccines include:

---

[3] Falk and Leslie (2001), p. 1569. https://doi.org/10.1016/S0264-410X(00)00353-4.

(1) selecting the appropriate control arm (e.g., separate injections of the components); Because combination vaccines are usually created after there are individual vaccines available, giving saline placebo is both unethical and inappropriate. It is unethical not to protect people from a disease when there already is an effective vaccine against it. And because the question before the regulators is whether the combined vaccine is as safe and effective as the individual ones, the clinical trial should reflect that. This may affect trial design, because it is still important for the trial to be blinded, if possible—participants and those running the trial should not know who received what;

(2) determining the safe dosage amounts of individual components; and

(3) selecting the proper endpoints to demonstrate the combination vaccine's effectiveness.

Emerging infectious diseases (*EIDs*) *and biothreat agents* (germs that can be used in terrorist attacks or as a weapon) pose challenges because they require a fast response, and may require a global response. Responding to these needs presents significant regulatory challenges. Vaccines designed to combat EIDs and biothreat agents may be developed with novel technologies involving more complex science. In response, the FDA and CBER engage in programs to enhance "regulatory science," which can expedite the development and licensure of new vaccines. One example of such a program—though the initiative was not the FDA's—was Operation Warp Speed (OWS), designed to accelerate the development of a COVID-19 vaccine. OWS was a partnership between HHS, the Department of Defense, and several private vaccine companies.[4] OWS adjusted the normal vaccine approval process by investing in the actual manufacturing of vaccines *prior to* approval from the FDA and CBER.[5]

An issue with responding to EIDs and biothreat agents is the possibility that the threat is rare or nonexistent when the vaccine needs to be developed. COVID-19 was around during the vaccine process; but SARS had not yet spread widely when a vaccine was considered, and a bioterrorism airborne anthrax attack has not yet materialized—and both involved efforts at finding vaccines. This challenges a manufacturer's ability to obtain clinical efficiency data, yet the manufacturer must establish safety and purity standards before licensure. Experts therefore realize that regulatory science needs to develop improved predictive models and alternative methods to determine vaccine efficacy.

---

[4] U.S. Government Accountability Office (2021) Operation Warp Speed: Accelerated COVID-19 Vaccine Development Status and Efforts to Address Manufacturing Challenges. https://www.gao.gov/products/gao-21-319 Accessed 15 Oct. 2022.

[5] Ho (2020), pp. 615–618. https://doi.org/10.1016/j.xphs.2020.11.010.

2.4 Conclusion

Safety in vaccine development and distribution is paramount. For the past 119 years, the federal government has been involved in ensuring vaccine safety, with primary authority currently resting with the FDA's CBER. To market and distribute a vaccine, a manufacturer must generally obtain FDA licensure after extensive clinical testing of the vaccine's safety, purity, and efficacy. But licensing can take years, so Congress and the FDA have created pathways for expeditiously granting a license or approving access to an unlicensed vaccine. In such cases, the vaccine manufacturer is required to conduct ongoing safety tests to ensure that the already distributed vaccine is actually safe and effective. Once a vaccine is licensed (or access to an unlicensed vaccine is approved), the ACIP and CDC issue official recommendations for the vaccine's use and provide such recommendations to health care professionals involved in administering the vaccine. As EIDs and biothreat agents remain an issue, regulatory science will need to constantly improve in order to quickly and efficiently respond to new threats.

References

Baylor NW, Marshall VB (2011) Food and drug administration regulation and evaluation of vaccines. Pediatrics 127:S24. https://doi.org/10.1542/peds.2010-1722E

Baylor NW, Marshall VB (2012) Regulation and testing of vaccines. vaccines 2013:1431. https://doi.org/10.1016/B978-1-4557-0090-5.00073-2

Bodie A, Sekar K (2021) Congressional Research Service: Vaccine Safety in the United States: Overview and Considerations for COVID-19 Vaccines 4. https://crsreports.congress.gov/product/pdf/R/R46593/5. Accessed 15 Oct 2022

Falk LA, Leslie BK (2001) Current status and future trends in vaccine regulation. Vaccine 19:1569. https://doi.org/10.1016/S0264-410X(00)00353-4

FDA, CDER (2022) Drug and biologic animal rule approvals. https://www.fda.gov/media/107839/download

Ho RJY (2020) Warp-Speed COVID-19 vaccine development: beneficiaries of maturation in biopharmaceutical technologies and public-private partnerships. J Pharm Sci 110:615–618. https://doi.org/10.1016/j.xphs.2020.11.010

U.S. Government Accountability Office (2021) Operation Warp Speed: Accelerated COVID-19 Vaccine Development Status and Efforts to Address Manufacturing Challenges. https://www.gao.gov/products/gao-21-319 Accessed 15 Oct 2022

Postmarket Vaccine Safety

3

Abstract

Vaccines are held to a very high safety standard because they are given to healthy individuals. To ensure this high level of safety, a great deal of effort is put towards vaccine development. This effort has several forms, including obtaining a license to develop the vaccine, post-marketing studies, monitoring by several surveillance systems and federal committees, and more. To get a license, vaccine manufacturers have to provide pre-licensure clinical trials and research, which help identify the vaccine's common safety risks. But this research may not identify *all* long-term effects and may not recognize rare adverse effects. This is for two reasons. Even the largest clinical trials enroll tens of thousands of people; that is not enough to identify events that are 1 per a 100,000 or 1 per 1,000,000. And clinical trials are of limited duration. Vaccines are unlikely to cause side effects after a few weeks of receipt, because by then the vaccine has left your body and its direct impact on the immune system is complete. However, because vaccine safety is so important, we do not want to ignore even the theoretical risk that a vaccine will have side effects later on. Therefore, the Food and Drug Administration (FDA) requires a vaccine manufacturer to conduct post-licensure (or postmarket) studies and clinical trials. These postmarket studies and trials cover the vaccine's manufacturing process and health risks associated with the vaccine's use (Bodie and Sekar, (Congressional Research Service: Vaccine Safety in the United States: Overview and Considerations for COVID-19 Vaccines, 4, 2021.). Other mechanisms also help monitor vaccine safety.

© The Author(s), under exclusive license to Springer Nature Switzerland AG 2023
Y. T. Yang, D. R. Reiss, *Vaccine Law and Policy*, Law for Professionals,
https://doi.org/10.1007/978-3-031-36989-6_3

3.1   Postmarket Vaccine Safety

3.1.1   Manufacturing Safety

The FDA monitors vaccine manufacturing facilities pre- and post-market. The Secretary of the Department of Health and Human Services (HHS) may authorize an HHS officer or employee to inspect a vaccine manufacturing facility "during *all* reasonable hours." A vaccine manufacturing facility is subject to this inspection requirement for as long as the manufacturer's license is valid. The inspections are designed to determine whether a licensed vaccine is manufactured and tested in compliance with the license and applicable regulations. If a manufacturing facility fails to meet certain standards, the manufacturer's license may be suspended or revoked.[1]

Vaccines are manufactured in groups called "lots," and manufacturers must test all lots to make sure the vaccine is safe, potent, and pure.[2] Additionally, a manufacturer must maintain records documenting the manufacturing process of each batch or lot. These records must document serious problems (if any) that occurred during a vaccine lot's manufacturing, and a lot cannot be distributed until released by the FDA.

3.1.2   Surveillance

Postmarket government surveillance is designed to monitor the number of adverse vaccine reactions discovered during the pre-licensure phase, as well as unidentified adverse effects that occur postmarket. Postmarket surveillance programs include: (1) the Vaccine Adverse Event Reporting System (VAERS); (2) the Vaccine Safety Datalink (VSD); (3) the Sentinel Initiative; and (4) other various monitoring systems. These surveillance programs are described as "passive" or "active." A passive surveillance program means someone has to voluntarily report an adverse health event that happens after a vaccine; while an active surveillance program involves a proactive search for adverse events.[3]

3.1.2.1 Vaccine Adverse Event Reporting System
VAERS is a national system used by the Food and Drug Administration (FDA) and Centers for Disease Control and Prevention (CDC) to collect information about adverse health events and side effects that occur after vaccination. Any individual

---

[1]Baylor and Marshall (2011), p. S28. https://doi.org/10.1542/peds.2010-1722E.
[2]CDC (2011) Ensuring the Safety of Vaccines in the United States 2. https://www.fda.gov/files/ vaccines,%20blood%20&%20biologics/published/Ensuring-the-Safety-of-Vaccines-in-the-United-States.pdf. Accessed 15 Oct. 2022.
[3]Griffin et al. (2009), pp. S346–S347. https://doi.org/10.2105/AJPH.2008.143081.

(physician, nurse, or the general public) can submit an online report to the VAERS system about an adverse event following vaccination.

VAERS is a passive surveillance system, because it makes no effort to search for individuals dealing with adverse effects and no data is *actively* collected. When VAERS receives a report, it is classified as "serious" or "non-serious," as defined by an FDA regulation. A "serious" report involves death, hospitalization, or other life-threatening event occurring after vaccination. After a report is received, VAERS may require additional information—such as medical records or death certificates—from the reporter; and information from each report is entered into an electronic database and sent to the FDA and CDC for analysis.[4]

Like all programs, VAERS has strengths and weaknesses. Because VAERS has a nationwide scope, it can rapidly detect safety problems and rare adverse events. For example, VAERS allowed us to detect a serious complication of a Rotavirus vaccine in 1998 that happened in about 1: 10,000 cases, and to detect rare blood clots from Johnson & Johnson COVID-19 vaccines in 2021.

By allowing individuals to make direct reports and provide supporting medical records, VAERS is not subject to the delayed access faced by other medical monitoring systems. The speed with which reports can be made means VAERS often provides the fastest information on potential vaccine safety problems.

But VAERS is subject to reporting bias. This means that VAERS could experience underreporting, where not all people facing a problem file a report, or *elevated* reporting in response to increased public awareness of potential adverse events. For example, if people read online or hear that a vaccine can cause heart problems, many vaccinated people who had heart problems may file a report - whether or not the problem is vaccine related, and sometimes, even when the problem happened long after the vaccine. Also, VAERS reports are often incomplete, but the volume of reports (approximately 30,000 annually) makes follow-ups for all reports impracticable. Finally, VAERS data generally cannot be used to determine whether the vaccine actually caused the adverse event, or whether the adverse event was merely associated with vaccination (some commenters present the reports as if it could; that is a mistake) (Fig. 3.1).

3.1.2.2 Vaccine Safety Datalink

The VSD is operated by the CDC in partnership with eight healthcare organizations around the country. VSD is an active surveillance program with each participating organization submitting electronic health data to the VSD. The data includes vaccine information (kind of vaccine, date of vaccination, other vaccines given the same day), and information about patients' medical diagnoses or hospital stays.[5] Currently, approximately 9.2 million patients are covered by the VSD.

---

[4]Shimabukuro et al. (2015), pp. 4400–4401. https://doi.org/10.1016/j.vaccine.2015.07.035.

[5]CDC (2020b) Vaccine Safety Datalink (VSD). https://www.cdc.gov/vaccinesafety/ensuringsafety/monitoring/vsd/index.html. Accessed 15 Oct. 2022.

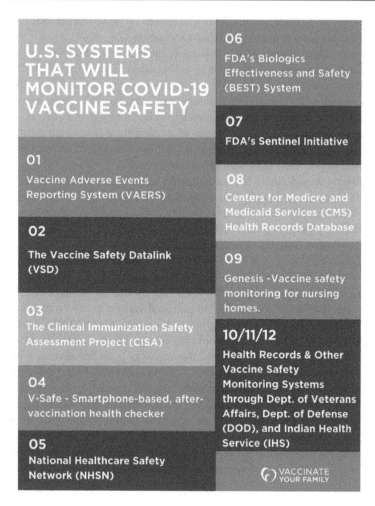

Fig. 3.1 The system in the U.S. for monitoring the safety of COVID-19 vaccines. Source: Vaccinate Your Family, https://vaccinateyourfamily.org/questions-about-vaccines/questions-and-answers-about-covid-19-vaccines/*

Unlike VAERS, VSD can serve to examine if there's a causal connection between a vaccine and an adverse event. The VSD data automatically includes a patient's full medical records, allowing a causal determination to be made through the system by comparing people who got a vaccine with people who did not.[6] VSD allows for rapid detection of large-scale adverse health events linked to vaccination. For example, VSD data was used to determine whether the measles-mumps-rubella vaccine had any association with autism (none).

---

[6]Nguyen et al. (2012), p. 292. https://doi.org/10.1002/pds.2323.

While VSD provides complete medical records allowing for almost real-time analysis, it is not without its limitations. The 9.2 million people covered by VSD do not completely represent the United States (U.S.) population in terms of geography, socioeconomic status, and other factors. The partnering healthcare organizations are private firms, generally over-representing people of higher socioeconomic status. Additionally, 9.2 million people may not be enough to detect extremely rare adverse events linked to vaccination.

3.1.2.3 Sentinel Initiative

In 2008, the FDA established the Sentinel Initiative. The Sentinel Initiative is a collaboration between FDA and various academic and private entities to develop methods for obtaining and analyzing vaccine safety data from multiple sources. As part of the Sentinel Initiative, the FDA has created two programs related to vaccines: the *Post-Licensure Rapid Immunization Safety Monitoring (PRISM) program* and the *Biologics Effectiveness and Safety (BEST) system*.

PRISM is an active surveillance program that monitors vaccine adverse health events, using data provided by insurance companies and state immunization registries. While VSD is a longer-established active surveillance program, PRISM is much larger (with data covering over 100 million people) and covers a wider geographic area. While VSD is limited by its size, PRISM's large population "enables more rapid evaluation of rare adverse events," and PRISM's data can "make its inferences fully generalizable." PRISM data also allows for analysis of vaccine adverse events based on subpopulation (e.g., race, ethnicity, age).

However, unlike VSD, PRISM cannot provide real-time information. Due to its size, PRISM data are updated less frequently than VSD (quarterly compared to weekly). Further, VSD allows for medical records access only days or weeks after a need for records is identified. Medical records associated with PRISM may not be available for several months after they are needed. This is because the FDA's partners are insurance companies (not healthcare providers like VSD) who do not *own* the medical records. Therefore, insurance companies must receive medical records from healthcare providers and contract with vendors to conduct reviews.

As its name suggests, BEST casts a wider net than PRISM. PRISM focuses solely on immunizations, while BEST covers vaccines and other biologics (such as blood products, tissue products, and other therapeutic biologic treatments). BEST is a relatively new program (established in 2017) and is designed to "build data, analytics, infrastructure for an active, large-scale, efficient surveillance system for biologic products."[7]

---

[7]U.S. Food & Drug Administration (2022) CBER Biologics Effectiveness and Safety (BEST) System. https://www.fda.gov/vaccines-blood-biologics/safety-availability-biologics/cber-biologics-effectiveness-and-safety-best-system. Accessed 18 Oct. 2022.

3.1.2.4 The Clinical Immunization Safety Assessment (CISA) Project

The Clinical Immunization Safety Assessment Project (CISA) is another CDC safety project, whose goal is to "improve understanding of adverse events following immunization (AEFI) AEFI at the individual-patient level".[8] CISA provides a few services. First, it offers two kinds of case-specific evaluations to healthcare providers. It can offer consultation and answers on whether a patient can be safely vaccinated. And it can offer consultation on whether a specific condition is vaccine related. In both cases, CISA acts as a final catchall, available for things not addressed by the CDC, and its consultations are limited to healthcare providers, not patients. In addition, CISA also conducts research studies related to vaccine safety focused on specific vaccines or specific populations (like individuals with autoimmune conditions or who are pregnant).

3.1.2.5 Other Safety Monitoring Systems

Along with FDA and CDC, other federal agencies conduct vaccine safety monitoring. The National Institutes of Health (NIH) is the primary federal agency supporting medical and health research, which includes vaccine research. The Centers for Medicare & Medicaid Services monitors vaccine safety among people 65 and older (*i.e.*, the Medicare population). The Agency for Healthcare Research and Quality (AHRQ) conducts vaccine safety reviews. The Health Resources and Services Administration (HRSA) administers the National Vaccine Injury Compensation Program (we discuss the program more fully in Chap. 5). And the Indian Health Service operates a database for vaccine safety monitoring of American Indian and Alaska Native people.[9] The aforementioned agencies fall under the purview of HHS, but other departments monitor vaccine safety too. The Department of Defense (DOD) has a database for monitoring vaccine adverse events for military service members and their families. Finally, the Department of Veterans Affairs (VA) has a similar database for veterans receiving care in the VA system.

3.2 Federal Research on Vaccine Safety

To determine whether a causal link exists between a vaccine and reported adverse events, scientists conduct various types of research regarding vaccine safety. There are three major types of research related to vaccines. *Biological research* explores how vaccines act in biological systems (animals, cell cultures, human tissue samples). This gives scientists an understanding of how adverse events may occur. *Epidemiological research* involves health data collected from human populations

---

[8]CDC (2020a) Clinical Immunization Safety Assessment (CISA) Project, Vaccine Safety Monitoring – CISA. https://www.cdc.gov/vaccinesafety/ensuringsafety/monitoring/cisa/index. html. Accessed 18 Oct. 2022.

[9]Indian Health Service Agency Overview. https://www.ihs.gov/aboutihs/overview/. Accessed 15 Oct. 2022.

(*e.g.*, VSD, VAERS, or PRISM) to explore statistical associations between vaccines and adverse events. Finally, *clinical research* involves actual patients and allows scientists to understand how adverse health events affect patients. Federal agencies—CDC, NIH, FDA, and others—conduct these various types of research to evaluate vaccine safety. This research is conducted by Scientists in U.-S. Universities, U.S. Agencies, and by scientists in foreign countries. We elaborate here on the research done by U.S. agencies.

3.2.1 CDC, NIH, & FDA

CDC research typically involves epidemiological and clinical studies. Its publications use data and findings from the safety monitoring systems mentioned above (VSD and VAERS). The CDC's research usually focuses on specific vaccines in specific populations, and hypothesized side effects or adverse events potentially attributable to vaccination. The NIH tends to focus on more biological research than the CDC. NIH research studies include physiological and immunological responses to vaccines, how generic variations respond to vaccines, and risk factors for adverse responses to vaccinations. Within the NIH, the National Institute of Allergy and Infectious Diseases supports the Human Immunology Project Consortium (HIPC). HIPC was established in 2010 to collect biological data over time on the immune systems of a diverse group of patients. HIPC data is used to study whether relationships exist between short-term vaccine adverse events and long-term health effects.

The FDA conducts regulatory science (the scientific and technical foundations upon which regulations are based in various industries—particularly those involving health or safety), which is used to evaluate vaccine safety and support the development of new vaccines. The FDA also studies adjuvants (which enhance a body's immune response)[10] and vaccine availability. For example, FDA research has focused on influenza vaccine production and ensuring a sufficient supply of a safe influenza vaccine.

3.2.2 Other Federal Research

As mentioned above, other federal agencies and departments like DOD and VA support vaccine safety research. Additionally, the National Vaccine Program Office within HHS offers grants to support vaccine safety research; and the AHRQ (also within HHS) has conducted safety reviews.

Federal agencies (primarily HHS) conduct periodic comprehensive scientific reviews of vaccine safety. These reviews evaluate and synthesize evidence from a

---

[10]CDC (2022) Adjuvants and Vaccines. https://www.cdc.gov/vaccinesafety/concerns/adjuvants. html. Accessed 18 Oct 2022.

large number of studies to assess vaccine safety. In 2011, the National Academy of Science, Engineering and Medicine (then, the Institute of Medicine), a private non-profit with acknowledged expertise, was contracted by HHS to assess the safety of 8 pediatric vaccines. This comprehensive review has been used to inform vaccine safety and compensation programs and has been updated several times since its inception.

3.3   Vaccine Safety Review Challenges

Ultimately, postmarket safety studies try to assess causality between an adverse health event and a specific vaccine. In other words, does the data show that condition X (stroke, heart attack, etc.) is caused by vaccine Y? However, as compared to pre-licensure clinical trials, postmarket safety poses unique challenges. Clinical trials are conducted as well-controlled scientific experiments: one group gets the vaccine, and the other gets a valid control—saline, or something that is well known, or the buffering formula for the vaccine without the active ingredient. Postmarket safety studies deal with a large population of vaccinated individuals that may be demographically different from the population of unvaccinated individuals in the society. This can make it difficult to draw comparisons of outcomes between both groups. To address this, researchers use a variety of methods to assess causality. For example, researchers may use predetermined time intervals to determine whether a certain adverse event is related to a certain vaccine: if a problem develops within a certain time after the vaccine has been given, there may be a causal connection. This may capture short-term side effects, but may not capture others beyond that time frame. It is even harder for common events. For example, time intervals may show an increased rate of heart attacks after increased use of a certain vaccine. Yet heart attacks are relatively common during people's lifetimes. So, a trend showing this increased rate of heart attacks suggests that there may be an *association* between heart attacks and the vaccine, but does not show *causality*. Researchers need to conduct comprehensive scientific reviews mentioned earlier to truly establish causality.

When there is a question on whether a vaccine causes a long-term side effect, studies need to address that. For example, to research whether infant vaccines cause asthma or allergies, some studies looked at children 8–13 to see if there were differences between those who received certain vaccines and those who did not.[11]

---

[11] Bernsen et al. (2006), pp. 463–469. https://doi.org/10.1002/ppul.20397.

*We discuss key systems in the text. There are additional safeguards that are introduced since covid vaccines became available.

3.4   Safety in Vaccine Distribution

Taxpayer money funds over 50% of vaccines in the U.S. Therefore, federal agencies are involved in the supply and distribution of vaccines. Vaccines are distributed via healthcare providers, health centers, pharmacies, and government health departments. State governments vary in requirements for providers who are able to distribute or administer vaccines. This decentralized process can lead to vaccine distribution problems. In response, the CDC manages several programs designed to improve the vaccine supply chain. One such program is the Vaccines for Children (VFC) program (the program's funding aspects are discussed in Chap. 8). Under the VFC, a provider receives VFC-covered vaccines, so long as state or local coordinators certify that the provider meets program requirements.

The CDC manages two other important programs involved in vaccine distribution. First, the Vaccine Management Business Improvement Plan (VMBIP), which started in 2003. VMBIP is a coordinated effort between the CDC and state and local partners designed to improve management of the vaccine supply chain, particularly vaccines distributed through VFC. Over time, VMBIP has adjusted the forecasting for supply needs and improved inventory tracking among vaccine providers. The second program, Vaccine Tracking System, is an information technology program designed to manage the publicly funded vaccine supply chain.

3.5   Conclusion

If pre-licensure research is important to ensuring vaccine safety before the vaccine is distributed, postmarket safety monitoring and research is important to ensure the vaccine remains safe and to quickly respond to unforeseen adverse health events or to problems too rare to be identified during clinical trials. Postmarket safety includes the vaccine's effects on the body and the vaccine's safe and proper distribution. The government has numerous tools designed to ensure vaccine safety and respond to negative events.

References

Baylor NW, Marshall VB (2011) Food and drug administration regulation and evaluation of vaccines. Pediatrics 127:S28. https://doi.org/10.1542/peds.2010-1722E

Bernsen RMD et al (2006) *Haemophilus influenzae* type b vaccination and reported atopic disorders in 8-12-year-old children. Pediatr Pulmonol 41:463–469. https://doi.org/10.1002/ppul.20397

Bodie A, Sekar K (2021) Congressional research service: vaccine safety in the United States: overview and considerations for COVID-19 vaccines 4. https://crsreports.congress.gov/product/pdf/R/R46593/5. Accessed 15 Oct 2022

CDC (2011) Ensuring the Safety of Vaccines in the United States 2. https://www.fda.gov/files/vaccines,%20blood%20&%20biologics/published/Ensuring-the-Safety-of-Vaccines-in-the-United-States.pdf. Accessed 15 Oct. 2022

CDC (2020a) Clinical Immunization Safety Assessment (CISA) Project, Vaccine Safety Monitoring – CISA. https://www.cdc.gov/vaccinesafety/ensuringsafety/monitoring/cisa/index.html. Accessed 18 Oct 2022

CDC (2020b) Vaccine Safety Datalink (VSD). https://www.cdc.gov/vaccinesafety/ensuringsafety/monitoring/vsd/index.html. Accessed 15 Oct 2022

CDC (2022) Adjuvants and Vaccines. https://www.cdc.gov/vaccinesafety/concerns/adjuvants.html. Accessed 18 Oct 2022

Griffin RM et al (2009) What should an ideal vaccine post licensure safety system be? Am J Public Health 99:S346–S347. https://doi.org/10.2105/AJPH.2008.143081

Indian Health Service Agency Overview. https://www.ihs.gov/aboutihs/overview/. Accessed 15 Oct 2022

Nguyen M et al (2012) The food and drug administration's post-licensure rapid immunization monitoring program: strengthening the federal vaccine safety enterprise. Pharmacoepidemiol Drug Saf 21:292. https://doi.org/10.1002/pds.2323

Shimabukuro TT et al (2015) Safety monitoring in the vaccine adverse event reporting system (VAERS). Vaccine 33:4400–4401. https://doi.org/10.1016/j.vaccine.2015.07.035

U.S. Food & Drug Administration (2022) CBER Biologics Effectiveness and Safety (BEST) System. https://www.fda.gov/vaccines-blood-biologics/safety-availability-biologics/cber-biologics-effectiveness-and-safety-best-system. Accessed 18 Oct 2022

Vaccines and Intellectual Property

4

Abstract

Intellectual property (IP) is "any product of the human intellect that the law protects from unauthorized use by others" (Cornell Law School Legal Information Institute Intellectual Property. https://www.law.cornell.edu/wex/intellectual_property. Accessed 18 Oct. 2022.) or "creations of the mind, such as inventions; literary and artistic works; designs; and symbols, names and images used in commerce." (World Intellectual Property Organization What is Intellectual Property. https://www.wipo.int/about-ip/en/. Accessed 18 Oct. 2022.) In the world of biopharmaceutical technology, the two most important forms of IP protections are *patents* and *trade secrets*.

Patents are property rights granted by the government providing an inventor with exclusive rights to a process, design, or invention. In return, the inventor is required to disclose the invention to the public, though the public cannot use (or more accurately profit off) the invention without a license (Kenton, What is a Patent in Simple Terms? With Examples, 2022). *Trade secrets* complement patent protections and are defined as "information that derives economic value from not being generally known or readily ascertainable," meaning that the inventor has gone to reasonable efforts to remain unknown (United States Patent and Trademark Office, Trade secrets/regulatory protection, 2022; Bandyopadhyay et al., Trade Secrets and Patents: Similarities, Differences, and Interplay, 2020). In the United States (U.S.), obtaining a patent requires applying to the U.S. Patent and Trademark Office while a trade secret does not require an application to a governmental entity (Bandyopadhyay et al., Trade Secrets and Patents: Similarities, Differences, and Interplay, 2020).

The underlying theory behind IP protections is utilitarian; it views them as necessary to promote "socially desirable innovation." (Rutschman, Mich Law Rev Online 118:172, 2020.) This is because IP protections should incentivize inventors and firms to engage in research and development in areas that might otherwise be underfunded and underrepresented, because the patent gives them a

© The Author(s), under exclusive license to Springer Nature Switzerland AG 2023

Y. T. Yang, D. R. Reiss, *Vaccine Law and Policy*, Law for Professionals,
https://doi.org/10.1007/978-3-031-36989-6_4

monopoly for a period of time and protects them from competition (Rutschman and Barnes-Weise, The COVID-19 Vaccine Patent Waiver: The Wrong Tool for the Right Goal, 2021.). This utilitarian theory suggests that unless inventors and firms can protect the return on their investment, there is no motivation to produce certain products—why invest just for someone else to profit from it? In other words, investors fund research and development for goods that are expected to produce economic returns, and economic returns can only be guaranteed through IP protections (Rutschman, Mich Law Rev Online 118: 172, 2020.).

4.1   Vaccines and IP

The rest of the chapter addresses how the general economic framework applies to vaccines, given several important and unusual aspects of vaccine creation and distribution. Vaccine research and development is a critical component of public health preparedness, and vaccines have long been recognized as cost-effective measures to prevent and mitigate burdens of disease. This means that society has a strong interest in developing vaccines, but much of the work of actually doing that is done—and funded—by private companies. As mentioned above, investors and manufacturers fund research and development for goods that are expected to produce economic returns. So, how does vaccine development fit into this incentives-based IP regime? History has shown that investors have faced a "split landscape," where some vaccines fare quite well and other vaccines struggle,[1] with the majority of vaccines fitting into the latter category.[2] In this section we look at that reality. Then, in the subsequent sections we address the reality under which vaccine patents exist both for profitable and less profitable vaccines, and limited access to these vaccines. Our assumption there is that while rewarding innovation in vaccines is important, so is access. We address the potential use of vaccine patent waivers to improve access, the limits of that, and other approaches.

4.1.1   Positive Examples

The U.S. Department Health of Human Services (HHS) recently characterized vaccine research and development as "successful" and "well established."[3] Vaccine development has long been a priority in the U.S. and some vaccines—specifically polio, tetanus, and measles, mumps, and rubella (MMR)—continue to have stable and sizable markets. This is due in part to federal recommendations and free (or insurance-covered) access to vaccines, which in turn fuels research and development of said vaccines and demand for them. Further, some vaccines do well beyond

[1] Rutschman (2021), p. 113.
[2] Rutschman (2020), p. 172.
[3] Rutschman (2021), p. 113.

stable but limited markets. For example, human papillomavirus (HPV) vaccines generated substantial revenue for Merck. [4] Similarly, Pfizer's pneumococcal vaccine, Prevnar, was a blockbuster seller, doing as well as other drugs. [5] These are examples of vaccines that do well, attract research and development, and benefit from patents for at least some time.

4.1.2 Negative Examples

Unfortunately, economic success is not the norm in vaccine development. Scholars have noted several reasons why vaccines are a poor match for incentives-based IP regimes. *First*, many vaccines are regarded as unappealing goods to invest in. This is because it is difficult to quantify the savings generated by an effective vaccine. A vaccine is preventative, so success leads to a nonevent; and vaccine developers do not always derive direct economic returns from their products. *Second*, vaccines typically deliver long-term immunity through a single use (or only a limited number of uses). And the longer the efficacy of a vaccine, the smaller the demand. Limiting the market size of a particular vaccine limits the investment appeal. This is somewhat countered by the fact that every year a new cohort is born, providing a new naive population, but vaccines still do not enjoy the market of a drug that is repeatedly given. *Third*, vaccines—unlike conventional drugs—can be difficult to successfully deploy. Vaccines typically require the maintenance of a "cold chain" which complicates vaccine delivery, particularly to remote areas with extremely hot climates. *Finally*, the supply side of vaccines has decreased dramatically. Between the 1940s and 1990s, the number of licensed vaccine manufacturers in the U.-S. dropped from over 50 to below 10. This is predominantly attributed to rising regulatory costs which leads to perceived unprofitability of vaccines.[6]

The aforementioned issues lead to vaccine development being characterized as unprofitable. As a result, vaccine research and development "has been significantly underfunded, particularly from the mid-twentieth century onwards."[7] Outbreak-spiked funding for vaccine development is likely to decline as soon as the pandemic begins to wane. This may cut short many of the development projects now underway, as was the case during the recent outbreaks of Ebola and Zika. For the vaccines that are fully developed, there is no guarantee that they will be made available at affordable prices to all populations in need.

---

[4] Songane and Grossmann (2021), p. e0244722. https://doi.org/10.1371/journal.pone.0244722.

[5] Ward (2016) Vaccines are among big pharma's best-selling products. https://www.ft.com/content/93374f4a-e538-11e5-a09b-1f8b0d268c39. Accessed 18 Oct 2022.

[6] Rutschman (2020), p. 172.

[7] Rutschman (2020), p. 172.

4.2   Patent Waivers and Why They Are the Wrong Tool

On May 5, 2021, U.S. Trade Representative Katherine Tai announced that the U.S. would support waiving protections on COVID-19 vaccines, which represented a reversal of longstanding U.S. policy.[8] The World Trade Organization (WTO) is a non-governmental forum designed to resolve international trade disputes. As part of the WTO, the Trade Related Aspects of Intellectual Property (TRIPS) Agreement requires WTO-member countries to enact laws protecting various forms of IP. A related concept is *compulsory licensing*. Compulsory licensing occurs when a country that has issued an IP right authorizes another to utilize the IP-protected product without the original owner's permission. TRIPS allows countries to engage in compulsory licensing (but only of a patented product), so long as it is done to ensure domestic supply of a patent-protected product and the original owner is paid "adequate remuneration."

In October 2020, South Africa and India requested that the WTO issue a waiver allowing countries to not violate TRIPS if they suspended enforcement of IP rights "in relation to prevention, containment, or treatment of COVID-19." The TRIPS waiver would expand compulsory licensing authorization to cover *any* IP protections (not just patents) so long as it is for any use relating to COVID-19. This means that the waiver covers trade secrets. So, a country could suspend patent protections and mandate that a foreign company operating on the home country's soil disclose trade secrets—"something that would be unprecedented in the international arena."

When vaccine scarcity is an issue, patent waivers would certainly reduce the exclusivity held by certain manufacturers. So why do some experts feel that patent waivers are not the answer to vaccine scarcity? Why is the information that would be disclosed in patents not enough to increase the supply of vaccines? Because removal of exclusionary rights does not address two fundamental problems underlying vaccine scarcity, sufficient knowledge to replicate the vaccine and infrastructure and resources to produce the vaccine.

First, knowledge disclosed through patents may not be sufficient to allow a third-party to replicate the vaccine. Vaccine development can be highly dependent on specific manufacturing processes that may not be disclosed in a patent. Second, lifting IP protections for vaccines does not solve the problem of weak infrastructure and lack of raw materials necessary to effectively manufacture and distribute vaccines on a global scale. This includes a lack of qualified personnel available to instruct the recipient of newly-released information.

Countries have instituted compulsory licensing in the past—which is akin to the current patent waiver proposal—particularly for drugs needed to treat HIV/AIDS. Furthermore, many of those countries used compulsory licensing quite successfully. But the drugs at the center of successful compulsory licensing stories differ from

---

[8]Contreras (2021) US Support for a WTO Waiver of COVID-19 Intellectual Property – What Does it Mean? https://blog.petrieflom.law.harvard.edu/2021/05/07/wto-waiver-intellectual-property-covid/#more-30058. Accessed 18 Oct. 2022.

vaccines. Vaccines are much more difficult to replicate and third parties taking advantage of compulsory licensing did not face the significant knowledge deficits that may apply to vaccine development. An incentives-based IP regime is a problem for global vaccine development, but the primary issue is infrastructural and contractual in nature.

4.3 Other Approaches to Vaccine Distribution

If patent waivers are not the answer, then how can vaccine distribution improve? Experts and scholars have come up with several answers. These will be discussed in turn below.

4.3.1 Liability Regimes[9]

There has been a long debate about IP protections as property rights. To be sure, IP protections like patents are property rights, but experts have debated whether patents should be viewed differently than other types of property (for example, physical property). Judicial decisions linking patents and property rights have been predominately concerned with the economic benefits derived from IP protections. The following solution would allow patent holders to be rewarded economically, even if their exclusive use of a product is granted to competitors.

A liability regime (or "take-and-pay" regime) allows an inventor to use a patented product or idea, so long as the inventor pays an "objectively determined value" to the patent holder. Normally, a subsequent inventor seeking to quickly follow-up a patent holder's invention would need permission from the patent holder. Under a liability regime, the subsequent investor could "take" the technology needed for the subsequent invention, so long as proper value is paid to the patent holder.

Liability regimes are especially apt for (certain) vaccine development during times of public health crises (*e.g.*, the recent Ebola outbreak and the ongoing COVID-19 pandemic). This is because the subsequent inventor does not need to bargain with the patent holder up front, so vaccine development can be expedited. But a liability regime is not a cure-all for vaccine distribution issues. A liability regime is effective for simpler forms of vaccine technology but would not work for more complex versions. Additionally, liability regimes would be better suited for more developed vaccine technologies as opposed to emerging ones.

---

[9]Rutschman (2021), p. 113.

4.3.2 Public-Private Partnerships[10]

Partnerships between public and private actors have grown exponentially. Until the 1990s there were almost no public-private partnerships in drug development. But starting in the 2000s, the landscape began to change. By 2016, about 40 public-private partnerships were being developed annually. These partnerships are either "access" or "product development" partnerships.

Access partnerships pool resources to purchase and distribute biopharmaceuticals (including vaccines). The most prominent example is the Global Alliance for Vaccines and Immunizations (GAVI) which is supported by (at least in part) the Bill & Melinda Gates Foundation, governments, and international organizations like the World Health Organization. GAVI's mission is to increase equitable and sustainable use of vaccines in the world's poorest countries.[11] *Product development* partnerships sponsor early research and development for vaccines that otherwise may be underfunded.

Public-private partnerships are an answer to vaccine distribution and IP considerations. This is because an organization can award a vaccine developer a monetary grant for a project that a developer otherwise may not pursue. As part of the agreement, if the vaccine is economically successful, both the organization and developer can recoup economic benefits. Further, the organization will likely require the developer to make IP available to third parties and provide for "non-exclusive [and] royalty-free" licensing.

4.3.3 Intellectual Property, Technology, and Know-How Bank[12]

Patent waivers may not be the answer to vaccine allocation issues, in part because providing information to other developers is not sufficient. Rather, there needs to be a transfer of "know-how" and technology that is not otherwise included when patents are made non-exclusive.

An intellectual property, technology, and know-how (IPTK) bank could be a solution. An IPTK bank would pool IP rights and manufacturing information "that could be licensed as a package with associated training modules," and "could also offer assistance in navigating vaccine registration with national regulatory authorities." Like the aforementioned liability regimes, patent holders whose products become part of the IPTK bank would receive royalties.

The strongest barrier to creating an IPTK bank is agreement from vaccine manufacturers. To entice manufacturers, an IPTK bank would adhere to high regulatory standards, enforce IP rights, and ensure the availability of skilled workers. These characteristics of the IPTK bank would make manufacturers more willing to

---

[10]Rutschman (2020), p. 172.

[11]GAVI About our Alliance. https://www.gavi.org/our-alliance/about. Accessed 18 Oct. 2022.

[12]Crager (2018), pp. S414–S419. https://doi.org/10.2105/AJPH.2014.302236r.

transfer technologies, because it is something these manufacturers have done before. Vaccine manufacturers have engaged in numerous technology transfers with other vaccine manufacturers in developing countries. Allowing vaccine developers in developing countries access to an IPTK bank would lower those developers' production costs. This in turn, would reduce the cost of vaccines for citizens in developing countries.

4.4 Conclusion

IP is a major component of vaccine development. Unfortunately, the nature of vaccines means that a traditional incentives-based IP regime leads to underdevelopment of vaccines for numerous diseases and creates access barriers in some parts of the world. Some global organizations have suggested that patent waivers are the right tool to increase vaccine allocation across the country. But experts say that waiving patent rights is not the answer because there are infrastructural barriers to vaccine allocation that would not be answered by waivers. Alternatively, experts and scholars have developed other solutions to vaccine allocation including public-private partnerships and different regimes for handling IP rights.

References

Bandyopadhyay E et al (2020) Trade Secrets and Patents: Similarities, Differences, and Interplay. https://www.jdsupra.com/legalnews/trade-secrets-and-patents-similarities-20313/. Accessed 18 Oct 2022

Contreras J (2021) US Support for a WTO Waiver of COVID-19 Intellectual Property – What Does it Mean? https://blog.petrieflom.law.harvard.edu/2021/05/07/wto-waiver-intellectual-property-covid/#more-30058. Accessed 18 Oct 2022

Cornell Law School Legal Information Institute Intellectual Property. https://www.law.cornell.edu/wex/intellectual_property. Accessed 18 Oct 2022

Crager SE (2018) Improving global access to new vaccines: intellectual property. Technol Transf Regul Pathways 108:S414–S419. https://doi.org/10.2105/AJPH.2014.302236r

GAVI About our Alliance. https://www.gavi.org/our-alliance/about. Accessed 18 Oct 2022

Kenton W (2022) What is a patent in simple terms? With examples. https://www.investopedia.com/terms/p/patent.asp. Accessed 18 Oct 2022

Rutschman AS (2020) The intellectual property of vaccines: takeaways from recent infectious disease outbreaks. Mich Law Rev Online 118:172

Rutschman AS (2021) Property and intellectual property in vaccine markets. Texas A&M Prop Law J 7:113

Rutschman AS, Barnes-Weise J (2021) The COVID-19 Vaccine Patent Waiver: The Wrong Tool for the Right Goal. https://blog.petrieflom.law.harvard.edu/2021/05/05/covid-vaccine-patent-waiver/. Accessed 18 Oct 2022

Songane M, Grossmann V (2021) The patent buyout price for human papilloma virus (HPV) vaccine and the ratio of R&D costs to the patent value. PLoS One 16: e0244722. doi:https://doi.org/10.1371/journal.pone.0244722

United States Patent and Trademark Office (2022) Trade secrets/regulatory protection. https://www.
    uspto.gov/ip-policy/trade-secret-policy. Accessed 18 Oct 2022
Ward A (2016) Vaccines are among big pharma's best-selling products. https://www.ft.com/
    content/93374f4a-e538-11e5-a09b-1f8b0d268c39. Accessed 18 Oct 2022
World Intellectual Property Organization What is Intellectual Property. https://www.wipo.int/
    about-ip/en/. Accessed 18 Oct 2022

Vaccine Injury Compensation in the United States

5

Abstract

While vaccines have large benefits, they do have some risks. Anything that has an effect on the body has the potential to cause harm—if nothing else, an allergic reaction is often a possibility. Vaccines are safe because serious harms from them are very rare, and their risks are much smaller than the risks they prevent. This means that vaccines are not *perfectly* safe, and rare adverse events can lead to serious, and sometimes deadly, effects. This chapter addresses how to handle these rare effects. In essence, we argue that it is important to provide fast, generous compensation for the rare cases of serious harms from vaccines. We believe the United States (U.S.) chose correctly in making compensation for routine childhood vaccines easier to obtain through different processes than in civil court, and that it should do the same for COVID-19 vaccines.

This chapter sets out the case for no-fault compensation for vaccines, and then provides an overview of the main program used in the U.S., the National Vaccine Injury Compensation Program (VICP). This includes a historical overview of the creation of the program, a description of how it operates, and its strengths and weaknesses. We then provide an overview of the other vaccine compensation program in the U.S., the Countermeasures Injury Compensation Program (CICP), used to compensate people hurt by a product under emergency use authorization—like COVID-19 vaccines—and its strengths and weaknesses. While we refer shortly to other countries' compensation schemes, we leave most of this discussion for Chap. 7, which examines vaccine regulation in comparison. We conclude this chapter by suggesting both programs require reform.

© The Author(s), under exclusive license to Springer Nature Switzerland AG 2023
Y. T. Yang, D. R. Reiss, *Vaccine Law and Policy*, Law for Professionals,
https://doi.org/10.1007/978-3-031-36989-6_5

5.1   The Case for No-Fault Compensation of Vaccine Injuries

There are two major ways to compensate vaccine harms. One way is to direct them to the traditional court system, to be addressed under regular principles of tort law. The other is through a no-fault system. In both systems, claimants must demonstrate, to some required level, that their injury was caused by the vaccine, and prove their damages. But in regular courts, they will usually have to meet other conditions, as well.

By and large, claims for vaccine injuries in courts are going to fall into two broad categories. In the first, the person injured could try and sue the company that made the vaccine, alleging that the vaccine was not good enough. In the U.S. (and in most places, but this chapter focuses on the U.S.), this would usually be a product liability claim, and the claimant would be alleging that the vaccine is "defective." Defective is a legal term of art here, hence the quotation marks, and a vaccine can be defective in one of three ways. First, it could have been manufactured in a way that doesn't meet the manufacturer's own standard—what we call a manufacturing defect. In the 1950s, a major vaccine tragedy in the U.S.—the Cutter Incident—involved a polio vaccine that should have had an inactivated virus, and instead had a live one.[1] This defect requires discovering a real problem in the manufacture of the vaccine, which is uncommon.

More commonly, the claim would be that the vaccine's design is too dangerous—that the vaccine has more risks than benefits. Note, this does not mean that having risks makes a vaccine "defective" in this sense—otherwise, manufacturers of products like cars, knives, or any drug, really, would be sued all the time. Claimants would need to show evidence that the risks of the vaccine outweigh its benefits. This is difficult to do, as a vaccine's Food and Drug Administration (FDA) approval is based on demonstrating that the vaccine's benefits outweigh its risks. Finally, claimants may claim that the vaccine's manufacturers did not properly warn against its risks. This requires that the manufacturer did not include a warning—and after the initial claim, can be rectified by the manufacturer by simply adding a warning.

Showing a vaccine is "defective" in the ways described earlier can be hard or even impossible. Another claim claimants could make is to try and show negligence or fraud by the manufacturer—but that can be difficult, too. The other type of claim claimants can make is against the doctors that gave them the vaccine, claiming it was medical malpractice to vaccinate. Sometimes, there are circumstances supporting that. For example, if a doctor gave a live virus vaccine to a child with a known immune deficiency, that's malpractice. But most of the time, vaccinating children according to professional recommendations is not malpractice; arguably, not offering the vaccine and not advising the parents to follow the regular schedule would be malpractice. So, these claims can be hard, too.

The alternative to the different claims that could be made earlier are no-fault systems. No-fault systems would still require a claimant to show that the vaccine

---

[1] Offit (2005), pp. 1411–1412.

caused their injury, but the claimant would not have to show that anyone did anything wrong, or that the vaccine would be defective. Generally, no-fault systems remove individual defendants—companies or doctors—from the process. Compensation is through a fund that is managed either by the government or through an insurance scheme. By removing these other requirements, no-fault systems make compensation easier.

We believe there are very strong reasons to use no-fault systems for vaccine compensation, which makes compensation easier. First, vaccines provide both a private benefit to the individual as it immunizes them to a disease, and a public benefit, where more individuals are immunized, lowering the rates of disease in the population and increasing safety. There is an ethical argument that due to this, the rare cases of vaccine harms deserve compensation from a collective fund. Because the recipients contributed to the public good, the public should not leave them to bear the costs of harm alone. They deserve fast, generous compensation. Further, if a society imposes any mandate, that creates an even stronger argument for compensation. If society conditions any benefits on vaccinating, anyone who suffers a serious reaction should be compensated—that is the other side of mandates. It is unfair to require vaccines and leave an individual to bear any harmful consequences without financial support.

Similar arguments led multiple countries to adopt no-fault compensation programs.[2] Germany was the first to adopt such a program, in the 1960s, and as of 2011, nineteen countries have implemented one. Unfortunately, many countries still do not have such programs.[3]

Opponents would argue, especially in the U.S., that the torts system would allow for higher compensation, and that targeting companies or doctors who act wrong would provide accountability and deterrence. However, we believe that the increased difficulty in winning cases undermine those benefits, and that those with vaccine harms should be compensated even if they cannot show a defect or wrongdoing by a company. Further, targeting vaccine-making companies comes at a cost: because the profit margin of traditional vaccines is low, manufacturers facing unknown or high amounts of litigation may leave the market. Even if they can win most of the suits, the cost of litigation is not worth it. This means that even baseless litigation can deprive the populations of safe, effective vaccines.

This brings us to the U.S. system for vaccine injury compensation.

---

[2]Looker and Kelly (2011), pp. 371–78; Mungwira et al. (2020), p. e0233334.
[3]Mungwira et al. (2020), p. e0233334.

5.2   The Vaccine Injury Compensation Program (VICP)

5.2.1   Background and General Description

The U.S. saw proposals for vaccine injury compensation programs through the 1970s, but one was not adopted until the 1980s. This occurred when a rise in lawsuits led to vaccine manufacturers leaving the market.[4] In 1986, Congress passed the National Childhood Vaccine Injury Act, which, among other things, created the compensation program. Congress had two goals in creating the program: (A) To protect the vaccine supply. (B) To make compensation easier for claimants.[5] Manufacturers were leaving the market in response to a small number of high-profile litigation wins and increased litigation in response. Congress, seeking to avoid having no vaccines available, offered them limited immunity as part of the act; and claimants were offered an easier process to receive compensation.

VICP was a compromise between different interests. The no-fault scheme did not require claimants—now referred to as "petitioners"—to show fault. Petitioners need to show causation based on the conditions of the program, and there are three paths to showing it. First, a claimant may show that an injury found on the Vaccine Injury Table occurred in the prescribed time interval.[6] The table of injuries can be periodically revised by the secretary of Health and Human Services (HHS) based on the scientific literature, and often through recommendations by the National Academy of Medicine.[7] After a long period without updates (where most cases were off-table, slowing the process down and encumbering it),[8] the table was recently modified in 2017, and then again in 2018. This was in response to the twenty-first Century Cures act including pregnant women and unborn children in the list of people who can use VICP for compensation.[9] If a petitioner shows that the vaccine recipient suffered an injury of the type enumerated in the regulations at the "Vaccine Injury Table"—corresponding to the vaccination in question and that the onset of such injury took place within a time period also specified in the Table. If so, the injury is presumed to have been caused by the vaccination and the petitioner is entitled to compensation (assuming that other requirements are satisfied) unless the government respondent affirmatively shows that the injury was caused by some factor other than the vaccination.

---

[4] Barnes and Burke (2014).

[5] Kirkland (2016).

[6] Cook and Evans (2011), pp. S74–S77.

[7] Meissner et al. (2019), pp. 343–344.

[8] Kirkland, pp. 81–82, 130.

[9] The rule for the 2017 update can be found here: Health and Human Services Department (2017) National Vaccine Injury Compensation Program: Revisions to the Vaccine Injury Table. https://www.federalregister.gov/documents/2017/01/19/2017-00701/national-vaccine-injury-compensation-program-revisions-to-the-vaccine-injury-table. Accessed 20 Oct 2022.
   The Cures Act point is based on Meissner, Nair and Plotkin, id.

Second, a claimant may qualify for compensation for an injury not found on the Vaccine Injury Table ("off-table injury") if the claimant can prove that the vaccine caused the adverse event. The causation requirements here, too, are less than in the civil courts: in civil court, a claimant would have to show scientific evidence that there is a connection between the vaccine and the harm. However, in VICP, a plausible theory of causation backed by a credible expert can be enough, even if there is no good scientific data showing a link (though scientific data against a link would count). The third way a claimant may qualify for compensation through the VICP is by proving that the vaccine significantly aggravated a preexisting condition.

The second and third means of qualifying for compensation are more challenging for claimants because the claimant must establish causation for off-table injuries. However, these options make it so claimants are not necessarily limited to compensation for injuries found on the Vaccine Injury Table.

Most assessments of VICP suggest that while it is not perfect, it has achieved several of its goals, including stabilizing the vaccine supply and providing compensation, even in cases of doubt.[10] Unsurprisingly, in an area as contentious as vaccines, the program also has strong critics, both from the academic side[11] and from the anti-vaccine side.[12] We will address some of those criticisms in part C.

5.2.2 The Process

The procedure for obtaining compensation through the VICP has many steps and conditions. First, the claimant must file a petition with the U.S. Court of Federal Claims (Claims Court).[13] The petition must contain an affidavit and supporting documentation. Petitions must be filed within 3 years of the first symptom or significant aggravation of the injury, and petitions for vaccine-related deaths must be filed within 2 years of the death and within 4 years of the first symptom or significant aggravation of the injury from which the death resulted.

Unlike in civil court, the time is not stopped during the minority of the claimant: in the tort system, children can bring suit until they reach the age of 18 plus whatever time is allowed (usually 2–3 years), but in vaccine court, the three-year limit applies to children as well as adults.

After filing, the petition is sent to the chief special master to assign the petition to one of eight special masters. The special master conducts a proceeding which is, in essence, an administrative hearing, to evaluate the merits of the petition under the VICP. Manufacturers are not parties to these proceedings. Instead, claims are filed against the secretary of HHS who is represented by government attorneys. That apart, the procedure, like other administrative hearings, allows parties to submit

---

[10]Meissner, Nair, Plotkin, id. Kirkland.

[11]Engstrom (2015), p. 1631.

[12]Holland (2018), p. 418.

[13]Hickey and Ward (2021).

evidence and cross-examine each other's experts, and hearings can easily be very fact-heavy. The special master has 240 days to issue a decision that includes factual findings, legal conclusions, and, if the petition merits compensation, the amount of compensation.

After a special master decision, the petitioner has 30 days to appeal the decision to the Claims Court for review. Then, the Claims Court has 120 days to uphold the decision, issue a separate decision, or remand to the special master for further proceedings. Once the court issues its judgment, the petitioner has 60 days to appeal the judgment to the Federal Circuit (and there are further appeals, if the petitioner chooses to use them, to the relevant federal circuit court and then to the Supreme Court, if the Court is willing to take the case). If the petitioner does not appeal the decision, the judgment is final. After a final judgment, the petitioner has 90 days to inform the Claims Court whether the petitioner accepts the judgment or will file a civil action for damages in court. The time limits are often not adhered to.[14]

Claimants may choose to exit the VICP and bring a civil action in federal district or state court under one of two conditions: (1) the claimant can opt-out of the compensation program if the special master fails to hand down a decision within the statutorily prescribed period of 240 days, or (2) the claimant may reject the special master's decision if he is dissatisfied with it and file a civil suit if the Vaccine Act's other provisions do not preempt litigation.

Families must file a claim in the VICP within 3 years of the first manifestation of injury. The program allows families to exit (opt-out of) the process and bring a civil action in federal district or state court after the 240-day waiting period, or if the claimant rejects the special master's decision. However, the Supreme Court interpreted the act to limit access to the court for design defect claims.

In 2011, the Supreme Court, interpreting the Vaccine Act, concluded that claims of design defects are categorically preempted by the act.[15] In lay terms, what the court said is that for one kind of claim—the claim that the design of the vaccine is too dangerous to be allowed, because it has more risks than benefits—VICP is the only forum people can use. For other types of claims—claims that the vaccine did not have good enough warnings, or that it was manufactured badly, or that the manufacturer was negligent in some way or committed fraud—people can go to state or federal court if the program's deadlines are not met or if they are unhappy with the procedures. For a number of reasons, cases in which unhappy claimants then go to the courts are likely to be rare. First, because the requirements of the program are lower than civil courts, if someone cannot win in the program, they are very unlikely to win in civil court, and a competent, honest lawyer should tell them that. Second, the costs are much higher in the civil system; VICP is required to cover reasonable lawyer fees and all the costs, including expert fees, even if a party loses as long as bringing the case was reasonable. However, such cases are occasionally filed. Recently, a law firm partnering with anti-vaccine activist Robert F. Kennedy Junior

---

[14] Kirkland, 160–161.

[15] Bruesewitz v. Wyeth, 562 U.S. 223 (2011).

has filed a number of lawsuits against Merck over their Gardasil vaccine, for plaintiffs that first went through the program.[16]

Petitioners who successfully navigate the VICP may be entitled to compensation.[17] Compensation through the VICP includes: (1) actual and reasonably projectable reimbursable expenses directly related to the vaccine-related injury including cost of diagnosis, medical care, rehabilitation, counseling, and vocational training; (2) actual and anticipated loss of earnings; (3) actual and projected pain and suffering (capped at $250,000; these caps were set in the 1980s, and unfortunately not indexed. The caps should be updated and require reform); (4) vaccination-related death benefit (capped at $250,000); (5) reasonable attorneys' fees and other costs associated with proceeding on the petition. The VICP does not pay punitive damages. Additionally, under the Vaccine Act, manufacturers cannot be held liable for unavoidable injuries when a vaccine is properly prepared and a patient is adequately warned.

Successful claimants are paid through the Vaccine Injury Compensation Trust Fund (trust fund). The trust fund is funded through excise taxes imposed on covered vaccines (the VICP covers most vaccines routinely given in the U.S.). The trust fund may only be used to pay for vaccine-related injuries from vaccines subject to the excise tax at the time of payment and for certain government administrative expenses incurred when administering the program. The program has paid out approximately $4.5 billion in compensation since its inception.

5.2.3   Strengths and Problems of VICP

The VICP is a generally successful program. In a recent academic book, a scholar explained that VICP "has been successful not because it has managed to please both scientists and activists, but rather because it has compromised between a vision of scientific certainty and a duty to compensate individuals to uphold the immunization social order."[18] Positive results include the dramatic decrease in civil litigation against drug manufacturers, the stabilized vaccine supply in the U.S., the increase in the development of new vaccines, and the number of injured parties who have been compensated through the program. An article by two vaccine scientists with another doctor from the Division of Injury Compensation Program in the Department of HHS also claimed the program was successful.[19] Though their focus was on achieving high immunization rates, they saw such rates as dependent, also, on providing compensation "in an equitable, consistent, and timely manner" of the person harmed (or who perceives they were harmed) by vaccines.

---

[16] Jackson (2022).

[17] Hickey & Ward.

[18] Kirkland.

[19] Meissner et al.

However, the VICP is not without problems. One problem pointed out by multiple critics is that the program is much more adversarial than intended. The problem of addressing vaccine injuries was always going to be contentious. Furthermore, the adversarial nature of the proceeding, however unfortunate, is not surprising—especially since similar systems in the U.S., like workers compensation, have also become more adversarial than expected.[20] A combination of a topic that evokes strong reactions—vaccines—and a culture of adversarial legal battles, affected VICP.

VICP's institutional features have created other problems. The program suffers from delays and backlogs. This is partially due to special masters allowing cases with incomplete evidence—lack of experts, lack of records—to stay on the docket for a long time while the parties put the evidence together that the special master considers sufficient; part of this may be due to the need for more special masters.[21] A Government Accountability Office (GAO) report attempted to criticize the delay, but noted that there have been substantial improvements since 2009.[22]

Another problem is the low caps for compensation provided by VICP. Caps on compensation for death and non-economic harms—pain and suffering—were set in the 1980s at $250,000 for death and the same amount for pain and suffering. These caps should be adjusted. They have not been raised or adjusted for inflation, and are considered low in today's terms. In addition, the statute of limitations for the program is set at 3 years generally, and 2 years from a death. That is in line with torts statutes of limitations, but it does not stop for children, and for something as complex as a medical injury, a more generous statute might be appropriate. Both of these issues should be improved, but attempts to change them have been caught in battles around the vaccine court between anti-vaccine and pro-vaccine groups.

5.3   The Countermeasures Injury Compensation Program (CICP)

CICP creates a compensation scheme for persons injured by covered countermeasures and protects manufacturers, distributors, and dispensers of covered vaccines from liability for serious adverse injuries that result from administration of vaccines.[23] However, the CICP is a more restricted compensation scheme with much stricter limits and caps on compensation.[24]

CICP was created in 2005.[25] CICP has been used infrequently since its creation, but it was used for the H1N1 vaccine and is currently in use for the COVID-19

---

[20] Kirkland.

[21] Id, pp. 208–209.

[22] U.S. Government Accountability Office (2014).

[23] Meyers (2020), p. Issa082.

[24] Id, at 4.

[25] Hickey and Ward.

vaccines. The CICP was created by the Public Readiness and Emergency Preparedness (PREP) Act, and applies to measures covered by a PREP declaration—which
strongly limits liability of manufacturers, distributors, and administrators of any
covered product. For covered products, liability only attaches for a narrow set of
willful behaviors; there is no possibility to bring a product liability or negligence
claim (unlike VICP, where claims other than design defect claims are still available
after going through the program).[26] Willful misconduct under the act means that the
person "acted (i) intentionally to achieve a wrongful purpose; (ii) knowingly without
legal or factual justification; *and* (iii) in disregard of a known or obvious risk that is
so great as to make it highly probable that the harm will outweigh the benefit."[27] This
would not cover most cases of vaccine harms, so there is no access to the courts for
those cases. This is much narrower than for cases covered under VICP.

At the beginning of the COVID-19 pandemic, for example, the Secretary of HHS
issued a declaration under the Public Readiness and Emergency Preparedness Act—
a PREP act declaration, as it is called—limiting liability of manufacturers,
distributors and providers of any countermeasures against the disease.[28]
Countermeasures are any "drug or device, as defined in the Federal Food, Drug,
and Cosmetic (FD&C) Act or a biological product, as defined in the Public Health
Service (PHS) Act that is (i) manufactured, used, designed, developed, modified,
licensed or procured to diagnose, mitigate, prevent, treat, or cure a pandemic or
epidemic or limit the harm such a pandemic or epidemic might otherwise cause;
(ii) manufactured, used, designed, developed, modified, licensed, or procured to
diagnose, mitigate, prevent, treat, or cure a serious or life-threatening disease or
condition caused by such a drug, biological product, or device; (iii) or a product or
technology intended to enhance the use or effect of such a drug, biological product,
or device." This covers not just vaccines, but tests of COVID-19 and any treatments
authorized or approved for it.

These covered programs may be compensated through CICP, but there are real
limits.

The CICP uses the Countermeasure Injury Table that lists injuries and time
intervals. If a petitioner can show a listed injury was sustained in the relevant time
interval, the CICP will presume it is the result of a covered countermeasure.[29] For
off-table injuries, the petitioner must prove causation based on compelling, reliable,
valid, medical, and scientific evidence beyond temporal association. This is a very
high bar; much higher than civil courts, and of course, much higher than the VICP's

---

[26] CRS Legal Sidebar (2022) The PREP Act and COVID-19, Part 1: Statutory Authority to Limit
Liability for Medical Countermeasures. https://crsreports.congress.gov/product/pdf/LSB/
LSB10443. Accessed 20 Oct 2022.

[27] Id.

[28] Health and Human Services Department (2022) Declaration Under the Public Readiness and
Emergency Preparedness Act for Medical Countermeasures Against COVID-19. https://www.
federalregister.gov/documents/2020/03/17/2020-05484/declaration-under-the-public-readiness-
and-emergency-preparedness-act-for-medical-countermeasures. Accessed 20 Oct 2022.

[29] Hickey and Ward.

relatively low burden. Proving causation often requires hiring medical experts and lawyers.[30] To be considered for compensation, a petition needs to be filed within a year of first symptoms. The CICP is more limited than the VICP, and all petitions for compensation are decided in secret without petitioners interacting with decisionmakers. Lawyers are not expected to participate, though petitioners would likely do well to work with a lawyer. There are no time limits for HHS to issue a decision. Further, CICP is a program of last resort; so, if a petitioner is, for example, entitled to worker's compensation, the petitioner will not also get compensation from CICP—even if worker's compensation does not cover everything.

Available compensation is limited to reasonable medical expenses, a capped award for loss of employment income, and a capped death benefit. Attorney's fees and pain and suffering damages are not available, making it costly for petitioners to claim off-table injuries.[31] Critics of the CICP say the process is inhospitable for petitioners, and it offers overbroad protection for covered entities.[32] There are alternative models, but they would require congressional action. One scholar suggests the CICP should be remodeled to resemble the September 11th Victim Compensation Fund (the Fund).[33] The primary objective of the Fund was to protect the airline industry and the World Trade Center's owners from liability, but the Fund also compensated those who were injured or had a family member die in the 9/11 attacks.

The Fund used an informal adjudication process, allowing victims to advocate for appropriate compensation and required final decisions within 120 days. The Fund was largely successful in protecting the airlines and the World Trade Center's owners from uncertain litigation as well as providing fair and prompt compensation to petitioners. Other alternatives include moving vaccines as fast as possible from CICP to VICP, or reforming the CICP to look more like VICP.[34]

5.4   Conclusion

Before the Vaccine Act, costly litigation over vaccine injuries threatened vaccine supply and created significant barriers to compensation for injured parties. The VICP addressed both sides of the issue by streamlining the compensation process for petitioners and shielding manufacturers from liability. The CICP was intended to boost innovation in times of public health emergencies, and, like the VICP, protect manufacturers from liability while offering a compensation scheme for persons injured by covered countermeasures.

---

[30] Meyers (2020), p. Issa082.

[31] Hickey and Ward.

[32] Meyers.

[33] Id.

[34] Zhao et al. (2022), p. Isac008.

VICP offers a reasonable balance between justice to claimants and protecting the vaccine supply. However, some of its features—like the compensation caps and the statute of limitations—need reform. Even with those, however, a no-fault system is better for claimants—reducing the barriers to compensation—and better for preserving the vaccine supply. CICP is a much more limited program, and arguably does not adequately compensate claimants.

There is opportunity to reform both the VICP and the CICP, and should be explored further.

References

Barnes J, Burke TF (2014) How policy shapes politics: rights, courts, litigation, and the struggle over injury compensation. Oxford University Press, Oxford

Bruesewitz v. Wyeth, 562 U.S. 223 (2011)

Cook KM, Evans G (2011) The national vaccine injury compensation program. Pediatrics 127:375, S74–S77. https://doi.org/10.1542/peds.2010-1722K

CRS Legal Sidebar (2022) The PREP Act and COVID-19, Part 1: Statutory Authority to Limit Liability for Medical Countermeasures. https://crsreports.congress.gov/product/pdf/LSB/LSB10443. Accessed 20 Oct 2022

Engstrom NF (2015) A dose of reality for specialized courts: lessons from the VICP. Univ of Pa Law Rev 163:1631

Health and Human Services Department (2017) National Vaccine Injury Compensation Program: Revisions to the Vaccine Injury Table. https://www.federalregister.gov/documents/2017/01/19/2017-00701/national-vaccine-injury-compensation-program-revisions-to-the-vaccine-injury-table. Accessed 20 Oct 2022. The Cures Act point is based on Meissner, Nair and Plotkin, Id.

Health and Human Services Department (2022) Declaration Under the Public Readiness and Emergency Preparedness Act for Medical Countermeasures Against COVID-19. https://www.federalregister.gov/documents/2020/03/17/2020-05484/declaration-under-the-public-readiness-and-emergency-preparedness-act-for-medical-countermeasures. Accessed 20 Oct 2022

Hickey KJ, Ward EH (2021) Compensation Programs for Potential COVID-19 Vaccine Injuries 4. https://sgp.fas.org/crs/misc/R46982.pdf. Accessed 22 Oct 2022

Holland MS (2018) Liability for vaccine injury: the United States, the European Union, and the developing world. Emory Law J 67:418

Jackson I (2022) Gardasil Injury Lawsuits Consolidated for Pretrial Proceedings in Federal Court System. https://www.aboutlawsuits.com/gardasil-injury-lawsuits-consolidated/. Accessed 20 Oct 2022

Kirkland A (2016) Vaccine court: the law and politics of injury. NYU Press, New York

Looker C, Kelly H (2011) No-fault compensation following adverse events attributed to vaccination: a review of international programmes. Bull World Health Org 89:371–378. https://doi.org/10.2471/BLT.10.08190

Meissner HC et al (2019) The national vaccine injury compensation program: striking a balance between individual rights and community benefit. JAMA 321:343–344. https://doi.org/10.1001/jama.2018.20421

Meyers PH (2020) The Trump administration's flawed decision on coronavirus vaccine injury compensation: recommendations for changes. J Law Biosci 7:lsaa082. https://doi.org/10.1093/jlb/lsaa082

Mungwira RG et al (2020) Global landscape analysis of no-fault compensation programmes for vaccine injuries: a review and survey of implementing countries. PLoS One 15:e0233334. https://doi.org/10.1371/journal.pone.0233334

Offit PA (2005) The Cutten incident, 50 years later. N Engl J Med. 352:1411–1412. https://doi.org/
    10.1056/NEJMp048180
U.S. Government Accountability Office (2014) Vaccine Injury Compensation: Most Claims Took
    Multiple Years and Many Were Settled through Negotiation. https://www.gao.gov/products/
    gao-15-142. Accessed 20 Oct 2022
Zhao J et al (2022) Reforming the countermeasures injury compensation program for COVID-19
    and beyond: an economic perspective. J Law Biosci 9:lsac008. https://doi.org/10.1093/jlb/
    lsac008

Immunization Information Systems

6

Abstract

Immunizations are important tools for reducing vaccine preventable diseases (Scharf et al., Acad Pediatr 21:S57, 2021) and by two years of age, over 20% of children in the United States (U.S.) have typically seen more than one healthcare provider (HCP), resulting in scattered paper medical records (CDC, Immunization Information Systems, 2019). Immunization information systems (IISs) are confidential, population-based, computerized databases that record all immunization doses administered by participating providers to persons residing within a geopolitical area (Scharf et al., Acad Pediatr 21:S57, 2021.).

IISs need to be thought of in two ways: their value for patients, and their value for broader, social policy. IISs can be a valuable tool in supporting a patient from childhood to adulthood, and help ensure that a patient is fully immunized. Pediatric HCPs can access IISs to obtain a patient's immunization records, which helps ensure that a patient is not over- or under-vaccinated. When a patient moves from pediatric care to adult care, IISs may facilitate the adult caregivers' knowledge of which vaccines a patient needs. IISs also contain reminder recall functions which remind patients of upcoming vaccinations, helping those patients stay up to date. Also, for a patient, IISs can help simplify transfer of immunization records when a patient moves between facilities or has to get treatment outside their usual doctor's office. IISs are also very important for public health. IISs can help identify vaccination gaps in a community before an outbreak occurs, allowing public health to target immunization campaign and warning them of vaccination deserts (places where people have trouble accessing vaccines), which can help solve access problems. During an outbreak, IISs are critical in providing timely insight into vaccine coverage and areas where vaccines are more urgently needed. Opponents would have concerns about the effect of IISs on medical privacy—concerns about disclosure of the data or hacking—and some vaccine-hesitant or vaccine-resisting individuals will be concerned that IISs can be used in enforcing vaccine mandates against them.

© The Author(s), under exclusive license to Springer Nature Switzerland AG 2023
Y. T. Yang, D. R. Reiss, *Vaccine Law and Policy*, Law for Professionals,
https://doi.org/10.1007/978-3-031-36989-6_6

Currently, there are 61 IISs across the U.S. These IISs operate within state and city health departments, and are overseen by the Center for Disease Control and Prevention's (CDC) National Center for Immunization and Respiratory Disease (NCIRD) and Immunization Services Division (ISD) (Greenberger, The Imperative of Immunization Interoperability and Information Sharing, 2021.). Over two decades ago, a national immunization registry was explored but not ultimately enacted.

Filling its oversight role, the CDC has been publishing standards for IISs since the early 2000s. The most current version of these standards is Version 4.1, developed in 2019. The CDC also publishes the IIS Annual Report (IISAR) which measures progress towards meeting IIS standards. The IISAR is published annually, and assesses programs that receive funding under Section 317b of the Public Health Service Act (PHSA) (See Chap. 8 for a more thorough discussion of that program and other funding mechanisms. Over the years, IIS standards have focused on several core concepts. These are: data quality, provision of data to stakeholders, privacy and confidentiality, clinical decision support, data exchange with Electronic Health Records (EHRs), and support of immunization program operations. Currently, these core concepts focus on "system functionality," but as IISs improve functionally, the emphasis will be placed on "data quality." This is because HCPs "rely on high-quality data from IIS[s] to aid with clinical decisions, ensuring coverage estimates are reliable, and identifying vulnerable populations to target for interventions." (Scharf et al., Acad Pediatr 21: S57, 2021.)

6.1   Challenges in the Current State

Because there is no nationwide IIS, local and state governments largely govern IISs' implementation, leading to issues of overlapping or conflicting laws and regulations. HCPs may in turn utilize different information systems and data standards which may lead to inconsistencies and potentially inaccurate data.[1] This section will describe challenges to IIS implementation based on policy considerations and data sharing.

6.1.1   Policy

While the CDC publishes standards for IISs, there is no national reporting law for immunizations. Local governance of IIS implementation is subject to varying statutes and rules; and some jurisdictions that require IIS reporting do not have enforcement mechanisms in place. A recent study of numerous IISs demonstrated various jurisdictional laws governing IISs. For one, 58.5% of jurisdictions mandated

---

[1] Greenberger.

at least 1 type of HCP to report immunizations while 41.5% had no such mandate. Even within jurisdictions that mandate reporting, the mandate may be limited to certain age groups or certain vaccines. Jurisdictions also have varying requirements for patient consent to share immunization information. In 66.6% of studied jurisdictions, IISs relied on the *implied consent* of adult patients to share immunization information; unless an individual explicitly objected to being included, it was assumed that the individual agreed to his, her or their information being recorded. In contrast, 15.9% of jurisdictions required explicit consent, in other words, the individual had to explicitly agree to information being included, and 17.6% automatically recorded information without requiring any consent.[2] IISs across the country are far from standardized. In the first situation, individuals seeking not to have their information included need to actively ask their doctor how to avoid it. In the second situation, they will be asked. In the third situation there may not be an easy path to avoid having your information included, but patients who do not want to be included should ask. If there is no path, it may be something to raise with the patient's political representative.

Although the main direct regulation of IIS comes from state or local laws it is not solely state and local law that impacts IIS data quality. Federal laws like the Health Insurance Portability and Accountability Act (HIPAA) and Family Education Rights and Privacy Act (FERPA) impact immunization information reporting even if they do not directly focus on IISs. While HIPAA allows the disclosure of personal health information in certain circumstances—such as public health surveillance, investigations or when state law requires it—HCPs interpret HIPAA differently, which may limit the amount of information provided to an IIS.

FERPA restricts a school's ability to share information from a student's educational record without parental consent. Immunizations are part of a student's educational record, thus FERPA precludes the school from sharing immunization information with an IIS. However, FERPA does have an exemption in case of an emergency whereby the school can disclose a student's information—without parental consent—if there is an "articulable and significant" threat to public health.[3] The Department of Education (DOE), in March 2020, stated that the COVID-19 pandemic could qualify as such an emergency. According to the DOE,

> If the educational agency or institution determines that there is an articulable and significant threat to the health or safety of the student or another individual and that certain parties need [students' records], to protect the health or safety of the student or another individual, it may disclose that information to such parties *without consent*.[4]

---

[2] Martin et al. (2015), pp. 298–299.

[3] Scharf et al. (2021), p. S57.

[4] Department of Education (2020) Student Privacy Policy Office FERPA & Coronavirus Disease 2019 (COVID-19) Frequently Asked Questions (FAQs). https://studentprivacy.ed.gov/sites/default/files/resource_document/file/FERPA%20and%20Coronavirus%20Frequently%20Asked%20Questions.pdf. Accessed 20 Oct 2022.

It is not clear, however, that this would cover disclosing COVID-19 vaccine status to an IIS, as opposed to disclosing a diagnosis of COVID-19 to health officials tracking an outbreak or a medical facility requiring treatment.

Another policy challenge for IISs are they limit the ability to easily share data among jurisdictions. The technology exists for data exchange between IISs and EHRs. But current policies do not allow an IIS to share any data without establishing a "data sharing agreement" between the IIS and each individual entity with which data are to be shared.[5] These policies severely affect individuals who receive care in one jurisdiction but live in another, because the care-giving state's IIS cannot report to the IIS in the individual's home state. Varying jurisdictional rules impact HCPs' abilities to use IISs for clinical and public health decisions.[6]

6.1.2   Data Sharing and Use

The lack of nationwide, standardized IIS requirements can lead to ineffective data sharing and use even where there are no legal barriers for disclosure (for example, where it is in the same state, or across states when patient consents or even asks for disclosure). For example, effective IIS data use relies on patient matching and patient status. Currently, IISs independently develop identity algorithms to match persons from various records (*e.g.*, medical claims and vital records of individuals). But, simple clerical errors such as the misspelling of an individual's name can cause serious challenges for patient matching. Because there is no unique national patient identifier, systems operate under probabilistic algorithms to make matches, but the algorithms are far from perfect. This in turn requires human review, which is time-consuming and costly.

One solution is the federal Trusted Exchange Framework and Common Agreement (TEFCA). TEFCA is a set of nonbinding principles developed by the federal government intended to foster trust among data exchange partners and allow exchange of health data in a variety of contexts.[7] TEFCA aims to enhance IIS data quality by facilitating exchange of data across jurisdictions among trusted partners participating as Qualified Health Information Networks (QHINs). But there are barriers preventing IISs from realizing the full potential of TEFCA's benefits. For example, TEFCA requires QHIN's to comply with HIPAA privacy and security requirements. This requirement may limit an IIS's ability to share medical records unless one of the exceptions to HIPAA applies (for example, a public health need).

---

[5] Martin et al. (2015), pp. 296–303.

[6] Scharf et al. (2021), p. S57.

[7] The Office of the National Coordinator for Health Information Technology (2022) Trusted Exchange Framework and Common Agreement. https://www.healthit.gov/topic/interoperability/ trusted-exchange-framework-and-common-agreement-tefca. Accessed 20 Oct 2022.

6.2 Future State Considerations

The previous section demonstrates that local control and governance—along with federal statutory provisions—can limit the effectiveness of IISs. These inefficiencies prevent IISs from creating high-quality data that can be used to improve the allocation, distribution, and overall use of immunizations across the U.S., and can interfere with a smooth transfer of patients' records. So, what can be done?

6.2.1 Ways to Improve IIS Infrastructure and Facilitate Data Exchange

The CDC and the Department of Health and Human Services (HHS) are sponsoring pilot programs designed to combat barriers to IIS efficiencies. One such program is the Immunization Gateway (Gateway). The Gateway is designed to simplify the process for HCPs—operating across several jurisdictions—to connect with one another and exchange information.

Currently, HCPs operating across multiple jurisdictions must consider the differences in local reporting rules. The Gateway would connect IIS platforms to a single cloud-based hub, allowing for more complete and timely immunization data. This streamlined data process would create what is known as a *data lake*. A data lake "is a system or repository of all enterprise data for tasks such as reporting, visualization, and advanced analytics."[8] In other words, it's a collection of data from different sources that can then be used for a variety of things. An immunization data lake would provide the CDC and other authorized entities access to high-quality, streamlined immunization data that can be extracted and analyzed. It should also make transfer of information between systems smoother and easier, helping patients.

In addition, experts argue that a strong IIS requires complete demographic information, including race/ethnicity, occupation, and residence type (*e.g.*, long-term care). Some demographic data are included in the CDC's guidance on effective IISs but are not always included in an actual IIS. Experts also call for "increased linkage" between IISs and EHRs. This increased linkage would support more rigorous evaluations of IIS data increasing vaccine campaign awareness.[9]

6.2.2 Ways to Ensure Consistent Implementation and Lower IIS Costs

Again, IISs are subject to varying rules and laws based on the jurisdiction in which they operate. This means that IISs' technology infrastructures vary and are not based on any single platform. The uncoordinated development of IIS technologies leads to

---

[8]Scharf et al. (2021), p. S57.
[9]Benjamin-Chung and Reingold (2021), p. 1077.

sustainability challenges, which experts say can be mitigated by consistent collaboration and planning which would avoid redundant maintenance and unnecessary
infrastructure costs.

The Measurement and Improvement initiative is a project of the American
Immunization Registry Association (AIRA) and the CDC. The initiative measures
IIS functionality and capability in the various IIS standards described as core
concepts above. While participation in the initiative is voluntary, a significant
majority of IISs have participated. The initiative conducted baseline measurements
of IISs, and over the years significant progress has been made in each measurement
area.[10]

Additionally, efforts are underway to improve data exchange between Electronic
health records (EHRs) and IISs. At the most basic level, EHRs are computerized
versions of patients' paper charts. But when fully operable, EHRs are "real-time,
patient-centered records." EHRs can inform HCPs about evidence-based tools in
making decisions about a patient's care, streamline HCPs' workflows, and increase
organization and accuracy of patient information.[11]

The Immunization Integration Program (IIP) is sponsored by the CDC and is
designed to bring together EHRs and IISs in order to improve data exchange
between the systems. The IIP's goal is to develop solutions enabling clinicians and
IISs timely access to complete and accurate immunization data. Increased access will
improve the decision-making of HCPs and increase vaccine coverage across the
U.S. To improve access, the IIP is seeking to address variabilities in the way EHRs
and IISs communicate and seeking to promote standardization in data transport
methods across EHRs and IISs.[12]

6.2.3 Ways to Support the Needs of Immunization Data Stakeholders

The CDC is sponsoring two pilot projects related to IIS data access and use. The first
project includes a workgroup of stakeholders that will define business requirements
for data request and approval processes and data use agreement procedures. In turn,
the business requirements will facilitate access to IIS data and other analysis tools for
stakeholders.

The second CDC pilot project is focused on testing statistical models to estimate
population level vaccination coverage using "imperfect" IIS data. Potential
methodologies and considerations were developed during a 2019 panel of national

---

[10] American Immunization Registry Association Measurement & Improvement Initiative. https://www.immregistries.org/measurement-improvement. Accessed 20 Oct 2022.

[11] The Office of the National Coordinator for Health Information Technology What are Electronic Health Records (EHRs)? https://www.healthit.gov/topic/health-it-and-health-information-exchange-basics/what-are-electronic-health-records-ehrs. Accessed 20 Oct. 2022.

[12] Scharf et al. (2021), p. S57.

experts, and the CDC is now testing for feasibility. If successful, the project will lead to improved IIS data and increased access to the improved data. This in turn will significantly augment HCPs' abilities to focus interventions on vulnerable populations, monitor and respond to outbreaks of vaccine-preventable diseases, and provide comprehensive patient data to clinical providers.[13]

6.2.4   Sustainable Funding

Running and maintaining an IIS can be costly. One study found that the annual cost of running a large IIS network was $108 million.[14] If IISs are to improve, additional funding is needed to support infrastructure and manpower needs. IISs are currently funded by federal, state, and local governments, as well as foundations. Since 2014, section 317 of the PHSA has provided federal funding for immunization programs at roughly $611 million, far from enough to enact meaningful and lasting changes (as a reminder, there are 61 such programs across states and other entities. So even if over $600 million sounds high, for such a large range of programs, it is not a lot.

However, over the past year, the CDC has received significant funding to be used for vaccine development. In March 2020, the Coronavirus Preparedness and Response Supplemental Appropriations Act gave the CDC $500 million to modernize public health data systems. In December 2020, a coronavirus stimulus bill provided the CDC $8.75 *billion* in funding to support COVID-19 vaccine dissemination and measurement of vaccine coverage. These funding grants would go a long way towards ensuring IISs nationwide are improved, and may help create coordination between them. This funding may also be used to incentivize local health care entities to improve and standardize IISs in exchange for funding from the CDC. It remains unclear though whether the CDC will use any of its newly allocated funding specifically to enhance IISs.[15]

6.3   Conclusion

If immunizations are an invaluable tool in enhancing public health, IISs are important for properly allocating vaccines and achieving good coverage, as well as providing data that would allow us to address problems. IISs ensure that patients are provided with all immunizations required from childhood through adulthood and can take their records with them as they move; IISs also can help determine when certain geographical areas are in need of increased vaccine dissemination. But IISs face a host of challenges in their effective implementation. They are largely governed by state and local rules, which makes it challenging for HCPs who operate

---

[13] Scharf et al. (2021), p. S57.

[14] Patel et al. (2015), pp. 253–262.

[15] Benjamin-Chung & Reingold.

across several jurisdictions. Additionally, federal rules limit HCPs' ability to share health information, hampering an IIS's effectiveness. Because IISs operate in jurisdictions with varying rules, there is a substantial lack of standardization in IIS technologies and data.

Currently, the CDC and partners are implementing various projects designed to address these needs. The projects are designed to enhance the data sharing required for an effective IIS and the standardization of IIS technologies and data. These changes and implementations will require funding to sustain IISs going forward, but the improved effectiveness of IISs can only serve to enhance public health.

References

American Immunization Registry Association Measurement & Improvement Initiative. https://www.immregistries.org/measurement-improvement. Accessed 20 Oct 2022

Benjamin-Chung J, Reingold A (2021) Measuring the success of the US COVID-19 vaccine campaign—it's time to invest in and strengthen immunization information systems. Am J Public Health 111:1077. https://doi.org/10.2105/AJPH.2021.306177

CDC (2019) Immunization Information Systems (IIS). https://www.cdc.gov/vaccines/programs/iis/index.html. Accessed 20 Oct 2022

Department of Education (2020) Student Privacy Policy Office FERPA & Coronavirus Disease 2019 (COVID-19) Frequently Asked Questions (FAQs). https://studentprivacy.ed.gov/sites/default/files/resource_document/file/FERPA%20and%20Coronavirus%20Frequently%20Asked%20Questions.pdf. Accessed 20 Oct 2022

Greenberger M (2021) The Imperative of Immunization Interoperability and Information Sharing. https://www.himss.org/resources/imperative-immunization-interoperability-and-information-sharing. Accessed 22 Oct 2022

Martin DW et al (2015) Immunization information systems: a decade of progress in law and policy. JPHMP 21:298–299. https://doi.org/10.1097/PHH.0000000000000040

Patel M et al (2015) Economic review of immunization information systems to increase vaccination rates: a community guide systematic review. J Public Health Manag Pract 21:253–262. https://doi.org/10.1097/PHH.0000000000000100

Scharf LG et al (2021) Current challenges and future possibilities for immunization information systems. Acad Pediatr 21:S57. https://doi.org/10.1016/j.acap.2020.11.008

The Office of the National Coordinator for Health Information Technology (2022) Trusted Exchange Framework and Common Agreement. https://www.healthit.gov/topic/interoperability/trusted-exchange-framework-and-common-agreement-tefca. Accessed 20 Oct 2022

The Office of the National Coordinator for Health Information Technology What are Electronic Health Records (EHRs)?. https://www.healthit.gov/topic/health-it-and-health-information-exchange-basics/what-are-electronic-health-records-ehrs. Accessed 20 Oct 2022

Vaccine Regulation in Global Comparison

7

Abstract

Vaccines are one of the most cost-effective public health measures ever taken by the scientific community, and no doubt provide irrefutable benefit to societies across the globe. This benefit, however, does not come without consequences, and public panic over rare adverse effects has limited the impact that vaccine programs can have, especially during emerging pandemics and epidemics. Nearly every country grapples with the challenges to achieve the perfect balance between the need to provide vaccines for the greater good of society, against the need to provide safe, effective, and accepted vaccination for each individual. However, not every country approaches this challenge with the same strategy. In this chapter, we provide an overview of the differing ways in which countries handle vaccine rollout and regulation. As with our other global chapters, we do not provide an in-depth discussion of each country's approach. Rather, we paint in broad strokes, describing the themes across countries and using examples to demonstrate, while sometimes highlighting a country whose approach sheds light on new possibilities that may be applied in a global manner.

As we discussed in the previous chapters, vaccine regulation covers several areas, including bringing the vaccine to market, monitoring vaccine safety, intellectual property, and compensation for vaccine harms. We structure this chapter to mirror that: first, addresses vaccine authorization/approval; second, addresses safety monitoring, and third, compensation. We addressed intellectual property from a global perspective in Chap. 4, and therefore will not be evaluating that point in this section.

© The Author(s), under exclusive license to Springer Nature Switzerland AG 2023
Y. T. Yang, D. R. Reiss, *Vaccine Law and Policy*, Law for Professionals,
https://doi.org/10.1007/978-3-031-36989-6_7

7.1   Bringing a Vaccine to Market

Vaccine manufacturing capacity is not distributed evenly across the globe, and therefore countries vary on whether they produce their own vaccines or must import inventory from abroad. Of the variety of countries that do manufacture their own vaccine supply, the majority also export excess supplies to countries abroad in order to meet demands where vaccine manufacturing is not feasible or possible. Since 2013, China, for example, makes vaccines not just for itself, but for the global market.[1] Whether countries manufacture vaccines or import them, it is imperative that there is an infrastructure in place to ensure that the vaccines provided are safe. Most do so by entrusting vaccine approval and oversight to administrative agencies, such as The World Health Organization (WHO), for example. The WHO maintains a list of countries that have "National Regulatory Authorities" that it considers functional.[2] These regulatory authorities oversee the approval, manufacturing, and safety of each vaccine brought to market.

Within these regulatory authorities, the operational foundation is quite different from country to country. For example, political persuasion can play a role in how vaccine oversight is carried out, though the degree of political influence varies. Some regulators lean more towards an expert model of decision making, while others rely more heavily on a politicized model, where political authorities control the regulators' discretion.[3] Some countries work to pool data—for example, countries in Africa created the African Vaccine Regulatory Forum to allow collaboration between national regulatory authorities in developing and assessing vaccines.[4] In addition, the WHO provides a list complete with recommendations for vaccines.[5]

Generally speaking, regulators approve vaccines based on a risk/benefit analysis, however the process of analysis and approval is not always consistent. For example, although the European Medicines Agency (EMA, the agency that approves or provides emergency authorization for vaccines for the 27 members of the European Union[6]), is typically responsible for approving vaccines for European countries, the United Kingdom (UK) regulator went ahead and approved the temporary authorization of COVID-19 vaccines before the EMA completed its process.[7] An editorial in Nature explains that the Food and Drug Administration (FDA) usually does its own analysis of pharmaceutical companies' raw data, while EMA

---

[1] Li (2013).

[2] WHO List of vaccine producing countries with functional NRAs. https://www.who.int/initiatives/who-listed-authority-reg-authorities/list-of-vaccine-prod-countries. Accessed 23 Oct 2022.

[3] Heims and Tomic (2021).

[4] WHO African Vaccine Regulatory Forum (AVAREF). https://www.afro.who.int/health-topics/immunization/avaref. Accessed 23 Oct 2022.

[5] Nature (2020), p. 195.

[6] European Medicines Agency Science Medicines Health. https://www.ema.europa.eu/en/about-us. Accessed 23 Oct 2022.

[7] Mahase (2020), p. m4759.

relies more on the companies' analysis.[8] That said, regulators typically look for clinical trials, and assess their results on safety and effectiveness—for example, the FDA, the EMA, and Health Canada all did that for COVID-19 vaccines.[9]

Vaccine regulation surrounding authorization and approval don't always play out smoothly; in fact, some countries, like China, have seen several scandals surrounding regulatory approval. In 2018, a rabies vaccine manufacturer was found to have submitted falsified data for its vaccine.[10] In the same year, authorities discovered that hundreds of thousands of children were given ineffective diphtheria, tetanus and pertussis (DTP) vaccines.[11] This led to a strong reaction both by the local and central government, highlighting a need for greater scrutiny upon vaccine approval evaluations moving forward.[12]

7.2   Post-Market Safety Monitoring

Before a vaccine enters the market, it undergoes several phases of clinical trials in humans to observe efficacy, safety, and the outcome of potential adverse effects, among other evaluations. These trials typically enroll thousands, or even tens of thousands, of individuals to collect data and often follow those enrollees for signs of adverse reaction for up to 6 to 9 months following injection. The statistical power of this data is considered strong enough to approve most vaccines for nationwide rollout, however, the presence of rare adverse events, especially for individuals prone to vaccine reactions or living with comorbidities, may not become apparent until the vaccine is administered on a much broader scale, reaching millions of individuals across the general population. For this reason, it is essential that vaccine manufacturers and regulatory agencies conduct thorough and coordinated post-market safety monitoring.

Many, though not all, countries currently engage in this type of post-market vaccine monitoring. Many of these countries typically have systems that allow reports to be filed in the event of a negative occurrence following a vaccine, such as the Adverse Event Reporting System that is systematically reviewed by the FDA. Others have active monitoring systems[13]; A study from 2014 identified nine active monitoring systems, in the United States, Canada, Europe, and Asia.[14]

---

[8] Nature (2020), p. 195.

[9] Lythgoe and Middleton (2021), p. e2114531.

[10] BBC News (2018) Chinese Premier Li Keqiang calls for crackdown on vaccine industry. https://www.bbc.com/news/world-asia-china-44920193. Accessed 23 Oct 2022.

[11] Hernandez (2018).

[12] Tai (2022), p. 628.

[13] Iannelli (2017); Reiss (2017). The Immunisation Advisory Centre (2020) Stages of vaccine safety monitoring. https://www.immune.org.nz/vaccines/vaccine-safety/safety-monitoring. Accessed 23 Oct 2022.

[14] Huang et al. (2014), pp. 581–596.

As new organisms emerge, and vaccines for both new and old infectious diseases are continually developed, it is of key importance that vaccine safety protocols are not just effective but also consistent, and easily applicable to multiple vaccine schedules. In its guide about COVID-19 vaccines, the WHO explained the extensive system of oversight that exists for vaccines generally, and that would be available for COVID-19 vaccines, too.[15] In an even more recent development, the CDC issued further guidance for the JYNNEOS and ACAM2000 vaccines that are being rolled out for immunization against monkeypox to follow previously outlined safety reporting requirements.

Aside from the differences in monitoring systems, countries also vary in their tolerance of potential vaccine harm. The matter becomes complicated by the fact that the distribution of benefit and burden of risk is not shared by the individual and society proportionally. To elaborate, vaccination can benefit an individual by preventing illness, or in some cases decreasing the severity of illness. However, the greatest benefit is awarded to society as the spread of an illness is limited, moving closer to herd immunity and disease eradication. On the contrary, the risk of harm from a vaccine is shared only by the individual and not at all by society. Therefore, there is generally low tolerance from the general public for vaccine risks, and even a rare side effect may lead to a vaccine being taken off the market. This balance can be challenging for companies to manage and gauging the amount of risk that any healthy individual should be willing to tolerate for the reward of preventing illness upon themselves and their community is not a predictable feat.

Some countries bear an exceedingly low tolerance for adverse events of any kind that are linked to vaccination. For example, Japan has a history of responding strongly to vaccine safety concerns. In 1975, two infants died after receiving the DTP vaccine. In response to this tragedy, Japan suspended the DTP vaccine, leading to a whooping cough epidemic that killed at least 41 babies.[16] This tendency of little tolerance for adverse events became an apparent pattern in Japanese vaccine regulation. In 1989, after Japan introduced the measles, mumps and rubella (MMR) vaccine, they not long after withdrew it from the market by 1993 due to reports of aseptic meningitis—even though the rates of the problem are higher than the rates of natural mumps.[17] In spite of the availability of an MMR vaccine that does not cause aseptic meningitis (manufactured by the pharmaceutical company Merck), Japan regulatory authorities still do not recommend immunization against MMR, instead administering a measles-rubella vaccine approved since 2006 (and seeing repeated outbreaks of mumps and rubella).[18] Most recently, Japan removed the

---

[15] WHO (2022) Statement for healthcare professional: How COVID-19 vaccines are regulated for safety and effectiveness. https://www.who.int/news/item/17-05-2022-statement-for-healthcare-professionals-how-covid-19-vaccines-are-regulated-for-safety-and-effectiveness.   Accessed 23 Oct 2022.

[16] Watanabe and Nagai (2005), pp. 173–184.

[17] Tanaka et al. (2017), pp. 1859–1860.

[18] Id.

recommendation for human papillomavirus vaccines (HPV) based on reports of problems that occurred after the vaccine, even though causation was not shown, leading to a drop of less than 1% in vaccination.[19] Japan only recently started re-recommending HPV vaccines.[20] This pattern suggests a country with very low tolerance to reports of risks from vaccines, a country that reacts vigorously to such reports, even at the cost of disease outbreaks. Other countries do not react as strongly to such concerns.[21]

Tolerance towards adverse vaccine reactions is not necessarily consistent over the course of a pandemic or outbreak of disease. One study argues that tolerance can remain high as long as the threat of potential illness also remains high. In that scenario, recipients view the benefit of vaccination as greater than the risk of harm. As vaccination rates increase, nearing closer to achieving herd immunity, and rates of illness decline, the threat of infection becomes much lower and therefore, additional uptake of the vaccine may decline because the threat of an adverse event is perceived to be too high compared to the risk of disease. Aware of this, many vaccine safety monitoring groups focus their efforts on identifying patterns of adverse events to guide research efforts toward eliminating these occurrences. Also important is the necessary communication to the public about potential reactions, which can help earn trust from the public and thereby increase further vaccine acceptance.

7.3 Compensation Systems

As we discussed in Chap. 5, vaccines are a public good, and therefore are expected to inflict no harm on the individual receiving immunization. Unfortunately, serious harms, albeit rare, do occur and in these circumstances, it is important to provide compensation quickly and generously to people who suffer as a result. While many can agree upon the notion that compensation should be provided, the protocol for qualifications, approval process, and financial coverage of the compensation has led to an array of approaches from several different countries across the world.

By and large, there are two general ways to handle vaccine injury compensation. Each claim may be handled similarly to injuries occurring from other capitalistic goods—in the court, to be handled by the regular torts system; or a special no-fault vaccine injury compensation program can be created to provide immediate compensation for injuries and reactions that qualify.

Based on expert analyses and evidence review, we advocate for a no-fault compensation system as the better approach. When a previously healthy individual suffers complications as a result of a vaccine, which they have received as an act for the public good, we, and others, believe that society should compensate them

---

[19] Id.

[20] Ujiie et al. (2022), pp. 1–3.

[21] Katsuta et al. (2020), pp. 7401–7408.

whether or not someone else was at fault. Additionally, evidence shows that no-fault systems can provide fast, generous compensation, which can lead to increased trust in vaccines and hence, greater vaccine acceptance.

That said, vaccine injury compensation systems are a minority. A study published in July of 2021 identified only 27 countries with existing compensations programs, spanning only 4 continents, leaving Africa and South America completely without that kind of protection for vaccine recipients.[22] The first such system was adopted in Germany in 1961, as a result of a supreme court ruling that found that people harmed by a vaccine should be compensated regardless of whether they can show fault. Since then, other countries have adopted them, most of them high income countries, though one low-income country (Nepal) and one lower-middle income country (Vietnam) adopted programs accordingly.[23] Several high-income countries do not have them—for example, Canada (with the exception of the providence of Quebec) and Australia. The lack of compensation schemes in low or middle-income countries is further complicated by the fact that many of these countries use vaccines that were developed specifically for use in their countries, and not all of them have sufficient vaccine monitoring programs to record and track patterns of adverse events. Not only do the gaps in vaccine safety monitoring and lack of compensation programs put individuals at exceedingly higher risk for harm, but also the lack of data makes creating a program much more challenging moving forward.

Countries vary in every aspect of the compensation programs. Funding is sometimes provided by government, insurance, or private companies. Some countries have pre-approved lists identifying which vaccines may be covered under their specific program, many of which specify a specific timeline for applying for compensation. All systems require some show of causal link to the vaccine, and most use a balance of probabilities approach whereby it must be determined that the vaccine is more likely than not—i.e., more than 50% likely—to have caused the injury.[24]

Despite their varying differences, one thing all these systems have in common are the concerns about the lack of awareness of the program, the standards for showing causation, and the timing of compensation.[25] The process for individuals to provide evidence for the causal link between their injury and the vaccine can be lengthy and costly, and approval for compensation is not guaranteed. A global compensation system would eliminate this concern, providing greater guarantee in compensation on a more appropriate timeline.

One general concern is the lack of vaccine compensation in many countries despite widespread vaccine rollout. Addressing this, over the past few years prominent public health researchers have argued for the creation of a global compensation system for vaccine injuries.[26] Not only does a global no-fault compensation scheme

---

[22] Mungwira et al. (2020), p. e0233334.

[23] Id.

[24] Id.

[25] Id.

[26] Halabi and Omer (2017), pp. 471–472.

provide assurance to recipients of immunizations that any risk of harm will be sufficiently compensated in the event of injury, but also it offers protection to vaccine manufacturers as it removes the liability from private vaccine companies by eliminating the need for fault to be proven in order for compensation to be awarded. Recently, it has been argued that global compensation schemes are also necessary to provide equitable access to COVID-19 vaccines.[27] At this point, some of the major drawbacks in efforts to draft a global compensation scheme center on questions of funding. More research and deliberation are needed by public health scholars and economic experts to evaluate how a global no-fault system should be funded and how the cost of such a program should be fairly distributed among low, middle, and high-income countries.

7.4 Conclusion

Regulation of vaccines and post-market monitoring of vaccines vary drastically across countries, but some of the dilemmas faced by all remain the same. The process for quick, safe, and organized approval of new vaccines can be time consuming and costly. After approval, monitoring of vaccine safety requires highly coordinated data collection, and analyzing the balance of harm to an individual against potentially great benefit to society can be nearly impossible to predict. Furthermore, developing a global system for fair, quick, and adequate compensation to individuals who experience unfortunate harm from vaccination is a monumental task that will require input from experts in many fields. Careful attention should be focused on research efforts moving forward to maximize the impact of new vaccines and to preserve public trust in the scientific community surrounding immunization efforts.

References

BBC News (2018) Chinese Premier Li Keqiang calls for crackdown on vaccine industry. https://www.bbc.com/news/world-asia-china-44920193. Accessed 23 Oct 2022

European Medicines Agency Science Medicines Health. https://www.ema.europa.eu/en/about-us. Accessed 23 Oct

Halabi S et al (2020) No-fault compensation for vaccine injury - the other side of equitable access to covid-19 vaccines. N Engl J Med 383:e125. https://doi.org/10.1056/NEJMp2030600.2022

Halabi SF, Omer SB (2017) A global vaccine injury compensation system. JAMA 317:471–472. https://doi.org/10.1001/jama.2016.19492

Heims E, Tomic S (2021) Covid-19 vaccines and the competition between independent and politicised models of regulation. https://blogs.lse.ac.uk/europpblog/2021/03/11/covid-19-vaccines-and-the-competition-between-independent-and-politicised-models-of-regulation/. Accessed 23 Oct 2022

---

[27] Halabi et al. (2020), p. e125.

Hernandez JC (2018) In China, Vaccine Scandal Infuriates Parents and Tests Government. https://www.nytimes.com/2018/07/23/world/asia/china-vaccines-scandal-investigation.html. Accessed 23 Oct 2023

Huang YL et al (2014) A comparison of active adverse event surveillance systems worldwide. Drug Saf 37:581–596. https://doi.org/10.1007/s40264-014-0194-3

Iannelli V (2017) Global Vaccine Side Effect Reporting System. https://vaxopedia.org/2017/10/22/global-vaccine-side-effect-reporting-systems/. Accessed 23 Oct 2022

Katsuta T et al (2020) Comparison of immunization systems in Japan and the United States – what can be learned? Vaccine 38:7401–7408. https://doi.org/10.1016/j.vaccine.2020.09.028

Li J (2013) China Enters Global Vaccine Marketplace for the First Time. https://www.scientificamerican.com/article/china-enters-global-vaccine-marketplace-for-the-first-time/. Accessed 22 Oct 2022

Lythgoe MP, Middleton P (2021) Comparison of COVID-19 vaccine approvals at the US food and drug administration, European Medicines Agency, and Health Canada. JAMA Netw Open 4: e2114531. https://doi.org/10.1001/jamanetworkopen.2021.14531

Mahase E (2020) Vaccinating the UK: how the covid vaccine was approved, and other questions answered. BMJ 371:m4759. https://doi.org/10.1136/bmj.m4759

Mungwira RG et al (2020) Global landscape analysis of no-fault compensation programmes for vaccine injuries: a review and survey of implementing countries. Plos One 15:e0233334. https://doi.org/10.1371/journal.pone.0233334

Nature (2020) COVID vaccines: the world's medical regulators need access to open data. 588:195. https://doi.org/10.1038/d41586-020-03458-z

Reiss DR (2017) Ginger Taylor writes a letter about vaccines – this will be interesting. https://www.skepticalraptor.com/skepticalraptorblog.php/ginger-taylor-writes-letter-vaccines-will-interesting/#Governments_support_vaccines_because_they_are_very_safe%20for%20passive%20monitoring%20systems. Accessed 23 Oct 2022

Tai YC (2022) Determinants of Chinese Provincial Governments' responses to the 2018 vaccine scandal: policy orientation and neighbor effect. Asian Surv 62:628. https://doi.org/10.1525/as.2022.1693011

Tanaka Y et al (2017) History repeats itself in Japan: Failure to learn from rubella epidemic leads to failure to provide the HPV vaccine. Hum Vaccin Immunother 13:1859–1860. https://doi.org/10.1080/21645515.2017.1327929

The Immunisation Advisory Centre (2020) Stages of vaccine safety monitoring. https://www.immune.org.nz/vaccines/vaccine-safety/safety-monitoring. Accessed 23 Oct 2022

Ujiie M et al (2022) Changing trends in HPV vaccination in Japan. Hum Vaccin Immunother 18:1–3. https://doi.org/10.1080/21645515.2021.1986333

Watanabe M, Nagai M (2005) Acellular pertussis vaccines in Japan: past, present and future. Expert Rev Vacc 4:173–184. https://doi.org/10.1586/14760584.4.2.173

WHO (2022) Statement for healthcare professional: How COVID-19 vaccines are regulated for safety and effectiveness. https://www.who.int/news/item/17-05-2022-statement-for-healthcare-professionals-how-covid-19-vaccines-are-regulated-for-safety-and-effectiveness. Accessed 23 Oct 2022

WHO African Vaccine Regulatory Forum (AVAREF). https://www.afro.who.int/health-topics/immunization/avaref. Accessed 23 Oct 2022

WHO List of vaccine producing countries with functional NRAs. https://www.who.int/initiatives/who-listed-authority-reg-authorities/list-of-vaccine-prod-countries. Accessed 23 Oct 2022

Part II

Equity and Vaccines

This part of the book is dedicated to exploring equity in access to vaccines. Chapter 8 delves into how the U.S. provides access to vaccines through comprehensive funding schemes. It discusses the current scheme for funding vaccines for children, while acknowledging the need for improvements. Furthermore, it highlights the significant gaps in vaccine access for adults in the U.S. Chapter 9 examines the role of government in promoting vaccine equity. It discusses the various ways in which government policies and actions can impact equitable access to vaccines. Lastly, Chap. 10 provides a comparative perspective, looking at vaccine access issues beyond the U.S., with a focus on equity considerations. Together, these chapters emphasize the importance of ensuring equitable access to vaccines, both in the U.S. and in a broader global context. They also highlight the progress made towards that goal, as well as the challenges and barriers that still exist.

Funding Vaccinations in the United States

8

Abstract

Vaccines are an important tool in promoting public health; they provide public and private health benefits and their economic returns are 16 times greater than the initial costs (Scharf et al., Acad Pediatr 21:S57, 2021.). Likewise, child immunization has been consistently ranked as one of the greatest public health achievements of the twentieth century. But vaccines work best when there is widespread coverage of a vaccine, which gives countries an incentive to solve access problems and fund vaccines for all. For that reason, in the United States (U.S.), vaccines are funded at a level unlike any other drug.

There are several aspects of vaccine development that influence funding. One is that the development of new vaccines requires the use of more sophisticated technologies. Using more sophisticated technologies costs more money—which can exacerbate access issues and creates more need for public funding (Hinman et al., Clin Infect Dis 38:1440, 2004.).

Since the passage of the Affordable Care Act (ACA) in the U.S., coverage of vaccines and vaccine recommendations for adults and children are set by the Centers for Disease Control and Prevention (CDC). The CDC's Advisory Committee on Immunization Practices (ACIP) is a federal advisory committee that develops recommendations for using vaccines to control disease in the U.-S. ACIP's recommendations consider the disease and its burden, vaccine safety and efficacy, the quality of the evidence reviewed, economic cost-benefits, and implementation challenges. After ACIP makes a recommendation, it is reviewed by the CDC director. Although the director is not bound by ACIP's recommendation, it is very rare for the director not to accept them. If ACIP's recommendation is adopted, it is published by the CDC and this affects vaccine coverage as we detail below (Schwartz et al., Vaccine Coverage, Pricing, and Reimbursement in the U.S. 2020.). In addition to this general framework, the U.S. has several programs to cover vaccines costs for those who may be left without vaccines.

© The Author(s), under exclusive license to Springer Nature Switzerland AG 2023   73
Y. T. Yang, D. R. Reiss, *Vaccine Law and Policy*, Law for Professionals,
https://doi.org/10.1007/978-3-031-36989-6_8

Part I of this chapter introduces the various programs offered by public and government agencies designed to provide access to vaccines—including how some of these programs have been impacted by the COVID-19 vaccines. These include: (A) the Vaccines for Children Program (VFC); (B) Medicare; (C) Medicaid and the Children's Health Insurance Program (CHIP); (D) Section 317 of the Public Health Services Act (PHSA); and (E) the Department of Veterans Affairs (VA). Part II further examines how vaccine access is accomplished via private insurance. Part III discusses shortfalls of vaccine financing in the U.S. and its implications, and Part IV concludes that Americans can access vaccines through various government and private insurance programs.

8.1   Public & Government Programs

8.1.1   Vaccines for Children Program[1]

Between 1989 and 1991, an especially large measles epidemic sickened tens of thousands of children and killed 123 people.[2] The vast majority of the victims were young inner-city children of color left unvaccinated because of access issues.[3] In 1993, Congress responded by enacting the VFC program.[4] Under the VFC, the CDC purchases vaccines directly from manufacturers and distributes them to *grantees* (state health departments and some local health agencies). The grantees in turn distribute the vaccines—for free—to private physicians' offices and public health clinics registered as VFC providers.[5] As the name suggests, an individual must be a *child* (younger than 19 years of age) to access the VFC program. The child must also be either Medicaid-eligible, uninsured, underinsured (have health insurance that does not cover vaccines or has a fixed dollar limit for vaccines), or an American Indian or Alaska Native.

If there are multiple manufacturers of a vaccine, the Secretary of the Department of Health and Human Services (HHS) is authorized to contract with more than one manufacturer. This helps avoid shortages in the event that one manufacturer experiences problems in the supply chain. Additionally, the Secretary is required to purchase six months of additional vaccine supply beyond what would otherwise be required for a specific time period, as part of the effort to assure that there is always an adequate supply of vaccines.[6]

What is the cost to patients under the VFC program? It depends. Children get vaccines for free through the VFC program, but VFC providers can charge for other

---

[1] Schwartz et al. (2020).
[2] Gastanaduy (2019).
[3] Atkinson et al. (1992), pp. 451–463.
[4] CDC (2016).
[5] Schwartz et al. (2020).
[6] CDC (2016).

services.[7] This may include a fee to administer the shot—though a VFC-eligible child cannot be refused a vaccination due to a parent's or guardian's inability to pay this fee. Additionally, VFC providers can charge for office visits and other non-vaccine services such as an eye exam or blood test. If a child has Medicaid and is VFC-eligible, then Medicaid covers any office visit or administrative fees with no cost-sharing responsibilities for the child's parent or guardian. An uninsured VFC-eligible child—who is subject to an office visit or administrative fee—may be eligible for free or reduced costs through a community health center.[8]

The HHS Secretary is statutorily authorized to negotiate a discounted price for vaccines purchased from manufacturers under the VFC program. The negotiated prices obviously impact the federal government, but can impact States as well. This is because States can purchase vaccines at the negotiated VFC price for children who otherwise are not VFC-eligible. The average discounted price for a vaccine purchased under the VFC is 30% below the vaccine's list price; and the overall range of the discounted price stretches from 15% to 72% below list price.[9]

The VFC is a large program. It covers a large fraction of the vaccines given to children in the U.S., and in recent years its annual cost is around $4 billion. [10] It has several important positive impacts, including saving lives and preventing diseases and costs. [11] It also contributed to decreasing racial differences in vaccines coverage, thus contributing to racial justice. [12]

8.1.2   Medicare[13]

Medicare covers vaccines for more than 60 million people ages 65 and older, and younger adults with long-term disabilities. Medicare covers vaccines under Part B (which covers primarily outpatient care) and Part D (which covers retail prescription drugs). Medicare Part B covers vaccines for influenza, pneumococcal disease, hepatitis B, and vaccines needed to treat an injury or exposure to disease. All other commercially available vaccines needed to prevent illness are covered under Part D.

Whether a vaccine is covered by Part B or Part D affects a vaccine's cost to patients. Patients receiving vaccines for influenza, pneumococcal pneumonia, and hepatitis B are not liable for any costs related to the vaccine or its administration. For other drugs and services under Part B, Medicare covers 80% of the cost while beneficiaries are responsible for the remaining 20%. Most—but not all—

---

[7] Schwartz et al. (2020).

[8] Schwartz et al. (2020).

[9] Schwartz et al. (2020).

[10] Chen et al. (2017), pp. 252–265.

[11] Whitney et al. (2014), p. 352. (Financially, vaccines in these years will result in "net savings of $295 billion in direct costs and $1.38 trillion in total society costs.").

[12] Walker et al. (2014), pp. 7–12.

[13] Schwartz et al. (2020).

beneficiaries of Part B have supplemental insurance to cover their financial responsibilities. Part D—which covers all other commercially available vaccines—affords flexibility in determining how much beneficiaries are required to pay for vaccines. For example, income status can impact a beneficiary's cost sharing responsibilities; and cost sharing can either be a flat dollar requirement or a percentage of the vaccine's list price.

Unlike the VCF program, Medicare does not involve the federal government in buying vaccines. Rather, health care professionals (HCPs) administering vaccines to Part B beneficiaries are reimbursed by the federal government. Reimbursement for influenza and pneumococcal vaccines covered under Part B is set at 95% of the Average Wholesale Price (AWP) for the vaccine. For other Part B covered drugs, reimbursement is 106% of the vaccine's Average Sales Price (ASP). The ASP is the average price of a vaccine for all non-federal purchasers in the U.S. including all discounts and rebates resulting from negotiations. Part D is administered by private drug plans sponsored by private insurers and pharmacy benefit managers. This means that vaccine pricing and reimbursement will vary based on negotiations between manufacturers and insurance plans. Hence, different Part D plan sponsors can pay a different price for the same vaccine, which in turn can affect the amount of cost sharing among Part D beneficiaries.

The COVID-19 vaccines are covered by Part B, which means that Medicare beneficiaries have access to the vaccines with no cost sharing. Part B coverage means broader access to the vaccines because not all Medicare beneficiaries are enrolled in a Part D plan. As of December 2022, Medicare will not pay for initial doses of the COVID-19 vaccines already purchased by the government. However, if Medicare does ultimately reimburse HCPs providing the vaccines, it will do so at 95% of the AWP.

8.1.3 Medicaid and the Children's Health Insurance Program[14]

Medicaid is "the single largest source of health coverage in the U.S."[15] Medicaid and CHIP—joint federal and state programs—provide health coverage to 75.5 million Americans. Medicaid coverage for vaccines varies based on age, eligibility, and state. For certain adult populations—including low-income parents or caretakers, pregnant women, and the elderly or disabled—vaccines are an optional benefit.

Additionally, states may provide "alternative benefit plans" for adults enrolled under the ACA Medicaid expansion. Such benefits are subject to certain requirements in the ACA, including coverage of ACIP-recommended vaccines with no cost sharing. All adults who are enrolled in Medicaid but not covered by

---

[14] Schwartz et al. (2020).

[15] Medicaid.gov Eligibility. https://www.medicaid.gov/medicaid/eligibility/index.html. Accessed 23 Oct. 2022.

the ACA's expansion have some state-provided vaccine coverage, though not every state covers all ACIP-recommended vaccines.

Each state has the option to cover its "CHIP population" (*i.e.*, children in families with low to moderate incomes) within the state's Medicaid program or under a separate CHIP program.[16] If a child is Medicaid-eligible, and the state's Medicaid program encompasses the CHIP program, then the child's vaccines are covered by the VFC. But if the child falls under a separate CHIP program, their vaccines are not covered by the VFC. However, age-appropriate vaccines are a required CHIP benefit, so children in separate CHIP programs receive ACIP-recommended vaccines without cost sharing. The only difference is that states must purchase vaccines for these children using CHIP program funds rather than use vaccines bought by the CDC through VFC funds.

In terms of patient costs, federal Medicaid rules allow states to impose nominal cost sharing, but only for specific populations. Adults for which a state has provided an alternative benefit plan must receive preventative vaccines with no cost sharing. Populations generally exempt from cost sharing include pregnant women, people in hospice, and people receiving Indian HCP services. As mentioned above, children in CHIP programs are exempt from cost sharing too. Some young Medicaid-covered adults are eligible for the Early, Periodic, Screening, Diagnostic, and Treatment (EPSDT) benefit. The EPSDT benefit includes vaccine coverage, but participants may face cost sharing (depending on the state) if not enrolled in an alternative benefit plan.

The Medicaid Drug Rebate Program (MDRP) requires Medicaid programs to cover all U.S. Food and Drug Administration (FDA) approved drugs from participating manufacturers in exchange for rebates to offset the cost of prescription drugs. While vaccines are excluded from the MDRP, states are still required to reimburse HCPs for administering vaccines. As expected, reimbursement varies widely across states. For example, reimbursement for an HPV vaccine in Missouri in 2019 was about $5.27. Reimbursement for the *same vaccine* in the *same year* in Mississippi was $491.38! States generally set reimbursement through fee-for-service (FFS) schedules—where reimbursement for each vaccine is given when it's administered—and most states reimburse for both the vaccine cost and its administration fee.

How has COVID-19 impacted Medicaid? Coverage of testing and treatment for COVID-19—including vaccines—is required with no cost sharing in order for states to access temporary enhanced federal funding for Medicaid. States must also provide continuous coverage for Medicaid enrollees through the end of the month in which the COVID-19 public health emergency (PHE) ends. The enhanced federal funding available for Medicaid will expire at the end of the quarter in which the PHE ends. This means that coverage for a no cost COVID-19 could expire for Medicaid

---

[16]National Academy for State Health Policy Virginia CHIP Fact Sheet. https://www.nashp.org/virginia-chip-fact-sheet/. Accessed 23 Oct. 2022.

enrollees—with coverage reverting back to the pre-pandemic Medicaid provisions described above—if the PHE is not extended.[17]

8.1.4   Section 317[18]

There is no VFC-like program for uninsured adults. But, the federal government does purchase a limited number of vaccines directly for uninsured and other qualifying adults. The funding for these purchases comes from PHSA Section 317. Section 317 is a discretionary funding program, with a budget of $611 million in 2020. When the ACA was passed, the CDC updated eligibility criteria for adults to receive vaccines through Section 317. To be eligible, an adult must be: (1) uninsured; (2) insured but with no vaccine coverage; or (3) being vaccinated as part of a public health response.

Adults receiving vaccines through Section 317 get the vaccines for free through their state or local health department. But, Section 317's yearly budget is fixed and does not automatically increase in response to an increased uninsured population or rising cost of vaccines. States can supplement federal funding they receive from Section 317 in order to reach more people.

Like the VFC program, the CDC negotiates prices for vaccines purchased through Section 317. The discounted prices for these vaccines varies from 24% to 59% below list price—with the average discount around 40%. In addition, section 317 funds support state and city immunization programs in other ways, allowing those states and cities to provide additional adult immunization programs, but the details vary dramatically. [19]

8.1.5   Department of Veterans Affairs[20]

Within the VA, the Veterans Health Administration (VHA) is an integrated healthcare system serving qualifying veterans. To receive VA healthcare, a veteran must generally meet certain minimum service requirements; though exceptions can be made in certain circumstances (*e.g.*, discharge due to a service-connected disability). Preventative care—including vaccinations—is provided by the VA at no cost to eligible veterans.

In terms of costs to the government, the VA benefits from drug manufacturers' wishes to participate in Medicaid and Medicare Part B. This is because those manufacturers must sell their medicines at a discount to the VA (along with several other government agencies). The price for a drug sold to the VA is lower than the

---

[17] Becerra (2022).

[18] Schwartz et al. (2020).

[19] Reiss and Yang (2020), pp. 50–51.

[20] Schwartz et al. (2020).

two formulae. The first—Federal Ceiling Price—starts with a minimum 24% off the "non-Federal Average Manufacturer Price" (non-FAMP) then adds any statutorily required discounts if necessary to prevent the federal ceiling price from rising faster than the rate of inflation. The second formula—the Federal Supply Schedule (FSS)—is negotiated between the VA and manufacturers. The FSS price is based on the prices that manufacturers charge their "most-favored" commercial customers under similar terms and conditions. These formulae result in an average discount of about 40% off of the vaccine's list price—within a discount range of 24% to 63%.

8.2   Private Health Insurance[21]

Approximately 55% of the American population is privately insured, predominately through employer-sponsored insurance plans. All health insurance plans—unless otherwise grandfathered—are subject to certain coverage standards and requirements included in the ACA. However, the Trump Administration recently expanded access to *short-term health insurance plans* which are not subject to any federal coverage standards. Short-term health insurance plans provide individuals with temporary medical coverage when they are between health plans or outside enrollment periods and need coverage in case of an emergency.[22]

Private health insurance plans subject to the ACA must provide coverage for ACIP-recommended vaccines without cost sharing. When ACIP recommends a new vaccine, insurance plans must update their coverage within approximately one year to include the new vaccine. Even if an insurance plan beneficiary has not met his deductible, the insurance plan sponsor must still provide the vaccine without cost sharing. Again, short-term health insurance plans are not subject to federal requirements, so short-term plans could require cost sharing or exclude ACIP-recommended vaccines altogether.

Unlike the government programs described above, there are no federal limits or rules regarding the price of vaccines. However, because ACIP recommendations include an economic analysis, manufacturers and HCPs have a starting point for negotiations that may help keep prices down. Manufacturers provide rebates and other price considerations based on various factors, though that information is not made publicly available. This makes it difficult to ascertain the average price private insurance plan sponsors pay for vaccines.

---

[21] Schwartz et al. (2020).
[22] Cigna (2019).

8.3   Implications and Shortfalls of Vaccine Financing[23]

New vaccines developed with new technologies are more expensive than "traditional" vaccines. This has highlighted weaknesses in the current system for financing vaccines and raises concerns about how newer vaccines can be paid for. One such weakness is vaccine delivery. None of the government programs mentioned earlier reimburse manufacturers and developers for delivery of vaccines, which in the early 1990s averaged $15 per dose. Manufacturers naturally pass these costs onto others. These costs have to be borne by insurance plans, parents, or absorbed as a loss for the HCP.

The introduction of the pneumococcal conjugate vaccine (PCV7) demonstrated other weaknesses in the system. At the time of its introduction, the PCV7 vaccine was the only vaccine that was not cost-saving to society. The cost of PCV7 doubled the public sector cost of vaccines for children and increased the private sector price by roughly fifty percent. Funding for VFC-eligible children was sufficient, but Section 317 and state funding was not adequate to cover non-VFC-eligible children. For the first time in a decade, some children coming to health department clinics could not receive ACIP-recommended vaccines. These issues led the CDC to ask the Institute of Medicine (IOM) to review the vaccine financing system.

After conducting a study involving original research and testimony on vaccine financing, the IOM made several recommendations. First, that there should be an insurance mandate for ACIP-recommended vaccines combined with a government subsidy and voucher plan. The mandate would apply to all private and public health plans and a voucher system for the uninsured population. Second, the IOM recommended creating a process to distinguish between vaccines that have strong and weak societal benefits and a process to calculate subsidy levels based on the vaccine's societal benefits.

The IOM's recommendations would provide significant advantages over the current financing system. This includes: (1) a guarantee of federal financing for vaccines with a societal benefit; (2) a financing system that covers the cost of a vaccine and its administration; (3) a "seamless financing system for private providers;" (4) elimination of underinsurance; (5) more rapid financing of new vaccines; and (6) a predictable pricing system through calculation of vaccine subsidies.

8.4   Conclusion

Vaccines are an extraordinary tool in promoting public health. Americans can access vaccines through various government and private insurance programs. But while an individual may not have to pay for the vaccine itself, that individual may have to pay other costs like an administrative fee or office visit fee. The development of new

---

[23] Hinman et al. (2004), p. 1440.

vaccines is obviously a good thing for the promotion of public health, but that development can be very expensive. As development prices increase, access may decrease. Therefore, arguments have been made for a federal vaccine mandate coupled with an increase in federal funding and subsidies. Proper funding regimes will ensure that new vaccine development is coupled with adequate access for all Americans.

References

Atkinson WL et al (1992) The resurgence of measles in the United States, 1989–1990. Annu Rev Med. 43:451–463. https://doi.org/10.1146/annurev.me.43.020192.002315

Becerra X (2022) Renewal of Determination that a Public Health Emergency Exists. https://aspr.hhs.gov/legal/PHE/Pages/covid19-15jul2022.aspx. Accessed 23 Oct 2022

CDC (2016) Vaccines for Children Program (VFC) About VFC. https://www.cdc.gov/vaccines/programs/vfc/about/index.html. Accessed 23 Oct 2022

Chen W et al (2017) Factors associated with the pricing of childhood vaccines in the U.S. public sector. Health Econ 27:252–265. https://doi.org/10.1002/hec.3539

Cigna (2019) What is Short Term Health Insurance? https://www.cigna.com/individuals-families/understanding-insurance/what-is-short-term-health-insurance. Accessed 24 Oct 2022

Gastanaduy PA (2019) Chapter 7: Measles. https://www.cdc.gov/vaccines/pubs/surv-manual/chpt07-measles.html. Accessed 23 Oct

Hinman A et al (2004) Financing immunizations in the United States. Clin Infect Dis 38:1440. https://doi.org/10.1086/420748

Medicaid.gov Eligibility. https://www.medicaid.gov/medicaid/eligibility/index.html. Accessed 23 Oct 2022

National Academy for State Health Policy Virginia CHIP Fact Sheet. https://www.nashp.org/virginia-chip-fact-sheet/. Accessed 23 Oct 2022

Reiss DR, Yang YT (2020) How congress can help raise vaccine rates. Notre Dame Law Rev Refl 96:50–51

Scharf LG et al (2021) Current challenges and future possibilities for immunization information systems. Acad Pediatr 21:S57. https://doi.org/10.1016/j.acap.2020.11.008

Schwartz K et al (2020) Vaccine Coverage, Pricing, and Reimbursement in the U.S. https://www.kff.org/coronavirus-covid-19/issue-brief/vaccine-coverage-pricing-and-reimbursement-in-the-u-s/. Accessed 23 Oct 2022

Walker AT et al (2014) Reduction of racial/ethnic disparities in vaccination coverage, 1995-2011. MMWR Suppl 63:7–12. PMID: 24743661

Whitney CG et al. (2014) Benefits from immunization during the vaccines for children program era – United States, 1994–2013. MMWR Morb Mortal Wkly Rep 63:352. PMCID: PMC4584777 (Financially, vaccines in these years will result in "net savings of $295 billion in direct costs and $1.38 trillion in total society costs.").

Vaccine Equity

9

Abstract

Vaccine equity ensures that everyone has fair and just access to vaccinations regardless of social, geographic, political, economic, and environmental factors (CDC, COVID-19 vaccine equity for racial and ethnic minority groups, 2022a.). When systemic factors create challenges to vaccine access or acceptance, vaccine inequity occurs—sometimes with serious consequences (*Id.*). Vaccine equity issues disproportionately impact racial and ethnic minority groups, making it harder for people in these groups to be vaccinated against infectious diseases like COVID-19. This was made apparent at the start of the pandemic, where people of color were two to three times more likely to be hospitalized and more than twice as likely to die from COVID-19 as white, non-Hispanic people (Underhill and Johnson, Yale Law J Forum 131:53, 2021.).

This chapter discusses the problem of inequitable access to vaccines, the factors that influence vaccine equity, governmental methods to address vaccine equity, and other issues that play a role in vaccine equity.

9.1 Inequitable Access to Vaccines

Some scholars say that vaccines, like other health innovations, "widen the gap between the rich and the poor." While inequality subsides as access increases over time, communities of color disproportionately suffer serious health consequences in the interim.[1] Inequitable access to vaccines is heightened by factors such as: education, income, and wealth gaps; job access and working conditions; systemic racism and other forms of discrimination; gaps in healthcare access; transportation and

---

[1] *Id.*

© The Author(s), under exclusive license to Springer Nature Switzerland AG 2023
Y. T. Yang, D. R. Reiss, *Vaccine Law and Policy*, Law for Professionals,
https://doi.org/10.1007/978-3-031-36989-6_9

neighborhood conditions; lack of trust as a result of past medical racism and experimentation.[2]

These factors not only make certain groups less likely to get vaccinated, but also make racial and ethnic minority groups more likely to get seriously ill and die from COVID-19.[3] Surveillance data in the early months of COVID-19 vaccination have shown "a consistent pattern" of lower vaccination rates in communities of color.[4] Furthermore, people of color have been more likely to experience COVID-19-related hospitalization, morbidity, or mortality.[5] These findings suggest there are various populations that have inequitable access to vaccines.

Different definitions are used to identify populations who may have inequitable access to vaccines.[6] These groups include protected classes under the Civil Rights Act of 1964, individuals with disabilities, individuals with health disparities, individuals with access and functional needs, and communities identified by the Centers for Disease Control and Prevention (CDC)/Agency for Toxic Substances and Disease Registry (ATSDR) Social Vulnerability Index.[7] During COVID-19, the CDC recommended states use the Social Vulnerability Index (SVI) to identify communities who may be at greater risk of unequal access to COVID-19 vaccination. The SVI considers variables including socioeconomic status, household composition and disability, minority status and language, and housing type and transportation to measure risk of inequity.

While the CDC's SVI is a useful tool, scholars researching the "inverse equity hypothesis" say that healthcare innovations amplify inequality.[8] Often, new health technologies, such as vaccines, are limited in supply and only accessible to the wealthy. As supply catches up and exceeds the demand of wealthy and middle-income people, poor people begin to gain access to the technology.[9] The delayed access creates health-status gaps between the rich and the poor. Data shows that these health gaps track racial disparities in wealth and healthcare between the rich and the poor. This means that racial and ethnic minorities are disadvantaged the most by vaccine inequity.

Vaccine inequity among racial and ethnic minorities also occurred during the COVID-19 vaccine rollout. When COVID-19 vaccines were released as new health technology, the government managed the limited vaccine availability by conducting vaccine distribution in phases.[10] The phases of vaccine rollout targeted populations at higher risk of contracting COVID-19 (like health care workers) or facing serious

---

[2]CDC (2022a).

[3]*Id.*

[4]Underhill and Johnson (2021), p. 53.

[5]Lister et al. (2021).

[6]Lister et al. (2021).

[7]*Id.*

[8]Underhill and Johnson (2021), p. 53.

[9]*Id.*

[10]Lister et al. (2021).

health outcomes as a result of infections (like elderly or immunocompromised people). The phased-in vaccine rollout disproportionately limited access to the vaccine for certain racial and ethnic groups.[11] The COVID-19 vaccine was first made available to priority groups, but now that it is more widely available, "disparities have narrowed."[12] During the early phases of vaccine rollout, disadvantaged communities still had lower rates of vaccines and thus remained at a higher risk. Data from the COVID-19 vaccine rollout shows that, at least in the first crucial months, White people accessed COVID-19 vaccinations "at rates that exceed their share of cases," while Black and Hispanic people have been vaccinated at lower rates.[13]

COVID-19 vaccine inequity was not limited to the priorities set in the vaccine roll-out. Indeed, the method of accessing vaccines once they were available also disadvantaged certain groups. For example, some researchers suggest that voluntary opt-in approaches can increase inequality. The COVID-19 vaccine requires individuals to seek out the vaccine rather than bringing vaccines to them. Depending on a person's circumstances, they may have personal barriers, such as financial constraints or lack of information, that prevent them from seeking out the COVID-19 vaccine. Financial constraints could also include people who cannot afford to lose paid work to get the vaccine or rest due to its side effects.

Further, physical access is also an issue. Some people may not have a car, and unless vaccine centers are accessible from public transportation, they would have problems getting there. Other components that can create barriers include a lack of internet access, preventing scheduling appointments online—and for some people, age or language may also make scheduling appointments more difficult. Beyond the limitations to access discussed above, there are other factors that are not unique to COVID-19 which can prevent access. For example, a report from 2018 documented access problems of childhood vaccines for children covered by Medicaid or in rural areas, among others.[14]

The discussion above focuses mostly on vaccine inequity in the United States (U.S.), but another important area of inequity that we discuss in several chapters is inequity among countries. During COVID-19, some scholars described the policies around COVID-19 vaccines as "vaccine apartheid."[15] Our discussion of recommendations touches on both types of inequities.

---

[11] Lister et al. (2021).

[12] Underhill and Johnson (2021), p. 53.

[13] Id.

[14] Hill et al. (2018), pp. 1123–1124, 1127.

[15] Bajaj et al. (2022), pp. 1452–1453.

9.2   Laws, Policies, and Regulatory Tools to Address Vaccination-Related Disparities

The government uses different laws, policies, and regulatory tools to address vaccine-related inequities. Before COVID-19, policies were put in place to protect certain groups from discrimination during public health emergencies.[16] During COVID-19, the government used funding, communication, and educational resources to address vaccine inequity and raise awareness and confidence in vaccines.[17] Despite these efforts, some populations are still disproportionately harmed, and experts recommend additional actions.

9.2.1   Existing Laws, Policies, and Regulatory Tools

This section describes what is already in place. However, we suggest that not all of it is sufficient—we discuss these gaps in the following sections.

The government has various tools to track data on vulnerable communities and reduce disparity in access to resources like vaccines during public health emergencies. The CDC uses the Social Vulnerability Index to assess the potential negative effects on communities caused by external stresses on human health. In addition to tracking data, federal laws like the Civil Rights Act, Rehabilitation Act, Homeland Security Act, Patient Protection and Affordable Care Act, and Stafford Act include provisions prohibiting discrimination, or restricting funding of state and local government programs to those that ensure the protection of certain populations. During COVID-19, the federal government provided specific funding for organizations that target and improve vaccine equity efforts for racial and ethnic minority groups.

The federal government also created dedicated offices and policies to address inequity. The Health and Human Services (HHS) Office of Minority Health, for example, develops health policies and programs to eliminate health disparities among racial and ethnic minority communities.[18] There have been several pandemic-specific authorities, entities, and policies created to address vaccine inequities during COVID-19. Notably, the COVID-19 Health Equity Task Force provides specific recommendations to the President regarding resource allocation, distribution of relief funding, communications, and other mitigation strategies to help protect access to vaccines for at-risk and minority communities.

While we focus on the U.S. here and will address global vaccine access in Chap. 10, we wanted to discuss a few important issues here. There have been a number of global initiatives aimed at providing vaccine access across the globe, but more could be done. Providing access to vaccines in other countries is not always

---

[16]Lister et al. (2021).

[17]CDC (2022a).

[18]Lister et al. (2021).

done out of a desire to address equity or even for humane reasons: in a globalized world, infectious diseases can travel. Therefore, more contagious diseases that can travel to rich countries encourage an interest in achieving global coverage. The smallpox eradication program was a global collaboration aimed at combatting a highly dangerous airborne virus that could travel, and the World Health Organization (WHO) and member states worked together to address it.[19] In 1988, the WHO adopted a polio eradication initiative that had substantial—if incomplete—success.[20] In 2012, the WHO endorsed a goal of eliminating measles and rubella across five world regions.[21]

The challenges of these last two programs also highlight how hard it is to achieve broad immunization.[22] Furthermore, some diseases have never been targeted globally, even though they kill many children in developing countries—for example, diphtheria, tetanus, or rotavirus were never the goal of global campaigns, though there have been efforts to support vaccinating against them. For COVID-19, there also have been collaboration efforts, but they, too, ran into trouble.[23]

9.2.2 Recommendations

While advances have been made, this does not mean that enough is being done or that the equity problem is solved—far from it. Real gaps still remain in vaccine access within the U.S. and globally. A large literature examines what should be done to decrease these gaps.

Some experts recommend increasing investments to expand equitable access to vaccines.[24] For example, a state health administrator suggested that making "disproportionate investments" in communities of color is "critical in trying to get equitable outcomes through vaccine allocation."[25]

Another proposed solution is through improvements in vaccine rollouts. Scholars recommend five categories of federal regulatory options that could increase equity from the outset of vaccine rollout: "(1) providing specific guidance regarding equity goals and obligations, (2) providing default equity plans for state adoption, (3) collecting equity outcome data, (4) publicly disseminating and ranking state equity outcomes, and (5) facilitating information sharing among states."[26] Equity directives should specifically address race, ethnicity, and social vulnerability in

---

[19] Henderson (1987), pp. 535–546.

[20] CDC (2022b).

[21] Mulders et al. (2016), pp. 438–442.

[22] Patel and Cochi (2017), pp. S1–S8. Davis and Mbabazi (2017), p. 11. Serdobova and Kieny (2006), p. 1554.

[23] Harman et al. (2021), p. e006504. Asundi et al. (2021), p. 1036.

[24] Gardner (2021).

[25] Id.

[26] Underhill and Johnson (2021), p. 53.

guidance. Default equity plans would require states to submit a plan to the CDC to evaluate the equity-enhancing factors of their plans, or the federal government would propose a default plan that states can opt into or modify. This could be enforced by tying federal funding to the equity plans. These equity plans would be designed to encourage compliance and transparency.

To further improve equity, data collection could be enhanced by having the federal government increase and refine data collection on race and ethnicity.[27] Once the federal government improves data on equity-related outcomes, the CDC should report the data on a state-by state level to encourage transparency through the comparison and ranking of states. Finally, a platform for states and localities to share strategies to improve equity should be provided. This would increase the flow of information so states can develop best practices and share evidence-based strategies to promote equitable vaccine distribution.

Similar to these U.S. efforts, one nonprofit called for a comprehensive global response to promote vaccine equity.[28] Their proposal focuses on raising money to support the rollout of vaccines, supporting global vaccine distribution, avoiding vaccine nationalism, sharing COVID-19 health technology-related knowledge and data, and ensuring full transparency around the distribution and development of COVID-19 vaccines.

9.3   Other Issues

9.3.1   Federalism

Vaccine-related disparities impact different demographic groups, including the geographic location of certain groups.[29] Federalism contributes to the complications from vaccine disparities across the country because non-uniform approaches to public health emergencies prevent equitable responses across state lines. For example, requiring countermeasures in some states but not others leads to a patchwork response. According to some scholars, "[H]eterogeneous state distribution programs prioritize[e] equity . . . differently."[30]

Federalism "places states and territories in the lead for most exercises of public health authority."[31] In other words, control over public health measures is historically a state police power, and the federal government does not typically impose nationwide policies. In the context of COVID-19 vaccinations, the federal government made recommendations (not requirements) for vaccine priority groups, but it

---

[27] Underhill and Johnson (2021), p. 53.

[28] Save the Children, Vaccine Equity, Save the Children. https://www.savethechildren.org/us/charity-stories/what-is-vaccine-equity. Accessed 15 Oct. 2021.

[29] Lister et al. (2021).

[30] Underhill and Johnson (2021), p. 53.

[31] Lister et al. (2021).

was ultimately the state and local governments who designated vaccine priority groups in their respective jurisdictions. This led to different priority groups being recognized in different places, which may have contributed to appearances of inequity. To avoid this type of inequity in the future, we can use incentives to assure equity in future public health emergencies.

Priorities were not the only issue. State and local governments sought to distribute the vaccine rapidly, and in doing so depended on information and technology infrastructures that failed to mitigate inequities.[32] The government used systems that relied on the internet for sign-ups, and based vaccine allocation on demand. Communities of color, low-income communities, and rural communities are less likely to have access to the internet, and may not have the knowledge or time to complete the vaccine appointment sign up. Access to vaccination sites was also a potential barrier for at-risk communities. Language barriers, transportation, and physical access are all factors that should have been part of the pandemic response and vaccine rollout. And while some states offered paid leave for workers taking time off to get vaccinated and workers suffering a day or two of vaccine side effects, many did not.[33] This would be a serious barrier for workers who cannot afford to lose paid work time.

Some states specifically designed the later phases of their vaccination rollout plans to reach communities that had lower vaccination rates relative to the general population. Some scholars say that while this approach likely helped address inequities, it highlights the disadvantage these populations had in the early vaccine rollout phases.[34] We understand the criticism, but worry that it can discourage action to correct inequities. We believe addressing these inequities later is better than not addressing them at all. While we agree that acknowledging systemic injustice and the history that led to it is important, we believe the government is right when it acts to prioritize access for previously under-served groups. However, we think the government needs to work with community leaders to do so.

Another recommended strategy for the federal government is to partner with neighborhood and nonprofit groups, community providers, and faith-based organizations to encourage outreach and access for disadvantaged groups.[35] Because "federal systems have a comparative advantage in collecting and rapidly analyzing data, publicizing information with credibility, disseminating expertise through guidance, enforcing civil rights violations, and supporting information networks,"[36] partnerships are an effective way to funnel resources to groups that can facilitate outreach efforts to vulnerable communities.

Scholars criticized the federal government for not utilizing existing authority and influence to address vaccine inequity during the COVID-19 vaccine rollout.

---

[32] Underhill and Johnson (2021), p. 53.

[33] Reiss and Caplan (2021).

[34] Underhill and Johnson (2021), p. 53.

[35] Underhill and Johnson (2021), p. 53.

[36] *Id.*

Although states control most public health policy, the federal government purchased the vaccines available in the U.S.[37] This gives the federal government more authority in directing the use of vaccines, including requiring providers to agree to vaccinate according to priority group. Others said the federal government could have been more active early on in the COVID-19 vaccine rollout to improve equity.[38] According to these critics, the government could have provided different incentives or given more specific guidance to take equity into account when creating the priority groups. A limit on this is that, for example, direct race-based distribution would run afoul of our constitutional equal protections as they stand; but allocation based on proxies—like neighborhoods with high rates of COVID-19 infection— likely would not.[39]

Despite criticisms of the patchwork vaccine rollout at the state level, the federal government did take some steps to address vaccine inequity. The Federal Emergency Management Agency established the Civil Rights Advisory Group "to help ensure equity in the allocation of scarce resources, including to ensure that Community Vaccine Centers in the Federal pilot program are located in areas that help serve historically disenfranchised and vulnerable populations."[40] In addition, the CDC has allocated $3.5 billion in funding to address inequities in vaccine administration.[41] Recipients of this grant money must tailor their vaccination programs to: (1) racial and ethnic minority groups, specifically Non-Hispanic American Indian; Alaska Native, Non-Hispanic Black; and Hispanic; (2) those living in communities with a high social vulnerability index; (3) those living in rural communities; (4) individuals with disabilities; (5) those who are homebound or isolated; (6) those who are underinsured or uninsured; (7) those who are immigrants and/or refugees; and (8) those with transportation limitations.

9.3.2 Data Gaps

While the federal system may have posed a disadvantage for unifying response efforts to reduce vaccine inequity across the country, it was not the only barrier that contributed to this problem.

Data gaps pose a serious challenge for the government to understand and address health care inequities. The COVID-19 Health Equity Task Force specifically addressed the need for better information about health disparities. The Task Force noted that data gaps impede efforts to help at-risk and underserved communities. Data on certain groups may be incomplete or obscured, making it more challenging to address health care inequities in certain groups.

---

[37] Lister et al. (2021).

[38] Underhill and Johnson (2021), p. 53.

[39] Persad (2021), p. 1085.

[40] Lister et al. (2021).

[41] Id.

Despite its efforts, HHS has trouble collecting data on characteristics that demonstrate disparities.[42] Individuals are not required to self-report information, and individuals often choose not to provide the information on a voluntary basis. People who have good historical reasons to mistrust government may be even less likely to share information with it. Privacy laws and "infrastructure gaps that impede data sharing" also create barriers to access information on disparities.[43] There are various proposals to improve data collection to better serve communities, but until these initiatives become effective, the data gaps remain a challenge during public health emergencies. Without better data, proposals to improve equity and access to vaccines may fall short.

9.4   Conclusion

Vaccine inequity poses a serious risk to vulnerable groups, making them more likely to get seriously ill or die from a vaccine-preventable disease. Many factors contribute to vaccine inequity, and existing systems and policies do not always effectively address inequity. Federal regulatory tools exist "to encourage delivery mechanisms involving trusted local organizations, opt-out systems to supplement or replace demand-based enrollment strategies" to broaden access to disadvantaged individuals, but the problem persists. The federal government should utilize the lessons learned from the COVID-19 pandemic to improve data, programs, and policies to better serve vulnerable populations and encourage vaccine equity across the country.

References

Asundi A et al (2021) Global COVID-19 vaccine inequity: the scope, the impact, and the challenges. Cell Host Microbe 29:1036. https://doi.org/10.1016/j.chom.2021.06.007
Bajaj SS et al (2022) Vaccine apartheid: global cooperation and equity. Lancet 399:1452–1453. https://doi.org/10.1016/S0140-6736(22)00328-2
CDC (2022a) COVID-19 vaccine equity for racial and ethnic minority groups. https://www.cdc.gov/coronavirus/2019-ncov/community/health-equity/vaccine-equity.html.   Accessed 24 Oct 2024
CDC (2022b) Global Polio Eradication Initiative Information. https://www.cdc.gov/polio/gpei/index.htm. Accessed 24 Oct 2022
Davis R, Mbabazi WB (2017) Challenges to global measles eradication: is it all in the timing? Pan Afr Med J 27:11. https://doi.org/10.11604/pamj.supp.2017.27.3.12553
Gardner B (2021) Vaccine equity: why it matters and how to achieve it, Data-Smart City Solutions. https://datasmart.ash.harvard.edu/news/article/vaccine-equity-why-it-matters-and-how-achieve-it. Accessed 28 Oct 2022
Harman S et al (2021) Global vaccine equity demands reparative justice — not charity. BMJ Global Health 6:e006504. https://doi.org/10.1136/bmjgh-2021-006504

---

[42] Lister et al. (2021).
[43] Id.

Henderson DA (1987) Principles and lessons from the smallpox eradication programme. Bull World Health Organ 65:535–546. PMID: 3319270

Hill HA et al (2018) Vaccination coverage among children aged 19–35 months—United States, 2017. MMWR Morb Mortal Wkly Rep 67:1123–1124, 1127. https://doi.org/10.15585/mmwr. mm6740a4

Lister SA et al (2021) Health equity and disparities during the COVID-19 pandemic: brief overview of the federal role – Congressional Research Service 5. https://crsreports.congress.gov/product/ pdf/R/R46861/1. Accessed 24 Oct 2022

Mulders MN et al (2016) Global measles and rubella laboratory network support for elimination goals, 2010–2015. MMWR Morb Mortal Wkly Rep 65:438–442. https://doi.org/10.15585/ mmwr.mm6517a3

Patel M, Cochi S (2017) Addressing the challenges and opportunities of the polio endgame: lessons for the future. J Infect Dis 216:S1–S8. https://doi.org/10.1093/infdis/jix117

Persad G (2021) Allocating medicine fairly in an unfair pandemic. Univ Ill Law Rev 3:1085

Reiss DR, Caplan AL (2021) Workers with COVID-19 vaccine side effects deserve time off to recover, health affairs. https://www.healthaffairs.org/do/10.1377/forefront.20210204.959004/ full/. Accessed 28 Oct 2022

Save the Children, Vaccine Equity, Save the Children. https://www.savethechildren.org/us/charity-stories/what-is-vaccine-equity. Accessed 15 Oct 2021

Serdobova I, Kieny MP (2006) Assembling a global vaccine development pipeline for infectious diseases in the developing world. Am J Public Health 96:1554. https://doi.org/10.2105/AJPH. 2005.074583

Underhill K, Johnson OC (2021) Vaccination equity by design. Yale Law J Forum 131:53

Vaccine Access in Global Comparison

10

Abstract

What began as a novel coronavirus outbreak in Wuhan, China in late 2019 soon erupted into an unprecedented global health crisis, as the COVID-19 outbreak emerged into a pandemic that spread across nearly every nation worldwide. Among the list of nations hit the hardest, developing countries are disproportionately represented, demonstrating an inequitable distribution of the harms that resulted from the pandemic. Shortage of resources and healthcare personnel led to overwhelmed hospitals, overcrowding, rapidly drained funds, and 'infodemic' (a rapid and far-reaching spread of both accurate and inaccurate information about something, such as a disease), all of which were exacerbated by the lack of clear leadership, worsening the situation in developing countries (Bong et al., Anesthesia Analgesia 131:86–92, 2020.). An immediate recognition of the need for a vaccine from the very beginning prompted global research efforts in an attempt to curb the pandemic. In December 2020, less than one year after COVID-19 wreaked havoc on the modern world, the first Emergency Use Authorization (EUA) was approved for the Pfizer-BioNTech COVID-19 Vaccine. Soon after, in 2021, a number of other vaccines were developed and approved by various regulatory authorities in some developed countries. Although more than 10 billion doses of COVID-19 immunizations have been administered by mid-2022, the pandemic, and its subsequent consequences, continue to persist. With new strains evolving every few months, ongoing vaccine hesitancy, and lack of coordinated global distribution, the development of an effective vaccine has proven to be only the first in a long series of steps toward achieving global herd immunity and halting the pandemic. In addition to the aforementioned challenges, emerging evidence reveals that the vaccines may be associated with clot formation and other unexplained illnesses, fueling the public's lack of trust in manufacturing companies and their rapid, unconventional mode of development.

© The Author(s), under exclusive license to Springer Nature Switzerland AG 2023   93
Y. T. Yang, D. R. Reiss, *Vaccine Law and Policy*, Law for Professionals,
https://doi.org/10.1007/978-3-031-36989-6_10

Apart from the trials of vaccine distribution, experts have recognized a basic human right regarding vaccination, advocating that access to a lifesaving medical intervention, such as a vaccine, should be provided as a core human rights obligation. To guarantee this access worldwide, and to achieve the anticipated success that a vaccine hopes to bring, the procurement, allocation, distribution, administration, and uptake of vaccines will be essential steps in the process. With many preexisting health care challenges, developing countries are likely to face increasing difficulty at vaccine distribution efforts in comparison to the developed world. Since a majority of the global population resides in these nations, and international travel to and from these countries is likely to extend the pandemic, there is a crucial need for serious consideration to overcome the challenges faced in the developing world.

10.1 Vaccine Development

Effective vaccines for COVID-19 have been developed rapidly, indeed much more promptly than has been seen historically for other diseases, drawing concerns from the public over safety and efficacy. Several factors have contributed to the rapid timeline that occurred. First, the global nature of disease and widespread coverage in mass media helped garner support from both government and philanthropic organizations to invest in research and development efforts. Lessons learned from prior pandemics led to the swift establishment of international collaborations, such as the Coalition for Epidemic Preparedness Innovations (CEPI), which were quickly able to support vaccine research and development. Decades of research into vaccine technology such as genome sequencing, previous mRNA vaccine candidates, adenovirus vectors, etc., gave researchers an instrumental head start in the successful development of COVID vaccines.

These vaccine development efforts have been a costly affair. From a global perspective, more than $39 billion was committed for vaccine development. The United States (U.S.) alone contributed more than U.S. $9 billion under operation warp speed. The top five companies have each received between $957 million and $2.1 billion in funding commitments, mostly from the U.S. Government and the CEPI. The Chinese and Russian governments have similarly invested in several vaccine candidates being developed by private companies or government enterprises. In contrast, however, many developing nations lack the financial and technological resources to invest in vaccine development, and will therefore be reliant on vaccines manufactured abroad or through global cooperation. Efforts at knowledge sharing through temporary waivers of intellectual property rights have been impeded by the opposition of developed nations and pharmaceutical companies, interfering with the need for global vaccine availability.

With several efficacious vaccines now available, the next major challenge has been to scale up the production of vaccine doses to meet the global need. Contributing to the monumental challenge of scaling up production is the fact that multiple components needed for vaccine production are manufactured at different locations across the globe and vaccine production capabilities are unevenly distributed. Supply chain disruptions of any component in manufacturing or packaging could set back production efforts. However, partnerships have emerged between vaccine developers and manufacturers to scale up production rapidly. For example, Oxford–AstraZeneca projected a production of approximately 3 billion doses of vaccine in 2021 with manufacturing partnerships in various nations, most notably with Serum Institute of India, which planned to manufacture 1 billion of these doses.[1]

Not all COVID-19 vaccines are the same, and therefore require different storage, handling, and transportation conditions. Several stimulate a host response against spike protein of SARS CoV2 virus. Those produced by Moderna and Pfizer are mRNA vaccines, whereas the vaccines developed by Oxford–AstraZeneca and Johnson & Johnson are viral DNA vaccines using adenovirus vectors. Inactivated viral components and recombinant vectors are also being used in many, including Sinopharm and Sputnik V. Although the widely used and approved vaccines are the mRNA vaccines, inactivated vaccines such as Sinopharm from China and Covaxin from India, are being used or planned for use in many developing countries across Europe, Asia, Latin America, Middle East, and Africa.

10.2 Procurement

As introduced above, the majority of developing countries do not have the financial and technological capabilities to develop novel vaccines and will likely have to purchase these vaccines from open markets. However, a large number of available global vaccines have been purchased by wealthier nations, pushing the developing world to the back of the queue regarding vaccine supply and delivery. In fact, high-income countries represent only about 16% of the world's population, but they have purchased more than half of all COVID-19 vaccine doses worldwide, demonstrating a clear imbalance in vaccine distribution.[2]

Fortunately, an alliance of 190 nations led by international organizations such as CEPI, the Vaccine Alliance (GAVI), United Nations Children's Fund (UNICEF), and World Health Organization (WHO) has been set up to improve global vaccine access. The aim of the organization, named COVID-19 Vaccines Global Access (COVAX), is to accelerate the development and manufacturing of COVID-19 vaccines, and to guarantee fair and equitable access for every country in the world.[3] COVAX aims to ensure equitable distribution such that the most vulnerable people are vaccinated first globally.

---

[1] Nature What It Will Take to Vaccinate the World Against COVID-19. 2021. https://www.nature.com/articles/d41586-021-00727-3/. Accessed 19 Oct. 2022.

[2] Yamey (2021), p. 529.

[3] World Health Organization (2021).

10.3   Administration

Providing enough vaccine supplies to each country is only the first hurdle. Within these countries, it is additionally important that the vaccine doses are allocated to reach the entire population. This monumental task requires diligent consensus data and outlining of population demographics, real time tracking of vaccine uptake, as well as ongoing analysis to identify and rectify gaps in distribution, all of which may not be possible under the current infrastructure of the developing world. Developing nations would also need to factor in populations that have historically had poor access to healthcare, including remote, rural and migrant populations.

Distribution of the COVID-19 vaccine in particular is further complicated by the fact that several current vaccines require ultra-cold temperatures for storage and transportation. For example, mRNA vaccines like Moderna require -20 °C for storage up to 6 months, with its stability dropping to 30 days at temperatures of 2 to 8 °C, and even lower to 12 h at room temperature. COVID vaccines by Pfizer require even lower temperatures for storage up to 6 months (-80 to -60 °C).[4] Other vaccines have less stringent requirements, such as the Oxford–AstraZeneca vaccine which can be stored at normal refrigeration temperatures (2 to 8 °C), and may be a viable option for vaccination in more remote locations or in regions with limited equipment or reliable power supply to maintain ultra-cold storage.

10.4   Vaccine Hesitancy

COVID vaccine hesitancy has been an emerging problem in several nations even before the first vaccine was developed and approved. Although anti-vaccine rhetoric can be found in nearly every country, there is somewhat of a geographic pattern to the degree of opposition. According to recent estimates from a survey, some developing nations such as India reported a higher willingness for vaccination but other countries such as Serbia, Croatia, France, Lebanon, and Paraguay were on the lower end of the acceptability spectrum.[5]

The consequences of vaccine hesitancy result from the convergence of numerous complicating elements. Perhaps one of the most prominent concerns stems from the speed with which vaccines were developed and subsequently purchased. Individuals across many countries feared the trials were rushed, or that regulatory standards may have been relaxed,[6] despite public officials and scientific experts speaking out to convey that the opposite was true, in an attempt of reassurance. Another concern is that the pandemic brought on the use of the very first mRNA vaccine, which had never before been approved for human use. The novelty of the approach alone has

---

[4]Crommelin et al. (2021), pp. 997–1001.
[5]Wouters et al. (2021), pp. 1023–1034.
[6]Shah et al. (2020), pp. 931–932.

sparked some hesitancy, with many people lacking trust in manufacturing companies.

As anti-vaccine advocates audited every bad outcome of COVID-19 vaccination, some safety concerns were brought to light. The important role of Oxford's AstraZeneca vaccine was effectively undermined when scientists began to report cases of thrombosis. The trial for the Adenovirus 26 vector-based vaccine, being manufactured by Johnson & Johnson was similarly put on hold when one of the participants developed an unexplained illness. While these safety challenges placed many nations at risk, especially in countries where rates of vaccine hesitancy were high and likely to climb higher, underdeveloped countries were at grave risk due to these developments, as the most viable and cost-effective options were now no longer available.

For developing countries, where religion and faith are heavily prominent, concerns about composition of the vaccine and its acceptability for religious and ethnic groups are widespread. Aside from religion, additional factors can present as predictors for acceptance of COVID-19 vaccination. According to a recent survey, the most important predictor was the participant's vaccination against influenza.[7]

Lastly, political factors are also responsible for vaccine hesitancy among the masses. A few prior incidents such as the French government overestimating the need for vaccines and voting bias have created mistrust among the people and have thus broke down a strong communication network.[8] Tracing these political patterns and correlating population demographics can prove to be tactful in targeting vaccine uptake campaigns and strengthening strategies to improve immunization rates among certain geographic and demographic populations. In rural sectors, however, this proves to be difficult if not impossible, as there is limited epidemiological data available in primary healthcare systems. Although there have been previous attempts at vaccination by creating sociocentric networks, the question of villages not recognized on census still remains.[9]

10.5 Leveraging Existing Strengths

Improving global vaccine distribution does not rely solely on identifying and amending weaknesses. Rather, it becomes equally important to recognize the existing strengths of vaccine rollout and leverage these techniques to further increase vaccination efforts. Many developing nations have had recent or ongoing vaccination campaigns against communicable diseases, some of which have had great success. Eradication of wild polio in Africa is one such success story, achieved through regional cooperation, adequate infrastructure, and expertise building. These resources—surveillance networks, trained personnel, and operation centers—can be

---

[7]Dror et al. (2020), pp. 775–779.
[8]Barry (2021), p. 502.
[9]Yang et al. (2019), pp. 115–122.

utilized in supporting COVID-19 vaccination efforts in similar environments. Ongoing polio vaccination campaigns in Pakistan mean that healthcare workers are already present and familiar with local communities and should therefore be incorporated into the plan for the COVID-19 vaccine rollout. Not only will experienced healthcare workers be key for vaccine delivery, but also, they will be pivotal in the aim to boost uptake by acting as trusted sources through which targeted messaging about the safety of the COVID-19 vaccine can be spread. India's universal immunization program, the largest public health program in the world, and vaccine manufacturing facilities such as Serum Institute of India, also the largest of its kind, are robust and readily available resources that will pivot to support the vaccination efforts in the nation.

Strategies in other countries can also help reform the response to COVID-19 vaccination within specific demographic populations. For example, attempts to eradicate Hepatitis B in sub-Saharan Africa focused on promoting vaccination through antenatal discussions, urging pregnant women to get vaccinated and become advocates for others to vaccinate as well. Although intrauterine transmission of COVID-19 seems unlikely, it has led to detrimental outcomes in neonates. By engaging pregnant women to promote vaccination, as Africa did for Hepatitis B, a broadened scope of awareness may be reached across populations.[10]

While the tactic described above can be learned from and modeled for COVID-19, there are some differences that should be acknowledged. It should be explained that vaccination might not prevent neonatal infection, however, it can reduce infection rates in pregnant women leading to fewer complications in routine antenatal care, and therefore acts in protection of both the fetus and the mother. It will be important to explain these distinctions in the anticipated benefits of vaccination for pregnant women so that they have accurate expectations.

Developing nations have been able to learn from the missteps made in other public health interventions throughout history. For example, a disinformation (false information which is deliberately intended to mislead—intentionally making the misstating facts) effort in Pakistan resulted in significant setbacks in the nation's effort to eradicate wild polio. Learning from this, the nation proactively prepared to counter misinformation (false or inaccurate information—getting the facts wrong) against COVID-19 vaccines to prevent interference with rollout plans. Recognizing these shortcomings and adapting COVID-19 vaccination efforts accordingly can help avoid costly errors moving forward.

Another example can be found in Nigeria's efforts toward polio eradication. During the initial phases of the public health intervention, political leaders boycotted the movement believing that the vaccines contained antifertility chemicals, HIV, and carcinogenic agents.[11] This created a sense of mistrust with the public leading many parents to refuse vaccination for their children. At the time, religious scholars played an important role. They encouraged people to undergo vaccination because it did not

---

[10]Spearman et al. (2017), pp. 900–909.

[11]Jegede (2007), p. e73.

violate any principles related to their religion, culture, or basic human rights. In fact, they elaborated on the negative impact that such a boycott produces on the same religion globally. The intervention on behalf of these leaders is one of the ways in which the nation is tackling its polio crisis and should serve as inspiration for other nations to follow.

Political stability continues to be a cornerstone of effective eradication programs. A demonstration of its importance can be found in the historical example of smallpox eradication in Somalia. The years 1977 to 1979 were probably known as the deadly years because of the spread of smallpox. The Ethiopian war, among other factors, undermined the efforts of vaccine rollout programs at that time, thwarting eradication efforts and challenging public health leaders in these nations. In this case, the WHO had to intervene as a neutral third party in order to tackle the situation and recover resources.[12]

10.6 Conclusion

The COVID-19 pandemic highlighted and exacerbated pre-existing health inequities, hitting disadvantaged and marginalized communities the hardest. Developing countries experienced greater levels of harm as their healthcare systems struggled to obtain resources to test and treat individuals infected with the virus. As the pandemic raced on, a glimmer of hope appeared with the discovery and approval of the first COVID-19 vaccine. It soon became apparent, however, that the inequities of the pandemic extended to vaccine distribution, as major nations sequestered vaccine doses and developing countries faced storage and transportation challenges. Global public health experts acted swiftly, learning from the strategies implemented during the smallpox outbreaks. Although many global initiatives have taken up the responsibility of ensuring vaccine equity, these organizations not only need to scale up and strengthen their efforts, but also there is need to maintain the sustainability of these initiatives for future disasters. These organizations will need to garner international support and cooperation to ensure every nation is able to acquire the volume of vaccinations needed for their populations. They must involve religious, cultural, and social representatives to assist in appropriate administration and uptake of the acquired vaccines. Leveraging existing strengths, building on recognized weaknesses, and learning from past vaccine rollout efforts can help mitigate some of the challenges facing developing nations in vaccinating populations and bring the world closer to the end of this pandemic.

---

[12]Deria (2011), pp. D36–D40.

References

Barry DS (2021) Politicians must dial down the rhetoric over COVID vaccines. Nature 591:502. https://doi.org/10.1038/d41586-021-00769-7

Bong CL et al (2020) The COVID-19 pandemic: effects on low- and middle-income countries. Anesthesia Analgesia 131:86–92. https://doi.org/10.1213/ANE.0000000000004846

Crommelin DJA et al (2021) Addressing the cold reality of mRNA vaccine stability. J Pharm Sci 110:997–1001. https://doi.org/10.1016/j.xphs.2020.12.006

Deria A (2011) The emergency campaign for smallpox eradication from Somalia (1977-1979)--revisited. Vaccine 29:D36–D40. https://doi.org/10.1016/j.vaccine.2011.05.039

Dror AA et al (2020) Vaccine hesitancy: the next challenge in the fight against COVID-19. Eur J Epidemiol 35:775–779. https://doi.org/10.1007/s10654-020-00671-y

Jegede AS (2007) What led to the Nigerian boycott of the polio vaccination campaign? PLoS Med 4:e73. https://doi.org/10.1371/journal.pmed.0040073

Nature What It Will Take to Vaccinate the World Against COVID-19.2021. https://www.nature.com/articles/d41586-021-00727-3. Accessed 19 Oct 2022

Shah A, Marks PW, Hahn SM (2020) Unwavering regulatory safeguards for COVID-19 vaccines. J Am Med Assoc 324:931–932. https://doi.org/10.1001/jama.2020.15725

Spearman CW et al (2017) Hepatitis B in sub-Saharan Africa: strategies to achieve the 2030 elimination targets. Lancet Gastroenterol Hepatol 2:900–909. https://doi.org/10.1016/S2468-1253(17)30295-9

World Health Organization (2021) COVAX working for global equitable access to COVID-19 vaccines. https://www.who.int/initiatives/act-accelerator/covax. Accessed 19 Oct 2022

Wouters OJ et al (2021) Challenges in ensuring global access to COVID-19 vaccines: production, affordability, allocation, and deployment. Lancet 397:1023–1034. https://doi.org/10.1016/S0140-6736(21)00306-8

Yamey G (2021) Rich countries should tithe their vaccines. Nature 590:529. https://doi.org/10.1038/d41586-021-00470-9

Yang Y et al (2019) Efficient vaccination strategies for epidemic control using network information. Epidemics 27:115–122. https://doi.org/10.1016/j.epidem.2019.03.002

Part III

Individual Decision Making and Vaccines

This part of the book focuses on individual choices in the context of vaccines. The chapters explore individual decision-making regarding vaccines and how the law regulates and intersects with these choices. Chapter 11 emphasizes the importance of informed consent in the context of vaccines and discusses the legal aspects of this concept. Chapter 12 delves into the question of whether and under what circumstances adolescents can provide consent for vaccines when their parents disagree. Lastly, Chap. 13 addresses the potential civil liability associated with the decision not to vaccinate, proposing an approach that requires individuals to bear the consequences of their choices. Collectively, these chapters examine the legal aspects of individual decision-making related to vaccines, including informed consent, consent by minors, and potential legal consequences for not vaccinating.

Informed Consent

11

Abstract

Informed consent is the right to make an "intentional, free, and knowledge-based decision about" medical treatment (Reiss and Karako-Eyal, Am J Law Med 45: 357–363, 2019.). This idea is grounded in the moral principle that individuals have a right to make autonomous decisions and to control certain aspects of their lives, including decisions about their bodies. Informed consent is especially important in healthcare settings, including when it comes to vaccination. However, because vaccination is a preventative public health measure intended to reduce the spread of disease, the decision to vaccinate affects not only the individual, but others in a community, creating a discrepancy between personal autonomy to make vaccination decisions and the health of the community. This creates a question: how do we balance an individual's interest in informed consent and the public health interest in broad vaccine coverage? What happens when the state sees a need to mandate vaccines—how does that interact with informed consent?

This chapter explores the role of informed consent in vaccination, and then discusses how the concept interacts with vaccine mandates. We begin with a discussion on its background. Then, we lay out a theoretical model for informed consent, and what is needed for meaningful informed consent to vaccinate. Next, we discuss the United States (U.S.) legal framework for informed consent. Following this, we examine practical considerations for implementing the theoretical model for informed consent in the U.S. We conclude that although mandates may affect an individual's ability to voluntarily consent to vaccination, vaccine mandates should still incorporate the principles behind informed consent. Furthermore, they should require the sharing of adequate information about the benefits and risks of the vaccine. Therefore, this tension between informed consent and vaccine mandates is not as problematic as it might initially seem.

© The Author(s), under exclusive license to Springer Nature Switzerland AG 2023
Y. T. Yang, D. R. Reiss, *Vaccine Law and Policy*, Law for Professionals,
https://doi.org/10.1007/978-3-031-36989-6_11

11.1   Background

To be meaningful, informed consent requires competence, information, and voluntariness. *Competence* requires that the individual making the decision to vaccinate has the mental capacity to understand the information they are given in order to obtain their informed consent or refusal, and must be able to appreciate the consequences of the decision they make. We will discuss this further in Chap. 12, but in most states, children under 18 are considered not competent to make medical decision, including the decision to vaccinate, and the consent needs to be given by their parents. Some adults suffering from mental or physical illness or disability may also be considered incompetent, and the decision there would be made by their caretaker. In that case, the competence requirement is satisfied if the decisionmaker is competent.

The *information* given to the individual should include a description of the medically indicated treatment (e.g., vaccine) and the risks, harms, benefits, and potential benefits of the treatment, or refusal of all treatment. Some scholars also suggest that the risks and benefits disclosed should not only include material risks to the individual, but risks and benefits to the public, such as increasing the risk of outbreaks. Ultimately, informed consent requires the decision to receive or refuse vaccination to be *voluntary*. That is, the individual must be able to make their decision free of coercion, duress, or undue influence.

On the surface, vaccine mandates are at odds with the principles of informed consent; vaccine mandates do not require competence, information, or voluntariness.[1] Instead, vaccine mandates are imposed in situations where the vaccine is determined to be necessary to protect the public health. But this tension may be more apparent than real. First, everyone acknowledges that despite the benefits of vaccination, vaccines also have risks—though for most vaccines, the risks are small, and the benefits outweigh them. At least in democratic countries, no mandate involves restraining and forcing an adult to receive a vaccine; most of them impose consequences for the choice not to vaccinate. The process of vaccinating itself still needs to meet the requirements of informed consent—where all information needed to make a decision is provided to the adult. Therefore, we need to discuss to what degree a mandate makes consent less voluntary—and when is overriding consent justified. The next sections address these issues.

11.2   Theoretical Model

Vaccination is a medical intervention designed to prevent the spread of communicable disease.[2] Vaccinating any given individual has two benefits: protecting that individual, and contributing to herd immunity which protects the public. Beyond

---

[1] Parmet (2005), p. 74.
[2] Reiss and Karako-Eyal (2019), pp. 357–363.

providing protection to the vaccinated individual, widespread vaccination protects the public, including those who are unable to be vaccinated and those whose vaccinations did not work. In order to achieve the public health goals of widespread vaccination, scholars suggest that informed consent can promote trust between the public and health authorities by requiring health care providers to "(1) inform parents about vaccines; risks and benefits, (2) share with them uncertainties, (3) honestly answer their questions, and (4) seriously address their concerns." Although this quote addresses childhood vaccines, similar requirements should apply to adult vaccination where relevant information is shared with the adult considering vaccination. A recent article proposed a model for what the informed consent process for vaccines should look like. Note that this discussion addresses what should happen when the person comes in to be vaccinated; we will add a discussion of how mandates interact with that later in this chapter.

Informed consent for vaccination requires an individual to make an autonomous decision. Autonomous decision-making requires understanding, or an accurate interpretation of facts. To facilitate understanding, health authorities should ensure that patients will have an opportunity to accurately interpret the facts provided to them and avoid actions that may imperil such understanding. Autonomy is associated with the ability to resist external influences. This means that while reasonable efforts to persuade individuals with pro-vaccination information is in line with the principles of informed consent, employing methods such as threats, intimidation, fear tactics, and manipulation during the actual vaccination process prevents individuals from acting out of free will and exercising autonomy.

Physicians should provide relevant material and accurate information regarding purpose, benefits, risks, and side effects of vaccines. This includes disclosing information about what is not known about a vaccine. While it may sound counter-intuitive, being honest about the uncertainties surrounding a vaccine is important to maintaining trust in health authorities. In the context of COVID-19 vaccination, this is especially important because experts are still learning about the virus, its variants, and the effectiveness of the authorized vaccines.[3] Experts should not over-promise the vaccine's effectiveness or safety for the short-term benefit of increasing vaccination rates if in the long-term, misguided information will have a negative effect on public trust of experts and vaccines generally.

Individuals should be given information about the individual benefits as well as the social benefits of vaccination. In the context of COVID-19, individuals should be made aware of the empirical data surrounding chances of infection, chances of severe illness, chances of death, and transmissibility of the virus—and here, too, the uncertainties should be made clear. Experts should explain the effects COVID vaccination has on other people, especially sick and vulnerable people in the community.[4]

---

[3] CDC, Key Things to Know About COVID-19 Vaccines. https://www.cdc.gov/coronavirus/2019-ncov/vaccines/keythingstoknow.html. Accessed 20 Oct. 2022.

[4] Reiss and Karako-Eyal (2019), pp. 357–363.

Physicians and experts should not provide patients with false or inaccurate information and should not withhold critical information; this would result in a discrepancy between the interpretation made by the person being vaccinated or a caregiver and the facts that correctly describe the nature of the decision and its consequences; misleading information also influences trust in authority.

Information should be presented in a way that facilitates understanding. Information should be accessible and should create a dialogue between a patient and expert that encourages candid conversations. Information should be made available through healthcare providers, in community groups, through online forums, and other sources to increase the probability that individuals can access and understand information to be able to form informed consent.

Some scholars suggest that individuals, including parents who are making vaccination decisions on behalf of their children, have an obligation to be informed about the nature, benefits, and risks of vaccination regardless of their decision to vaccinate or not. This means an individual must be educated about the treatment, regardless of their decision whether to vaccinate or not, to provide both informed consent and informed refusal. This cooperation would prevent individuals from simply refraining from discussion about vaccination and encourages the opportunity to make an informed decision. Because individuals are required to be educated on the subject of vaccines, scholars believe this can help balance informed consent with the individual and public interest to be vaccinated. There are, of course, challenges in implementing this—for example, how do you ensure individuals comply with being educated? One way this was done is by adding an educational requirement to a mandate: you can opt-out, but only if a healthcare provider signed a document confirming that you discussed the risks and benefits of receiving or refusing a vaccine, or you have to complete an online education module.

11.3   United States Legal Framework

The U.S. recognizes informed consent as the right to make autonomous decisions. The U.S. also recognizes the state's power to protect the public health. Vaccination policies in the U.S. address both informed consent and protecting the public health. Some of these policies are discussed here.

11.3.1 Vaccine Information Statement

Case law does not treat informed consent to vaccination differently than informed consent for other medical decisions. However, there is a statutory difference in the way informed consent operates in the vaccination context. U.S. federal law requires a Vaccine Information Statement (VIS) prepared by the Secretary of Health and Human Services to be distributed "by health care providers to the legal representatives of any child or to any other individual receiving a vaccine set forth in the Vaccine Injury Table."

These materials include a description of the benefits of the vaccine, a description of the risks associated with the vaccine, a statement of the availability of the National Vaccine Injury Compensation Program, and other relevant information. Providing the information necessary to each individual to achieve informed consent can be time-consuming and a logistical challenge for healthcare providers. Requiring the VIS demonstrates the statute's intention, to balance providing an individual with information needed to make an informed decision to vaccinate with the public health desire to vaccinate as many people as quickly as possible, by producing a brief and accessible tool with pertinent information.

Current VISs are very clear, concise, and helpful, but the process could be improved to better serve its purpose. Scholars note that the law is unclear as to whether, and to what extent, an oral discussion of the VIS is required and how far in advance of vaccine administration a parent or individual needs to receive the VIS. Scholars have also suggested that the VIS should include information on the community benefits of widespread vaccination in addition to explaining the individual benefits of the vaccine.

11.3.2 State Educational Requirements

In 1905, the U.S. Supreme Court upheld vaccine mandates, citing a community's "right to protect itself against disease which threatens the safety of its members."[5] Despite the well-established principle that states can provide for the public health by imposing vaccine mandates, there is also a rich history promoting bodily autonomy and an individual's right to determine "what shall be done with his own body." A potential question is how school mandates interact with informed consent.

Today, all fifty states and the District of Columbia require that children receive certain vaccines before going to school.[6] Each jurisdiction with vaccine requirements also provides certain exemptions from the vaccine requirements, though these exemptions vary in each state. For example, although each state recognizes medical exemptions, the medical exemptions vary, and states may offer some or no non-medical exemptions (we discuss school mandates further in Chap. 15).

States implemented the school vaccination requirements to protect the public health by reducing outbreaks. However, requiring certain vaccinations for children to attend school limits parental freedom. Although, in theory, parents who choose not to vaccinate their children have the choice to homeschool their children, some commenters argue that this is not, in fact, a real choice, and therefore argue that there is a tension between informed consent and school vaccination requirements. On the other hand, there is, we believe, a good argument that this tension is often overstated. First, most states have non-medical exemptions available to parents who do not want

---

[5] Parmet (2005), p. 74.
[6] Reiss and Karako-Eyal (2019), pp. 357–363.

to vaccinate children before sending them to school—though not all. Second, many medical choices may have external consequences—for example, having a driver's license may be conditional on the medication an individual takes. Moreover, at the very least, the choice not to take a vaccine comes with a higher risk of preventable disease, and potentially with other limits. To travel to some countries, people may need to take a yellow fever vaccine. The external consequences do not absolve the doctor from going through an informed consent process. Absent direct coercion, this would not negate the choice to give informed consent, after learning the risks and benefits of the procedure. Finally, there is a history in the U.S. of limiting liberty to protect the public health—and for vaccines there is a clear public health benefit. Imposing consequences on the choice not to vaccinate should be done after consideration of both the public health needs and the importance of individual autonomy. Furthermore, to the degree possible, an opt-out should be available—even with consequences—to an individual refusing. However, imposing a consequence that limits access to employment or education is a very different interference in autonomy than imposing a jail sentence. Describing a consequence as negating informed consent is overstating the case. Choices have consequences. They are still choices.

Some scholars suggest that informed refusal policies may be an alternative way to encourage parents to vaccinate their children without requiring vaccination for school attendance. As mentioned already, informed refusal policies would allow parents to send a child to school unvaccinated, but would require a process—a discussion with the doctor or an online course—beforehand. Informed refusal would give doctors and healthcare experts the opportunity to provide individuals with information on the risks of their choice to refuse vaccination and would create an educational opportunity for open discussion.

11.3.3 Liability Protections

The National Childhood Vaccine Injury Act (NCVIA) requires the Department of Health and Human Services to create materials, like the VIS, describing the risks and benefits of vaccination and distribute them to patients before administering a vaccine. The law also limits liability through the National Vaccine Injury Compensation Program. Part of the purpose of the NCVIA was to encourage widespread childhood vaccination against certain vaccine-preventable diseases. The law intended to promote informed consent through the VIS and relieve fears of vaccine injury through the compensation program.[7] The law also intended to protect manufacturers from liability to incentivize them to continue to manufacture safe and effective vaccines. We addressed the compensation program in Chap. 5.

In terms of informed consent, the NCVIA incorporates the learned intermediary doctrine, which provides that manufacturers fulfill their duty of care when they provide all necessary information to a "learned intermediary" (such as a physician or

---

[7]Reiss and Karako-Eyal (2019), pp. 357–363.

other healthcare provider) who then interacts with the consumer of a product. The doctrine does not require manufacturers to provide direct warnings to patients. This, however, is not in tension with informed consent. The change in the law was adopted in response to findings of liability in the mass immunization context—and that itself was unusual; normally, manufacturers do not have to directly warn people about drug side effects, and the learned intermediary doctrine—making the doctor responsible to warn, was adopted to address that. The exception was adopted for mass immunization clinics because in those clinics, there was no individualized process between doctor and vaccinee, and the courts felt that absent manufacturer liability, there would be no recourse.[8] Outside mass vaccination clinics, there really is no reason to treat vaccines different than other products, where the informed consent process is between the doctor and patient—and the remedy towards the manufacturer is if there are warning defects in their materials, as provided to the doctor. The program preserves the ability to sue manufacturers for warning defects, but it does create a presumption that there were no warning defects if the manufacturer complied with Food and Drug Administration (FDA) requirements—in essence, creating a preemption regime.[9] That is a limit on manufacturer liability, but it's not directly part of the informed consent discussion: patients should still receive the full informed consent process.

11.4 Practical Considerations in the United States

11.4.1 General Considerations

Before vaccinating, an individual should go through an informed consent process, and be given the information that will allow them to assess the risks and benefits of vaccinating. Because vaccination is performed on healthy people, some individuals may hesitate to get vaccinated because of the associated risks.[10] If an individual believes that they have a low susceptibility to the disease or its severity, or if they doubt the vaccine's efficacy, they may be less likely to consent to vaccination. Vaccine hesitancy reduces vaccination rates, and lower vaccination rates have a negative effect on public health. This can cause, for example, a temptation to downplay vaccine risks or overstate their benefits—and that would be a serious error. To preserve trust, individuals need to learn that the information provided to them is as complete and accurate as possible, at the time it's given. There are, however, ways to decrease hesitancy within the context of full and accurate information—for example, by providing information about the community effects of vaccines. Providing adequate information and resources on both the individual

---

[8]Reyes v. Wyeth Lab., Inc., 498 F.2d 1264, 1277 (5th Cir. 1974).
[9]42 U.S.C. §300aa-22 (b)(2).
[10]Reiss and Karako-Eyal (2019), pp. 357–363.

and community risks and benefits of vaccination may foster a better sense of understanding.

In the context of COVID-19, a young, healthy person may believe that if they were to be infected, they will likely have mild symptoms and recover. Such an individual may be hesitant to get the COVID-19 vaccine if they think the vaccine risks or side effects are more dangerous than getting COVID-19. Information should be made available that explains not only the individual benefits and risks, but also the community risk for the refusal to vaccinate.

The spread of misinformation affects how individuals feel about vaccines. Inaccurate or misconstrued "facts" about vaccination contribute to vaccine hesitancy. Individuals may feel confused or uncertain about vaccines when they hear contradictory or frightening information about vaccine side effects or efficacy. Scholars suggest that the informed consent process is a tool to counter the effects of misinformation. Providing full, accurate, and clear information "from an authoritative, trusted source" can correct misconceptions and persuade more individuals to be vaccinated. In addition to providing information to counter the uncertainty surrounding vaccines, scholars note that the framing of pro-vaccination messages can affect how individuals receive the information. For example, studies show that "information about the risks posed by failing to vaccinate is significantly more effective than providing information aimed at dispelling myths about vaccines."

11.4.2 Benefits of Accessible Information

From a public health perspective, vaccine administration may be time-sensitive.[11] In the context of COVID-19, public health officials were promoting fast and widespread vaccination to reduce the spread of COVID-19 infection, relieve the stress on overwhelmed hospitals, and to reduce the risk of virus variants from evolving. Under these circumstances, the "cumbersome steps" to ensure individuals would have the information necessary to provide informed consent may have posed the risk of undermining efforts to increase vaccination rates quickly. However, some scholars suggest that incorporating the principles behind informed consent actually serves public health goals by promoting trust, preventing injuries, and recognizing choice. Scholars also provide a caveat for informed consent for vaccination in the context of a public health emergency; informed consent must shift from focusing on the individual to a broader, public health focus.

11.4.2.1 Promoting Trust
Informed consent is intended to "foster mutual trust and education between doctor and patient." Informing patients of the risks of vaccinations promotes and maintains trust between a patient and healthcare provider because it demonstrates the provider's interest in the health of the patient and respect for the patient's

---

[11] Parmet (2005), p. 74.

autonomous decision-making. Trust is essential to a patient's willingness to be vaccinated, and failure to warn of side effects or risks can deteriorate a patient's trust in their healthcare provider.[12] Patients who lose trust in healthcare providers may search for information elsewhere, leaving them susceptible to misinformation and anti-vaccination messages.

Hiding information from patients may be perceived as coercive, and may undermine a patient's trust in their own healthcare provider as well as in public health officials and government entities. In public health emergencies where time is of the essence, public health officials can promote trust and inform the public quickly and efficiently through large-scale public education campaigns that include means to ask experts questions and discuss concerns or uncertainties about vaccines.

11.4.2.2 Preventing Injuries

Preventing injuries is important for both informed consent and promoting the public health. Informing the public about vaccine risks and contraindications may help reduce vaccine-related injuries without reducing overall vaccination rates, thereby aiding the overall public health. It will let individuals who should not be vaccinated know that they, personally, should not be vaccinated (and should rely on herd immunity, and hence, should encourage those around them to vaccinate). Informed consent requires risks to be disclosed to the public, and therefore incentivizes the manufacture and administration of safer vaccines. If patients have a reduced risk of injury, they may be more likely to give informed consent for vaccination, or buy into mandatory vaccination policies.

11.4.2.3 Recognition of Choice

Although the goal of informed consent is intended to recognize autonomy, public health advocates note that autonomy is not absolute, and "[i]t must give way at times to the greater good of public health." This does not mean, however, that in public health emergencies such as COVID-19 that choice should not be respected. Even in the face of a vaccine mandate, individuals should still have the opportunity to be educated on the individual and public benefits of vaccination, express concerns and share information with their healthcare provider, and be able to make a choice.[13]

Choices may be supported by (1) the availability of exemptions, as appropriate, and (2) transparency about the consequences of the choice to refuse vaccination. Medical and non-medical exemptions may be available for individuals who have medical contraindications or religious and philosophical objections to vaccination, though these exemptions may vary across jurisdictions. Individuals need to know that refusing to vaccinate may have consequences like the forfeiture of certain activities such as education, employment, or access to public spaces. Although the choice may be burdensome, a choice of some degree may still exist for those who refuse to be vaccinated in the face of a mandate.

---

[12] Parmet (2005), p. 74.

[13] Parmet (2005), p. 74.

11.5   Conclusion

Informed consent is a human right, though it is not absolute. Informed consent requires the availability of clear and accurate information.[14] Without trust in health authorities, individuals may not be able to develop informed consent because there is confusion and uncertainty regarding what sources of information are reliable.[15] Trust in health authorities is essential to effectively communicate information about vaccines.[16] To encourage vaccination, public health officials and healthcare providers should provide individuals with information about the individual and public impact of the vaccine. Sharing adequate information about the risks and benefits may encourage trust in public health authorities, and demonstrate respect for the individual's interests, all while promoting the broader public health goal. Mandates should also consider individual autonomy and, where possible, provide options to refusers.

References

42 U.S.C. § 300aa-22(b)(2)

CDC, Key Things to Know About COVID-19 Vaccines. https://www.cdc.gov/coronavirus/2019-ncov/vaccines/keythingstoknow.html. Accessed 19 Oct 2022

Parmet WE (2005) Informed consent and public health: are they compatible when it comes to vaccines? J Health Care Law Policy 8:74. https://digitalcommons.law.umaryland.edu/jhclp/vol8/iss1/5/. Accessed 19 Oct 2022

Reiss DR, Karako-Eyal N (2019) Informed consent to vaccination: theoretical, legal, and empirical insights. Am J Law Med 45:357–363. https://doi.org/10.1177/0098858819892745

Reyes v. Wyeth Lab., Inc., 498 F.2d 1264, 1277 (5th Cir. 1974)

---

[14] Reiss and Karako-Eyal (2019), pp. 357–363.

[15] Parmet (2005), p. 74.

[16] Reiss and Karako-Eyal (2019), pp. 357–363.

Adolescent Consent

12

Abstract

State law generally controls whether parental consent is required for minors who may want to make their own health care decisions—including vaccination (English et al., J Adolesc Health 53:550–551, 2013.). This means that in many states, teenagers under the age of 18 cannot decide for themselves about whether or not to get vaccinated against diseases like diphtheria, measles, polio, or COVID. Lower vaccination rates put unvaccinated individuals and others in their communities at risk (Weithorn and Reiss, Conn Law Rev 52:771, 2020.).

One proposal to address this issue is to create a limited exception to parental decision-making authority by permitting certain older minors to legally consent to approved vaccinations, and protecting the confidentiality of minors who request vaccination without parental consent. The law allows similar exceptions for minors to make healthcare and treatment decisions independent of parental consent in other contexts. This chapter explores the issues related to adolescent consent to vaccination. We provide a brief overview of the legal landscape of health care decision authority for minors. We then discuss related issues and considerations. Next, we suggest a legislative solution for adolescent consent. Finally, we conclude that minors and the state have compelling interests for reform to vaccination consent laws.

12.1 Legal Landscape

The laws concerning minor health care decisions in the United States have developed to prioritize parental and caregiver consent. This precedent and the legal landscape surrounding adolescent consent to vaccination created a barrier to vaccination for teens. Specifically, if their parents refused consent, teens were denied the

© The Author(s), under exclusive license to Springer Nature Switzerland AG 2023   113
Y. T. Yang, D. R. Reiss, *Vaccine Law and Policy*, Law for Professionals,
https://doi.org/10.1007/978-3-031-36989-6_12

ability to receive a vaccination. [1] Experts say that allowing parents to block children's receipt of certain vaccinations "unfairly risks those children's right to health and life."[2] Although vaccines have risks, the risks of approved and recommended vaccines are relatively low. The government has an interest in the substantial benefits of vaccinations both for the individual and the community, and these interests are at odds with parental objections to vaccination.

12.1.1 Doctrine of Parental Consent

The well-established doctrine of parental consent is grounded in the idea that parents are responsible for the welfare of their children, and as part of this responsibility, parents should have discretion in how they support and nurture their children. Because children are immature physiologically and psychologically, the law generally views children as incapable of acting in their own best interests and treats their incompetence in making most personal decisions of legal import, including health care decisions, as presumptive. Because of this presumed incompetence, parents are the default proxy decision-makers for their children.

12.1.2 Competing Interests

When it comes to child vaccination, there are three main groups with interests at stake: parents with an interest as medical decision-makers for their children, the state as a regulator with interests in individual and general welfare, and the minors with interests in their own health and autonomous decision-making.[3] Each of these groups have overlapping interests when it comes to vaccination, making it difficult to balance the interests against one another.

Parents have a constitutionally protected interest in making decisions about their children's healthcare, but the minor's own constitutional rights may compete with parental claims. When a child's welfare interests are at stake, courts or legislatures may create exceptions to parental consent that use alternative decision-making structures to promote the child's best interests.

States have the power of *parens patriae*, paternalistic authority to regulate the lives of individuals who cannot protect themselves in the interest of that person's welfare. *Parens patriae* usually operates at the individual level and for the individual's best interests. The state police power, on the other hand, allows legislatures to regulate the conduct of individuals in order to promote the general welfare for society as a whole. This is understood and justified as the government

---

[1] English et al. (2013), pp. 550–551.
[2] Weithorn and Reiss (2020), p. 771.
[3] Weithorn and Reiss (2020), p. 771.

advancing the common good even when the action or regulation restricts individual liberty.

The state powers to intervene in the lives of children are greater than the power to intervene in the lives of adults because children are thought to be more vulnerable than adults and are presumed to be incompetent under the law. Like the rationale behind the parental consent doctrine, the state justifies stepping in to protect children because of their vulnerability. When parents' decisions are deemed to endanger their children's welfare or the public health, the legal system may override parental discretion. Recommended vaccines are usually in the best interest of both the minor and the community, since they involve protecting both from the harms of a contagious disease, and the risk from immunization is extremely low; therefore, the case for overriding parental discretion is strong, and the state may legally act under either its police power or its *parens patriae* authority.

12.1.3 Minor Consent Laws in States and Localities

State laws govern the consent requirements concerning vaccinations for minors.[4] Most states do not allow children to be vaccinated without parental consent, as of 2022. [5] However, states and localities have different laws regulating the consent process for teenagers. For example, in Oregon, minors 15 and up may consent to vaccination (and other medical treatments) without parental consent. Some states, like Minnesota, require parental consent with limited exceptions, for example when (1) the minor lives apart from their parent/guardian; (2) the minor is married; or (3) the minor has given birth. Other places, including some local jurisdictions in Arizona and California, allow minors to consent without being physically accompanied by a parent as long as the parent is able to consent (through a consent form, a notarized letter, etc.). One source found that 34 states and the District of Columbia allow minors "who are living on their own, including unaccompanied minors experiencing homelessness" to consent to "routine health care," including vaccinations. [6]

Most of these state laws are justified based on age and capacity of the adolescent, the legal status of the adolescent, the type of health care, and the disease for which vaccination is being administered.[7] Some of them are also based on convenience of parental consent. Most young children are vaccinated during regular wellness checkups, but data shows that adolescents and adults are less likely to keep up with annual preventative checkups. Despite the decline in annual preventative

---

[4]English et al. (2013), pp. 550–551.

[5]The Network for Public Health Law (2021) COVID-19 Vaccination State Minor Consent Requirements. https://www.networkforphl.org/wp-content/uploads/2021/05/Fact-Sheet-COVID-1 9-Vaccines-and-Minor-Consent.pdf (last accessed Jan. 19, 2022).

[6]School House Connection (2021).

[7]English et al. (2013), pp. 550–551.

checkups, teenagers do have contact with the medical system at least once a year at clinics, school-based health centers, etc. Because adolescents are not always accompanied by parents to these healthcare visits, parents would not be present to consent to vaccination if vaccination was offered at one of these visits. In these situations, the age of consent functions as a barrier to adolescent vaccine uptake, so some states have modified their laws to loosen restrictions on parental consent.

12.2 Related Issues

Although most states preserve the need for parental consent when it comes to health care decisions, this discretion is not absolute.[8] All states recognize certain exceptions to the doctrine of parental consent that allow older minors to consent to some medical interventions independent of parental consent.[9] Because of the sensitive nature of minors seeking health care interventions over parental rejection, it is recommended that confidentiality protections are incorporated into laws permitting minors to make certain medical decisions without parental consent.

12.2.1 Exceptions

State laws recognize various exceptions to parental consent for minor health care. As previously discussed, the state may limit parents' interests in exercising authority over the child's health care when those interests are outweighed by the state's *parens patriae* or police power interests in the child's welfare and/or the child's independent (and possibly constitutionally protected) interests in health care decisional auton-omy.[10] In other cases, the presumption that parents are acting, are capable of acting, or are situated to act to promote their children's best interests relative to a healthcare decision does not accurately reflect the circumstances. Finally, the presumption that minors are incompetent may not be supported by the evidence. Of particular relevance to the discussion surrounding adolescent consent to vaccination are the concepts of the "mature minor" and the treatment-specific statutory exceptions to parental consent.

The concept of the "mature minor" enables certain older minors to give informed consent, if they have the capacity to give informed consent, for care that is within the mainstream of medical practice, not high risk, and provided in a non-negligent manner.[11] Some scholars suggest that the "mature minor" concept may provide a basis for a minor to give consent for vaccinations.

---

[8]Weithorn and Reiss (2020), p. 771.
[9]English et al. (2013), pp. 550–551.
[10]Weithorn and Reiss (2020), p. 771.
[11]English et al. (2013), pp. 550–551.

Similarly, all states have laws allowing minors to consent to care for sexually transmitted diseases. These laws provide opportunities for minors to seek out and receive needed sensitive health care services confidentially that they might otherwise forego. Depending on the language of the state law, the laws may cover diagnosis, prevention, and services related to covered diseases. When these laws cover prevention, they typically extend to vaccinations against diseases such as human papillomavirus (HPV) and Hepatitis B. These laws serve as an example of existing exceptions to parental consent laws.[12]

12.2.2 Confidentiality

Scholars advocating for reform to adolescent vaccination consent laws also recommend that authorizing legislation require that minors' preferences regarding confidentiality be respected and that their vaccination status and vaccination-related medical contacts not be disclosed to their parents without their consent.[13] When states allow minors to consent to sensitive treatments independent of their parents, the information must be maintained in confidence if the minor does not authorize disclosure. Experts have expressed that "[r]esearch findings and clinical experiences reveal that minors' concerns about parental access to health care information can be a major deterrent to adolescents seeking, and therefore receiving, needed care for sensitive health matters".

The state has an interest in the minor's welfare, and protecting confidentiality encourages minors to seek out and receive care without fear of the consequences of their parents knowing about the treatment.

12.3 Reform

There is evidence that minors may have competence to make health care decisions, and that it is advisable to allow them to do so "if relying on parental consent alone would not achieve important interests." Specifically, studies show that competence to give informed consent for vaccination may not track the current common age-based laws of consent. Experts, including the Society for Adolescent Health and Medicine, recommend that reform is needed to maximize opportunities for minors to receive vaccinations when parents are not physically present, including opportunities for them to give their own consent.[14]

Such reform could be accomplished through judicial or state legislative action.[15] We recommend that reform be pursued via statute because this is a more effective

---

[12] Id.

[13] Weithorn and Reiss (2020), p. 771.

[14] English et al. (2013), pp. 550–551.

[15] Weithorn and Reiss (2020), p. 771.

mechanism than case-by-case judicial determination. Statutes create clear and specific criteria, and legislatures are better equipped to bring about law reform than courts. However, in the absence of legislative reform, experts suggest that courts should allow mature minors to consent independently to recommended vaccinations.

The state has an interest not only in the health of the minor, but in protecting the general public health. Creating a legislative exception to the doctrine of parental consent is a tool to combat low COVID vaccination rates, which has led to increases in serious illness and death.[16] In the era of COVID, vaccination status impacts many social, educational, and career opportunities. The minor's interests in their health, welfare, and other opportunities should hold value in this context. It may be in both the minor's and the community's best interest to consider an exception to parental consent for both routine and COVID-19 vaccines, at least for teens for whom COVID-19 vaccines are licensed, and not just under emergency use authorization.[17] Such a policy would mirror existing exceptions that allow minors to access medical intervention, like seeking treatment for sexually transmitted diseases. A statutory mechanism for adolescent consent to vaccination should include setting a minimum age based on empirical data regarding competence and psychosocial maturity, providing complete information regarding vaccination, and requiring the minors have the time to process, analyze, and discuss the information with health care professionals before providing consent.

One of the primary justifications for parental consent laws is that patients must be competent to give informed consent, and minors are presumed incompetent. Informed consent requires the patient's decision be informed, competent, and voluntary. In other words, the patient must have the capacity to understand the information provided about the vaccination. Older minors may have the capacity to make the decision to be vaccinated if they have the ability to communicate a choice, to understand relevant information, to reason about treatment options, and to appreciate the situation and its likely consequences.[18] In fact, empirical research shows that minors as young as 12 may have attained sufficient levels of capacity to meet legal standards of competence to consent to vaccination (though the age of competence varies among individuals). We suggest that based on data, minors ages 14 and older can be presumed to be competent to receive vaccinations without parental consent.

Older minors should be authorized to decide to be vaccinated when their psychological capacities have matured sufficiently to enable them to satisfy the legal requirements for competent informed consent. This would be "in line" with existing exceptions to the doctrine of parental consent. Reiss and Weithorn also advocate for protecting the confidentiality of minors who consent to vaccination independent of their parents to protect their privacy, avoid conflict, and encourage them to seek out vaccination rather than forego it.

---

[16] CDC (2021).

[17] Weithorn and Reiss (2020), p. 771.

[18] Weithorn and Reiss (2020), p. 771.

12.4 Conclusion

Competent adolescents who wish to be vaccinated despite parental resistance to provide consent for vaccination should be able to make this choice autonomously. A statutory change could permit older minors to independently and confidentially access certain vaccinations, including the COVID vaccine, without parental consent. This change would function similarly to existing exceptions to parental consent, and would advance the state's interests in promoting individual welfare and the public health.

References

CDC (2021) Science brief: COVID-19 vaccines and vaccination. https://www.cdc.gov/coronavirus/2019-ncov/science/science-briefs/fully-vaccinated-people.html. Accessed 19 Oct 2022

English A et al (2013) Adolescent consent for vaccination: a position paper of the Society for Adolescent Health and Medicine. J Adolesc Health 53:550–551. https://doi.org/10.1016/j.jadohealth.2013.07.039

School House Connection (2021) Minor consent to routine medical care. https://schoolhouseconnection.org/state-laws-on-minor-consent-for-routine-medical-care/. Accessed 19 Oct 2022

The Network for Public Health Law (2021) COVID-19 vaccination state minor consent requirements. https://www.networkforphl.org/wp-content/uploads/2021/05/Fact-Sheet-COVID-19-Vaccines-and-Minor-Consent.pdf. Accessed 19 Oct 2022

Weithorn LA, Reiss DR (2020) Providing adolescents with independent and confidential access to childhood vaccines: a proposal to lower the age of consent. Conn Law Rev 52:771. https://doi.org/10.2139/ssrn.3450277

Tort Liability for Failure to Vaccinate

13

Abstract

Despite the medical and scientific consensus that the risks associated with vaccinating with routine vaccines are smaller than the risks of not vaccinating (Reiss, Cornell J Law Public Policy 23:595–601, 2014; CDC, Who sets the immunization schedule, 2021; Reiss, Legal responsibilities in choosing not to vaccinate, 2013.), some parents refuse to vaccinate their children against vaccine-preventable diseases like measles. Parents might refuse to vaccinate their children on religious grounds—for example, opposition to the use of cell lines derived from old abortions in developing the rubella component of certain vaccines. They might also oppose vaccination for personal or philosophical reasons, including the belief that children are better protected if they contract certain preventable diseases and develop natural immunity. Parents may also be concerned that it is unsafe to vaccinate their children, for example buying into the popular (but debunked) myth that vaccines were linked to the development of autism in children (McKee and Bohannon, J Pediatr Pharmacol Ther 21:106–108, 2016.). Due to these, and other reasons, we should consider if the harms from non-vaccination can lead to tort liability (we address compensation for vaccine injuries in Chap. 5).

There are two potential questions here regarding tort liability. First, what if a child—who is unvaccinated against such diseases—infects other children? The unvaccinated child might infect other children who are too young to receive certain vaccines, children who cannot be vaccinated for medical reasons, or those who were vaccinated, but the vaccine did not work. Can the parents of the unvaccinated child be held legally liable to the child who has become infected? Some scholars argue yes—and this will be discussed in further detail later on regarding traditional negligence lawsuits or legislative statutes establishing liability. Second, can children who are harmed because their parents did not vaccinate them, sue their parents?

© The Author(s), under exclusive license to Springer Nature Switzerland AG 2023
Y. T. Yang, D. R. Reiss, *Vaccine Law and Policy*, Law for Professionals,
https://doi.org/10.1007/978-3-031-36989-6_13

To address these questions, we start with the case of an unvaccinated child infecting others. We describe how parents of unvaccinated children might be held liable under a traditional negligence lawsuit framework. Next, we discuss potential statutes establishing liability for parents of unvaccinated children. We also examine counter-arguments to imposing such liability. Finally, we discuss the possibility of children suing their own parents, and the limitations there. To note, this chapter will focus on vaccines that have been around for years (*e.g.*, polio, measles, etc.) and to a lesser extent the more recently developed COVID-19 vaccines. Furthermore, this paper solely focuses on tort liability for parents who refuse to vaccinate their children; it does not encompass adults who refuse to vaccinate themselves and then infect other members of the community.

13.1   Framework

Parents of a child infected by an unvaccinated child (the plaintiffs) may be able to establish a negligence lawsuit against the unvaccinated child's parents. A negligence lawsuit would allow the parents to sue for damages due to harms (their child becoming sick, cost of healthcare, etc.) In order to prevail in a negligence lawsuit against parents of an unvaccinated child (the defendants), five elements must be met. Those five elements are: (1) a duty of care on the part of the defendant; (2) a breach of that duty; (3) a causal connection between the conduct and the injury; (4) that the injury was within the scope of liability; and (5) a loss or damages as a result of the injury.[1]

13.1.1   Duty

A plaintiff cannot successfully maintain a negligence lawsuit if the defendant never owed the plaintiff a duty of care. In a negligence suit, a court must "decide not only who owes the duty, but also to whom the duty is owed, and what is the nature of the duty owed."[2] A problem that plaintiffs encounter when trying to establish the duty element is that our courts distinguish between *misfeasance* vs. *nonfeasance,* and not vaccinating may fall under nonfeasance, which usually does not lead to liability. Misfeasance is defined as "the improper performance of some act which a man may lawfully do," while nonfeasance focuses on not acting to prevent harm to others.[3] A person who commits misfeasance owes a duty to "others to exercise the care of a reasonable man" but generally "one who commits nonfeasance has no duty of care. . . ."[4] For centuries, the common law has never imposed a duty to act on individuals

---

[1] Behrendt v. Gulf Underwriters Ins. Co., 768 N.W.2d 568, 573 (Wis. 2009).

[2] Keller v. City of Spokane, 44 P.3d 845, 848 (Wash. 2002).

[3] Baccus v. Ameripride Servs., 179 P.3d 309, 313 (Idaho 2008) (quoting Rexburg v. Madison County, 764 P.2d 838, 842 (Idaho 1988)).

[4] Ramsey v. Ga. Southern Univ. Advanced Dev. Ctr., 189 A.3d 1255, 1265–66 (Ga. 2018).

unless their conduct creates some type of risk or there is a special relationship. For example, an individual who could safely rescue someone who is drowning is generally not liable for failing to rescue the drowning person.[5]

Parents who choose not to vaccinate their children could be seen as choosing not to act. This could reasonably be described as nonfeasance. While certain vaccines are generally required before a child can attend public school—every state allows parents to opt out of this requirement on various grounds. Furthermore, parents who do not qualify for exemptions generally have a choice to homeschool rather than vaccinate.[6] On the other hand, the decision not to vaccinate is not the same as passively allowing others to take a risk; parents who do not vaccinate, actively and deliberately make a choice, after claiming to have done research and sometimes having to act by resisting pressure from doctors or getting exemptions from school mandates.[7] Thus, it can be argued that the decision not to vaccinate and then place an unvaccinated child in the community is closer to misfeasance than to the traditional definition of nonfeasance.

Alternatively, courts can impose a duty to act, even in situations where one normally would not exist, if there are compelling policy reasons to do so. Making such a determination typically turns on several factors, including: (1) the foreseeability of harm to the plaintiff; (2) the moral blame attached to the defendant's conduct; (3) the policy of preventing future harm; and (4) consequences to the community of imposing a duty to exercise care with resulting liability for breach.[8] Here, because an unvaccinated child is at a higher risk of getting and transmitting an infectious disease than a vaccinated one, it is foreseeable that the unvaccinated child will contract and transmit a disease to others. There is also additional support for imposing a duty, because it can reduce harms to others and the community by encouraging vaccination. Furthermore, "the costs of the fact that a parent wrongly believes that the risks of vaccinating are higher than the risks of not vaccinated should not be borne by his neighbors."[9]

13.1.2 Breach

If a plaintiff can establish that the defendant owed a duty of care, the next step is proving that the defendant breached that duty.[10] Proving this breach element requires showing that the defendant acted in an objectively unreasonable manner under the

---

[5] Reiss (2014), p. 606.

[6] Dobbins Baxter (2014), pp. 103–104.

[7] Reiss (2014), p. 607.

[8] *Id.* at 609 (quoting Rowland v. Christian, 69 Cal. 2d 108, 113 (1968)).

[9] *Id.* at 612–13.

[10] Kirby v. NMC/Continue Care, 993 P.2d 951, 954 (Wyo. 1999).

circumstances.[11] In other words, the defendant's conduct is compared to that of a "hypothetical individual who is intended to represent a sort of 'average' citizen."[12] If the defendant does not exhibit the same level of care the "hypothetical individual" would under the circumstances, he has breached his duty of care.

Some argue that because states allow for exemptions from vaccine requirements, the decision not to vaccinate complies with state law and is thus reasonable. However, this argument is limited, because behavior can be legal and yet unreasonable.

One approach to negligence compares the burdens of taking a particular preventative measure with the probability and magnitude of injury that might occur absent the measure relevant here.[13] If the probability and magnitude of injury outweigh the burdens, then a defendant has breached his duty of care if he fails to take the particular preventative measure. Here, the particular preventative measure—vaccination—presents a very small risk or burden and is vastly outweighed by the probability and magnitude of injury related to not vaccinating.[14]

Furthermore, determining the reasonableness of a defendant's conduct would likely include comparing such conduct to the defendant's community as a whole. In 2015 just under 99% of children born in the United States (U.S.) received at least some Centers for Disease Control and Prevention (CDC)-recommended vaccinations. That statistic would lend credence to the notion that the decision not to vaccinate one's child is objectively unreasonable. However, there is a twist when discussing the recently released COVID-19 vaccines. A report in December 2021 found that only half of parents said that their adolescent child had received at least one dose of a COVID-19 vaccine, with significantly fewer parents of younger children expressing confidence in the COVID-19 vaccines.[15] Those numbers could certainly increase as COVID-19 vaccines become more established, and the report was published prior to the recent omicron surge. However, those numbers stand in stark contrast to the percentage of children receiving traditional vaccines recommended by the CDC. Therefore, it stands to reason that the decision not to vaccinate a child against COVID-19 would be viewed as much more objectively reasonable in the near future than not vaccinating against other vaccine-preventable diseases.

Finally, expert recommendations can reflect what is or is not reasonable, and an expert consensus supports giving children recommended vaccines.

---

[11] Pfenning v. Lineman, 947 N.E.2d 392, 404 (Ind. 2011).

[12] People v. Mendoza, 42 Cal. 4th 686, 703 (2007).

[13] Raab v. Utah Ry. Co., 221 P.3d 219, 232-33 (Utah 2009).

[14] Reiss (2014), p. 618.

[15] Palosky (2021).

13.1.3 Causation

After establishing a duty of care, and proving that the defendant breached that duty, a plaintiff must show that the defendant's conduct caused the plaintiff's harm. This requires "showing that the injury or harm would not have occurred 'but for' the defendant's action."[16] One problem here is that it is not always possible to determine where someone contracted an infectious disease. Even if a child contracts an infectious disease, and is classmates with another child unvaccinated against that disease, it may be impossible to prove that the child did not contract the disease from other sources.

However, establishing causation does not require a plaintiff to completely rule out other potential sources of harm. Instead, the plaintiff must simply show "facts and conditions from which the negligence of the defendant and the causation of the accident by that negligence may be reasonably inferred."[17] This will depend on the facts of the case, including how common is the disease, and how effective the vaccine is at preventing transmission. For example, if an unvaccinated American child travels to Europe and contracts measles, then after his return a classmate contracts measles, the classmate could reasonably imply that the unvaccinated child was the source of the infection. This is because the U.S. has had low levels of measles since the early 1990s, and most recent measles outbreaks are traced to unvaccinated individuals who have travelled abroad and then brought the disease back home.[18] On the other hand, causation will be much harder to show for COVID-19, where the disease is still highly prevalent in the community and the vaccines are less effective at preventing transmission. In this case, showing causation will require a special set of circumstances that would allow ruling out some of the other potential sources of infection.

In many circumstances causation may be impossible to prove, but the hypothetical shows that causation can in fact be proved in the right cases. The burden—as is the case with all elements required to establish a negligence claim—is on the plaintiff to prove causation by a preponderance of the evidence.[19]

13.1.4 Scope of Liability (Also Known as Proximate Cause)

Even if there is causation, scope of liability looks at whether the connection between an unreasonable behavior, not vaccinating, and the harm is too attenuated, unexpected, or remote to justify imposing liability. This will not be an issue in the usual

---

[16]Romain v. Frankenmuth Mut. Ins. Co., 762 N.W.2d 911, 917 (Mich. 2009) (Young, J., dissenting).

[17]Reiss (2014), p. 620 (quoting Ingersoll v. Liberty Bank of Buffalo, 14 N.E.2d 828, 829–30 (N.Y. 1938)).

[18]Reiss (2014), p. 619.

[19]Daniels v. Chesapeake & O. Ry., 94 W. Va. 56, 58–59 (1923).

case where someone is suing for their own exposure to disease via non-vaccinating. Nevertheless, in some cases, the infected person may infect others or cause indirect harm—and in those cases, there may be questions about the scope of liability. For example, if an unvaccinated child infects a baby with measles, and the baby infects their grandmother who has cancer, or other babies in their daycare, we may ask whether the connection to the parents' choice not to vaccinate is direct enough. Alternatively, if non-vaccination leads the infected child to infect another child with measles, and the infected child develops high fever that causes her to thrash and hit a baby in the hospital, can the baby's parents sue the non-vaccinating parents? These are the kind of situations where scope of liability might be relevant. In these cases, the question will be whether the harm was reasonably foreseeable from the initial negligence, and the question will be determined on a case-by-case basis by the jury, or if the facts are extreme, by the judge acting as the gatekeeper.

13.1.5 Damages

Finally, "[d]amages are an indispensable element of a common-law negligence claim."[20] One court has defined damages as "the word which expresses in dollars and cents the injury sustained by the plaintiff."[21] In this context, computing damages is relatively simple. On the one hand, a plaintiff's economic damages could include: past and future medical bills, lost wages and loss of earning capacity, age, and life expectancy. Additionally, a plaintiff could recover non-economic damages including pain and suffering, permanent impairment, and loss of enjoyment of life.[22]

Here though, a plaintiff may have difficulty recovering the damages actually awarded. That is because most defendants who are successfully sued rely on liability insurance to cover the damage awards. However, many insurance companies have a "Communicable Diseases Exclusion," which may preclude coverage for liability related to a defendant's transmission of a communicable disease to a plaintiff. In that case, a defendant may not have enough personal wealth and assets to cover the damages awarded to the plaintiff, meaning that plaintiff may only see a fraction of their recovery. While the danger of insolvent defendants arises in other contexts, we still allow plaintiffs to sue.[23]

---

[20] Walsh v. Advanced Cardiac Specialists Chtd., 273 P.3d 645, 648 (Ariz. 2012).

[21] Donovan v. Philip Morris USA, Inc., 914 N.E.2d 891, 899 (Mass. 2009) (quoting Turcotte v. DeWitt, 131 N.E.2d 195 (1955)) (internal quotations omitted).

[22] Meals ex rel. Meals v. Ford Motor Co., 417 S.W.3d 414, 420 (Tenn. 2013).

[23] Reiss (2014), p. 623.

13.2 Arguments

If courts are unwilling to impose a duty to vaccinate on parents, scholars argue for a legislative remedy. Many point to state laws creating duties to report accidents and child abuse, and contend that the same policy reasons behind creating those duties apply to creating a duty to vaccinate. Such statute provides exceptions if a child cannot be vaccinated due to age or other circumstances determined by the Advisory Committee on Immunization Practices (ACIP). Furthermore, parents can escape liability by proving that they made reasonable efforts to vaccinate their child, but were unable to due to events beyond the parents' control such as a vaccine shortage (or having to stay at home during a pandemic). Notably, qualifying for a religious or personal belief exemption from vaccination requirements under state law would not be a defense against civil liability.[24]

Such a statute balances the rights of parents to decide whether or not to vaccinate their child with the rights of those who could be harmed by that choice. The statute essentially codifies the notion that a parent has a legal duty of care to vaccinate the child. That notion is rebuttable—but the avenues of rebuttal are slim. Such a statue can draw on ACIP recommendations to identify when not vaccinating is a breach of duty. Ultimately, the rationale is "that absent a compelling reason, no one should bear the costs of the decision not to vaccinate beyond the deciding parent (and the child for whom they are making the decision)."

13.3 Counter-arguments

Despite arguments for imposing liability on parents who refuse to vaccinate their children, a number of arguments have been raised against the idea. The first argument is that imposing liability on parents who refuse to vaccinate their children will alienate those parents and possibly further jeopardize their children's health.[25] Proponents of this argument suggest focusing on research and education for those parents rather than imposing liability. Nevertheless, a study found that numerous parents claiming personal belief exemptions from pertussis vaccines in California "tended to be in neighborhoods with higher levels of education and income." Therefore, increasing education may not be as effective a tool as some may think.

The next argument against imposing liability rests on the U.S. Constitution and parental autonomy. Under the Fourteenth Amendment, people enjoy a significant amount of personal liberty. However, such liberty is subject to reasonable state regulation to promote the common good. For example, the Supreme Court in 1905 upheld a law passed by the city of Cambridge, Massachusetts requiring all citizens be vaccinated against smallpox. Relatedly, the Supreme Court has recognized that parents have broad discretion in raising their children—including making medical

---

[24] Reiss (2014), pp. 624–625.
[25] Dobbins Baxter (2014), p. 115.

decisions for the child. Nevertheless, this discretion can be curtailed, as it was by the Tenth Circuit when it endorsed actions taken by doctors to remove a cancerous growth from a child's mouth against the parent's wishes.[26]

Supreme Court cases support the notion that a state can mandate vaccinations in the face of vaccine-preventable disease outbreaks or specific and significant risks. But parents may in fact not have to provide certain medical treatments to their children. Further, even when it applies, parental freedom does not protect parents from consequences of that decision—"especially if that decision was based on faulty information, unless they took reasonable steps to protect others."[27] The other side of freedom is personal responsibility; parents can choose whether to vaccinate or not, but may face consequences if they choose not to vaccinate and that choice harms others.

13.4 Suing One's Own Parents

Unvaccinated children do have the option to sue their own parents for potential harms. A claim by a child against parents who did not vaccinate would, in several ways, be easier than a claim by a third party. First, while there is usually no duty to act, parents have a duty to act for the benefit of their children, including taking medical care of them. Further, for most vaccines, causation will be very straightforward: most routine vaccines are over 50% effective at preventing disease and harm, so it will be easy for the child to show that had the parents vaccinated the child, the harm would not have happened.

There are two main obstacles that allow a child to conduct a lawsuit against their parents, one practical and one legal. The legal obstacle is that in a majority of states, parents are still immune from lawsuits by their children over negligent medical care.[28] So a lawsuit for parental non-vaccination will only be viable in the states that allows children to sue parents in negligence for such choices, or will require a change of law in the state in question. This is another place where a legislative remedy may be needed.

The practical obstacle is that it is hard for children to sue their parents, absent a breakdown in the relationship. It causes strain, and for a young child, there is a need for external adult representation. The most likely situation where such suits would come up is either for a child that is now an adult or in a family after a breakdown like a divorce.

---

[26]Dobbins Baxter (2014), pp. 119–120.
[27]Reiss (2014), pp. 612–613.
[28]Reiss (2017), pp. 73–108.

13.5   Conclusion

Vaccines have made some previously devastating diseases either extremely rare or virtually non-existent. Their development has saved the lives of countless children who would not have survived to adulthood fifty years ago. Yet a small fraction of parents refuse to vaccinate their children—despite the clear benefits and safety of the vaccines. This decision can have deadly consequences for the child, and also for others, if a child of those parents contracts a vaccine-preventable disease and then spreads it to another child. That child may be too young to receive a certain vaccine or the infection may spread regardless of the child's vaccination status. The parents of the harmed child could face exorbitant medical expenses and potentially face the loss of a child—because other parents refused to vaccinate their child. In that situation, some scholars argue that the parents of the unvaccinated child should be held legally liable.

Holding those parents legally liable requires the law—either via courts or legislatures—to establish a duty on parents to vaccinate their children or face the consequences. The reasons offered by scholars for imposing a duty are compelling—and for diseases such as measles, one can see how parents of an impacted child could prevail on a negligence lawsuit. However, It is less clear that the negligence framework would be applied to cases involving the COVID-19 vaccines—as communities have remained significantly divided on whether to give their children such a vaccine. Therefore, determining if not vaccinating one's child against COVID-19 is an unreasonable choice would likely be difficult to swallow for courts, juries, and legislatures.

References

Baccus v. Ameripride Servs., 179 P.3d 309, 313 (Idaho 2008) (quoting Rexburg v. Madison County, 764 P.2d 838, 842 (Idaho 1988))

Behrendt v. Gulf Underwriters Ins. Co., 768 N.W.2d 568, 573 (Wis. 2009)

CDC (2021) Who sets the immunization schedule. https://www.cdc.gov/vaccines/parents/schedules/sets-schedule.html. Accessed 20 Oct 2022

Daniels v. Chesapeake & O. Ry., 94 W. Va. 56, 58–59 (1923)

Dobbins Baxter T (2014) Tort liability for parents who choose not to vaccinate their children and whose unvaccinated children infect others. Univ Cincinnati Law Rev 82:103–104. https://scholarship.law.uc.edu/uclr/vol82/iss1/3/. Accessed 20 Oct 2022

Donovan v. Philip Morris USA, Inc., 914 N.E.2d 891, 899 (Mass. 2009) (quoting Turcotte v. DeWitt, 131 N.E.2d 195 (1955)) (internal quotations omitted)

Keller v. City of Spokane, 44 P.3d 845, 848 (Wash. 2002)

Kirby v. NMC/Continue Care, 993 P.2d 951, 954 (Wyo. 1999)

McKee C, Bohannon K (2016) Exploring the reasons behind parental refusal of vaccines. J Pediatr Pharmacol Ther 21:106–108. https://doi.org/10.5863/1551-6776-21.2.104

Meals ex rel. Meals v. Ford Motor Co., 417 S.W.3d 414, 420 (Tenn. 2013)

Palosky C (2021) Half of parents of adolescents 12-17 say their child has gotten a COVID-19 vaccine, though uptake has slowed; 16% of parents of 5-11 year-olds say their child has gotten a vaccine. https://www.kff.org/coronavirus-covid-19/press-release/half-of-parents-of-

adolescents-12-17-say-their-child-has-gotten-a-covid-19-vaccine-though-uptake-has-slowed-1
    6-of-parents-of-5-11-year-olds-say-their-child-has-gotten-a-vaccine/. Accessed 20 Oct 2022
People v. Mendoza, 42 Cal. 4th 686, 703 (2007)
Pfenning v. Lineman, 947 N.E.2d 392, 404 (Ind. 2011)
Raab v. Utah Ry. Co., 221 P.3d 219, 232-33 (Utah 2009)
Ramsey v. Ga. Southern Univ. Advanced Dev. Ctr., 189 A.3d 1255, 1265–66 (Ga. 2018)
Reiss DR (2013) Legal responsibilities in choosing not to vaccinate. https://shotofprevention.
    com/2013/09/12/legal-responsibilities-in-choosing-not-to-vaccinate/. Accessed 20 Oct 2022
Reiss DR (2014) Compensating the victims of failure to vaccinate: what are the options? Cornell J
    Law Public Policy 23:595–601. https://pubmed.ncbi.nlm.nih.gov/25330552/ (last accessed Oct.
    20, 2022)
Reiss DR (2017) Rights of the unvaccinated child. Stud Law Polit Soc 73:73–108. https://doi.org/
    10.1108/S1059-433720170000073007
Romain v. Frankenmuth Mut. Ins. Co., 762 N.W.2d 911, 917 (Mich. 2009) (Young, J., dissenting)
Walsh v. Advanced Cardiac Specialists Chtd., 273 P.3d 645, 648 (Ariz. 2012)

Part IV

Vaccine Mandates

The chapters in this part explore the topic of vaccine mandates and the various legal aspects associated with them. Chapter 14 provides an introduction to vaccine mandates in the U.S. and discusses the roles of different levels of government in setting them. Chapter 15 focuses on school immunization mandates, which are commonly used to increase childhood vaccination rates in the U.S., and the exemptions available, including medical, religious, and philosophical exemptions. Chapter 16 examines workplace vaccine mandates, both by state actors and private employers, and the limitations in imposing them. Chapter 17 addresses the emergence of federal vaccine mandates during the COVID-19 pandemic and the legal challenges they faced. Chapters 18 and 19 broaden the discussion to a global perspective, examining mandates across different nations and for travel. Together, these chapters explore the legal framework and considerations related to vaccine mandates, including their types, exemptions, challenges, and global implications.

Introduction to Vaccine Mandates in the United States

14

Abstract

Since the invention of vaccines, the benefits of effective vaccination have become clear, and the more individuals who vaccinate, the greater the protection of the whole population. However, opposition to vaccination has threatened its success since the advent of the first immunization in the eighteenth century. Some view the decision to vaccinate as an individual one; they argue for the right to decline it as a medical choice. For communicable diseases, however, the decision not to vaccinate does not only affect the decisionmaker; it both directly and indirectly puts the population around an unvaccinated individual at risk, diminishing the effectiveness of vaccination in that population. First, vaccines can reduce the likelihood of transmission to another person (though many vaccines do not completely negate it). This means that the unvaccinated individual poses more of a risk of infection to others than the vaccinated one. Second, by reducing the number of available hosts in a community, vaccines reduce the ability of a germ to survive in the population; germs that require a host have a greater chance of spreading in populations where fewer people have immunity. This concept is referred to as community or herd immunity and has been a powerful tool of protection for individuals who cannot be vaccinated, such as children and immunocompromised people (Children's Hospital of Pittsburg. https://www.chp.edu/our-services/transplant/liver/recovery/life-after/vaccinations. Accessed 20 Oct. 2022.).

For highly communicable diseases, unvaccinated individuals pose a risk to the whole population. For this reason, policymakers—or private actors—may conclude that the need for high vaccination rates is important enough to limit individual freedom. In democratic countries, it is generally deemed illegal and unethical to vaccinate unwilling adults by force. As a less coercive alternative, governments may choose to enforce a vaccination mandate. A mandate functions by attaching a consequence to not being vaccinated. At the extreme end, that consequence would be a criminal penalty, but it can also come in the form of

© The Author(s), under exclusive license to Springer Nature Switzerland AG 2023
Y. T. Yang, D. R. Reiss, *Vaccine Law and Policy*, Law for Professionals,
https://doi.org/10.1007/978-3-031-36989-6_14

limiting access to a benefit such as education, employment, or public and private services. The next few chapters will be spent addressing the challenges surrounding mandates and how they are implemented.

Mandates are not a modern development; They have been employed in the United States (U.S.) since the nineteenth century, and other countries, such as England, have mandates that go even further back. By and large, there is sufficient evidence that suggests mandates increase vaccination rates. Literature also shows that mandates are an effective method of disease control (Gostin, Vaccine mandates are lawful, effective, and based on rock hard science, 2021.), and in the U.S., for example, states with stronger school vaccination mandates and enforcement have lower rates of infection (Salmon and Siegel, Public Health Rep 116(4):289–295, 2001.). However, vaccine mandates come with costs. They limit autonomy and harden opposition, prompting pushback and advocacy against not just mandates but vaccinations in general. Unsurprisingly, there has been extensive litigation around vaccine mandates.

The rest of this chapter will provide a basic overview of the power of state and local government, the federal government, and private actors to mandate vaccines as well as when mandates may be justified. The following chapters will then address, individually, school mandates, workplace mandates, and the federal vaccine mandates that came into prominence during the COVID-19 pandemic.

Freedom of religion is a central argument surrounding vaccine mandates. As such, we provide a general introduction to the topic in this chapter. A deeper look will be taken into the constitutional jurisprudence around freedom of religion in the chapter on school vaccine mandates, and the statutory protection of religion in the Civil Rights Act of 1964 in the chapter on workplace mandates. We then address separately vaccine mandates in global comparison and vaccine passports.

14.1 State and Local Authority to Mandate Vaccination

In the U.S. system, the federal government has always been one of limited authority, leaving powers not expressly given to the federal government to the individual states. Mandatory vaccination laws fall within what we call traditional state "police power".[1] The "police powers" are the state's general authority—within constitutional limits—to enact laws "to provide for the public health, safety, and morals" of the states' inhabitants.[2] Long ago, the Supreme Court ruled that this includes the authority to require mandatory vaccinations. In 1905, the U.S. Supreme Court upheld a state law requiring mandatory vaccination, reasoning that vaccine mandates fall directly within the states' discretion to provide for public health.[3] The Court pointed out that society cannot exist without some regulation for the common good,

[1] Malone & Hinman at 271–72.
[2] Shen (2019).
[3] *Id.* at 2.

and that individuals can successfully challenge arbitrary coercive orders, but need to accept reasonable ones—even if those laws inconvenience or burden them to some extent. The Court also states clearly that it will not intervene in scientific controversies, and Jacobson is—rightly—interpreted as allowing public officials wide latitude to act in public health, even if it limits individual rights.

Although courts give considerable deference to state power to protect public health, there are limits. For example, courts tell us that laws may not "contravene the Constitution of the U.S. or infringe any right granted or secured by that instrument."[4] Exact interpretations of this may vary, and we will discuss the specifics in more detail in the following chapters; but for now, it's important to remember that state power to require vaccines does have some loose, poorly defined limits. Within these limitations, all states have vaccine mandates, including compulsory vaccination laws for children,[5] while some states also have mandates for workers. Importantly, states reserve—as local governments may—the authority to require vaccines during an emergency—for example, during an unusually large measles outbreak in New York in 2019, New York City's mayor imposed a fine of $1000 on individuals not vaccinated with Measles, Mumps, and Rubella (MMR) in three neighborhoods, where the measles cases were especially high.[6]

The situation for local government is different. Under current U.S. law, local government by default only has the power that the state gives it.[7] That said, in many states, local government had, before the COVID-19 pandemic, broad powers to regulate in public health, often referred to by the legal term "home rule". These powers were sometimes embedded in the state constitution, sometimes in state law, and sometimes—for specific local government—in the charter the state gave the (usually) city, its founding document. Under these powers, some local governments have previously required vaccines. New York City, for example, has a history of requiring vaccines for school children.[8] But whether a local unit can, in fact, do this will depend on the state's specific laws, and unless the power is in the state constitution, a state can change its law and take away local power—in legal terms, "preempt" it. As demonstrated by this power of preemption, in the partnership between state and local government, the states are often the senior partner.

So local power to require vaccines depends on the state's goodwill in many—but not all—states. One development during the COVID-19 pandemic was that some states passed laws prohibiting local governments from requiring COVID-19 vaccines.[9]

---

[4]Cole and Swendiman (2015), p. 255.

[5]Shen (2019), p. 1.

[6]Paris (2019).

[7]Hunter v. Pittsburgh, 207 U.S. 161 (1907).

[8]Garcia v. New York City Dept. of Health & Mental Hygiene, No.07687, slip op. at (N.Y. App. Div. Dec. 23, 2020).

[9]Reiss (2022a), p. 788.

14.2   Federal Authority to Mandate Vaccination

If the default in our system is that states can mandate vaccines, but this may be (slightly) limited by constitutional rights, the default for the federal government is the opposite: the starting point is that it does not have general powers to act in the public health, only specifically delegated powers. Based on this, we have written in the past arguing that the federal government does not have the power to impose a universal vaccine mandate.[10] But in saying this, we had in mind a general vaccine mandate applied to all citizens of the U.S. We still think such a mandate is of dubious legality, at best. But a universal mandate is not the only option.

As discussed above, the power to regulate public health generally falls within state police powers.[11] The Tenth Amendment prevents the federal government from commandeering the states, or otherwise requiring officers of the states to carry out federal directives. Within constitutional constraints, the federal government has traditionally limited its role to promoting, facilitating, and monitoring the manufacture and use of vaccines. There are currently no federal laws requiring vaccination for the general population (such as mandating vaccination for school attendance).[12] However, the federal government has mandated vaccination of specific populations such as immigrants and the military.[13]

The federal government does have authority over public health measures, including regulating vaccines. The authority derives from the enumerated powers of the Constitution, specifically the Commerce Clause and the Spending Clause.

The Commerce Clause "grants Congress the power "[t]o regulate Commerce with foreign Nations, and among the several States." This authority empowers Congress to regulate "three broad categories of activities": (1) "channels of interstate commerce," like roads and canals; (2) "persons or things in interstate commerce, and (3) activities that substantially affect interstate commerce."[14] This may justify the federal government to require vaccines for interstate or international travel. Congress is also authorized to tax and spend for the general welfare through the Spending Clause. Within this power, Congress may condition the use of federal funds granted to non-federal entities. This power is broad, but is subject to certain limitations, including that funding conditions must be germane to the federal interest in the particular national projects or programs to which the money is directed.

During the COVID-19 pandemic, several federal agencies used existing regulatory powers to require vaccines in some specific contexts. These efforts, the litigation around them, and the legal conclusions will be discussed in Chap. 17.

---

[10] Reiss and Yang (2020a), p. 42; Reiss and Yang (2020b).

[11] Shen (2019), p. 2.

[12] Salmon and Siegel (2001), p. 1.

[13] Shen (2019), p. 3.

[14] *Id.*

14.3 Private Mandates

The largest difference between private and public mandates is that constitutional rights apply between citizens and government, but not between citizens and other private actors. This means that citizens are not protected against interference in their freedom of action, freedom of religion, or other things by private actors unless the state passes a specific and constitutional statute to protect citizens. For example, employers can and do fire employees for speaking—essentially punish them—in ways that, in the U.S., government cannot punish citizens for due to constitutional freedom of speech protections. As such, the limits on private mandates will not come from the constitution, but rather private actors, essentially, can do anything that the state or federal law did not make illegal. Therefore, private businesses can require vaccines for entry, as well as for employment, unless the state acted to forbid it (though there are limits, as discussed in the following chapters).

One of the most unusual developments during the COVID-19 pandemic was that a significant minority of states passed laws to limit vaccine mandates by private actors. We will discuss that as part of our discussion of workplace mandates.

14.4 Freedom of Religion

In some circumstances, a person may claim exemption from a public agency's vaccine mandate on the basis of conflict with a religious belief. Sometimes, however, someone with safety concerns about the vaccine may dishonestly claim the vaccine contradicts a religious belief, to avoid the mandate. Both situations raise the question of how the protection of freedom of religion interacts with a vaccine mandate. This draws into question first whether a religious exemption should be required, and second when a government may deny a person's claim of such exemption.

Historically, courts have not required a religious exemption from a vaccine mandate. Conversely, if a state did offer a religious exemption, courts limited the content of that exemption in several ways. First, courts across the U.S. have consistently struck down requirements for a letter from a clergy member on the basis that it discriminates against people who have sincere religious concerns about a vaccine, but their religious beliefs are personal, not part of an organized church. Second, although courts have not been fully consistent on this, generally, support for vaccines from the organized religion's leadership does not mean that a believer's exemption should be rejected. For example, if the Pope calls to vaccinate, an individual Catholic may still have a valid religious exemption, because the question in an exemption is whether the believer sincerely believes there's a conflict, not what the believer's religious leaders think. The challenge with such rules is that they make it difficult to identify people claiming a religious exemption in the absence of true religious belief. Our courts are historically hesitant to make such accusations against the validity of a person's religious beliefs, though this may change moving forward.

Separately, we may ask whether states have to provide a religious exemption from a vaccine mandate at all. The Supreme Court has moved to tighten protection of religious freedom since October 2020. Although we try to focus on the law as separate from the individual members of the Supreme Court, in this case, it is clear that the death of Justice Ruth Bader Ginsberg, and the appointment in her place of Justice Amy Coney Barrett, led to a change in the Supreme Court's approach to religious freedom in the context of pandemic measures, and to a more aggressive review of measures limiting religious freedom.[15] It is not quite clear how this will affect vaccine mandates; in two cases challenging mandates without religious exemptions from Maine and New York, the Supreme Court did not stay the mandates (although three justices dissented), and allowed the states to require mandates without religious exemptions.[16] The justices also refused to hear other challenges to decisions upholding mandates without religious exemptions.[17] The Court did not, however, directly address the question of whether vaccine mandates without religious exemptions are still constitutional, and may at some point go the other way.[18] It has not done so yet, though, and at this point, vaccine mandates without exemptions are still constitutional under existing jurisprudence.

14.5   Conclusion

The law provides a limit to what can be done, but it will not always tell you what should be done. As we mentioned, vaccines mandates work to prevent disease and increase vaccine rates. But they also have costs. Our view is that whether a vaccine mandate is a good or bad idea depends on a variety of factors, including the vaccine's risks and benefits, the body of evidence on this, the population affected by the mandate, the ability to enforce it, and other available tools. In other words, it's a case-specific question. Sometimes a mandate will be a very good idea; sometimes it will not be.

References

Children's Hospital of Pittsburg. https://www.chp.edu/our-services/transplant/liver/recovery/life-after/vaccinations. Accessed 20 Oct 2022
Cole JP, Swendiman KS (2015) Mandatory vaccinations: precedent and current laws. Curr Polit Econ 17:255
Doe v. Mills, No. 21A90 (U.S. Oct. 29, 2021); Dr. A. v. Hochul, No. 21A145 (U.S. Dec. 13, 2021) (Gorsuch, J., dissenting)
F.F., as parent of Y.F. v. New York, No. 21-1003 (U.S. May 23, 2022) (cert. denied)
Garcia v. New York City Dept. of Health & Mental Hygiene, No.07687, slip op. at (N.Y. App. Div. Dec. 23, 2020)

---

[15] Parmet (2021), pp. 564–579.

[16] Doe v. Mills, No. 21A90 (U.S. Oct. 29, 2021); Dr. A. v. Hochul, No. 21A145 (U.S. Dec. 13, 2021) (Gorsuch, J., dissenting).

[17] F.F., as parent of Y.F. v. New York, No. 21-1003 (U.S. May 23, 2022) (cert. denied).

[18] Reiss (2022b), pp. 552–563.

Gostin LO (2021) Vaccine mandates are lawful, effective, and based on rock hard science. Scientific American. https://www.scientificamerican.com/article/vaccine-mandates-are-lawful-effective-and-based-on-rock-solid-science/. Accessed 20 Oct 2022

Hunter v. Pittsburgh, 207 U.S. 161 (1907)

Malone & Hinman at 271–72

Paris F (2019) Judge upholds mandatory measles vaccinations as New York closes more schools. NPR. https://www.npr.org/2019/04/19/715016284/brooklyn-judge-upholds-mandatory-vaccinations-as-new-york-city-closes-more-schoo. Accessed 20 Oct 2022

Parmet W (2021) From the shadows: the public health implications of the Supreme Court's COVID-free exercise cases. J Law Med Ethics 49(4):564–579. https://doi.org/10.1017/jme.2021.80

Reiss DR (2022a) Laws prohibiting vaccine mandates: an overview. N Carolina J Law Technol 23: 788. https://ncjolt.org/articles/volume-23/volume-23-issue-4/laws-prohibiting-vaccine-mandates-an-overview/. Accessed 20 Oct 2022

Reiss DR (2022b) Vaccines mandates and religion: where are we headed with the current Supreme Court? J Law Med Ethics 49(4):552–563. https://doi.org/10.1017/jme.2021.79

Reiss DR, Yang YT (2020a) How Congress can help raise vaccine rates. Notre Dame Law Rev 96: 42. https://scholarship.law.nd.edu/ndlr_online/vol96/iss1/3. Accessed 20 Oct 2022

Reiss DR, Yang YT (2020b) A federal COVID-19 vaccine mandate: dubious legality, faulty policy. The Hill. https://thehill.com/opinion/healthcare/508773-a-federal-covid-19-vaccine-mandate-dubious-legality-faulty-policy/. Accessed 20 Oct 2022

Salmon DA, Siegel AW (2001) Religious and philosophical exemptions from vaccination requirements and lessons learned from conscientious objectors from conscription. Public Health Rep 116(4):289–295. https://doi.org/10.1093/phr/116.4.289

Shen W (2019) Cong. Rsch. Serv., LSB10300, an overview of state and federal authority to impose vaccination requirements

School Vaccine Mandates and Exemptions   15

Abstract

School vaccination mandates have a long history in the United States (U.S.) dating as far back as 1855, when the state of Massachusetts implemented the first mandate requiring a smallpox vaccine (Reiss and Weithorn, Buff Law Rev 63: 881–910, 2015.). Today, all fifty states have school vaccination mandates, and until recently, that decision had always been handled at the state level (Salmon, Unpublished commentary, mandatory immunization laws and the role of medical, religious and philosophical exemptions, 2003; Cole and Swendiman, Mandatory vaccinations: precedent and current laws, 2014.). Now, there is speculation that the federal government may have some authority to mandate vaccinations, however, scholars suggest federalism and the protection of individual rights act as key constraints limiting federal power from mandating vaccines. Unlike the federal government, states have the general authority to provide for public health, which protects their ability to implement school vaccine mandates for the greater safety of the public. In order to balance public health goals and civil liberties, all states permit exemptions for medical reasons, with the majority of states also providing some exemptions for non-medical reasons (Salmon, Unpublished commentary, mandatory immunization laws and the role of medical, religious and philosophical exemptions, 2003.). Exemptions play an important role in protecting those who are medically unable to receive the vaccine, and preserving individual rights (WebMD, What are the rules on vaccine exemptions?, 2020.). However, exemptions may lead to lower vaccination rates and may have implications for disease outbreaks. As such, it is important to evaluate all types of exemptions and the net effect they have on the population and individual health.

© The Author(s), under exclusive license to Springer Nature Switzerland AG 2023
Y. T. Yang, D. R. Reiss, *Vaccine Law and Policy*, Law for Professionals,
https://doi.org/10.1007/978-3-031-36989-6_15

15.1   Mandate Efficacy and Legal Justification

Vaccine mandates became prevalent amongst our nation's schools primarily because of evidence that they work. School mandates are one of the most effective methods of disease control,[1] and states with vaccination mandates and enforcement have lower rates of infection.[2] The success of a vaccine mandate lies within its ease of implementation, the strength of the consequence of forgoing vaccination, and the context of the population it's imposed on. Placing a mandate specifically within the school setting strategically utilizes vaccination as a condition to accessing an important service—schools—therefore providing a built-in enforcement mechanism. Additionally, the school system facilitates easy implementation of such a policy, as the enforcement authority, the school, already compiles and collects various documents of information from families of attendees. Lastly, they fit well within a school's mission since disease outbreaks can seriously disrupt education and harm children.

The second reason for widespread adoption of mandate policies, is that school vaccine mandates are backed by strong legal protections. The constitution grants states "police power" that gives them the authority to protect public health. The authority to mandate the vaccination of children, specifically, comes from *parens patriae*, the doctrine standing for the proposition that in the general interest of youths' wellbeing, the state may restrict parental control by regulating children. When both legal doctrines are combined, a school vaccine mandate is irrefutably justified to protect the public and the vulnerable from vaccine-preventable diseases, thereby reducing any barriers states may have when implementing their own mandates. This was proven in 1905, when the U.S. Supreme Court upheld a state law requiring mandatory vaccination, reasoning that vaccine mandates are not an arbitrary power, but fall directly within the states' discretion to provide for the public health.[3]

By and large, school mandates are within state powers. Rarely, however, attempts have been made by local governments to add a school or daycare mandate. For example, in 2013 New York city imposed an influenza mandate on children 6 months to 5 years in the city's daycares. Although this mandate was upheld in court despite challenges against it, such local mandates are rare and very likely to face legal challenges when they happen.

School vaccination laws have been a key factor in reducing the spread of communicable disease in the U.S. because they are far-reaching and easily enforceable. Therefore, courts have consistently upheld vaccination requirements as a condition to attend school, and vaccine mandates have since been used in daycares, public K-12 schools, as well as higher education. Although courts give considerable deference to state power to protect public health, laws may not "contravene the

---

[1] Gostin (2021).
[2] Salmon (2003).
[3] Shen (2019).

Constitution of the U.S. or infringe any right granted or secured by that instrument."[4] As such, exemptions do apply, and must therefore be carefully studied to identify how exemptions alter the implications of a vaccine mandate.

15.2 Exemptions

States recognize exemptions to school vaccination mandates for several reasons, including (but not limited to) the need to balance public health with individual freedom.[5] Exemptions vary state by state.[6] For example, as of 2022, all states permit medical exemptions, 44 states permit religious exemptions, and 19 states permit personal or philosophical exemptions. In addition to recognizing different types of exemptions, states have different restrictedness for individuals to opt-out of a mandatory vaccination by claiming a recognized exemption (for example, although both State A and B recognize religious exemptions, it can be more difficult to receive a religious exemption in State A than in state B.).[7]

Individual rights pose potential due process and equal protection concerns, although courts have limited these arguments.[8] The Supreme Court has said there is no absolute right in each person to be entirely free from restraint. In other words, the government can limit individual freedoms to protect the good of all its citizens— but within important constraints.

Vaccines are safe and effective, but they are not "perfectly safe or effective."[9] Most vaccine risks are low for the majority of people, but there are those with medical conditions that increase the likelihood of adverse effects. Because of this, states allow medical exemptions for those who are "immunocompromised, have allergic reactions to vaccine constituents, have moderate or severe illness, or other medical contraindications to vaccination."[10] Additionally, some states permit non-medical exemptions for individuals who do not believe in immunizations. Opt-out provisions and exemptions "further the integrity and sustainability" of vaccine mandates by accommodating civil liberty concerns, however, they also limit what vaccine mandates can achieve.

---

[4] Cole and Swendiman (2014).

[5] WebMD (2020).

[6] Cole and Swendiman (2014).

[7] WebMD (2020).

[8] Shen (2019).

[9] Malone & Hinman.

[10] Salmon (2003).

15.2.1 Medical

Medical exemptions prevent individuals from getting vaccines that are unsafe for them.[11] Few people actually need or qualify for these exemptions, so these exemptions protect vulnerable children without significantly impacting the overall rates of vaccination. Each state has its own process for granting medical exemptions, some of which can make it more difficult to opt-out of the vaccine requirements. For example, some states ask whether the exemption is temporary or permanent, and some states require doctors to sign a new exemption form every year. States requiring fewer or easier steps to get an exemption tend to have higher numbers of exemptions than those with more difficult laws. Medical exemptions to vaccine mandates are typically non-controversial because public health interventions should not pose a high health risk to its subject.[12] In fact, the correct way to think about a vaccine mandate is "everyone who can vaccinate without a high risk, should, in part to protect those who cannot safely vaccinate." Medical exemptions thus fit into the logic of mandates.

15.2.2 Non-medical

For religious, personal, or philosophical reasons, some individuals may object to vaccine mandates.[13] Individuals may also be concerned about vaccine safety or side effects. Although it's hard to separate these in reality, the law treats these reasons differently, with respect to religious opposition in particular. Forty-four states allow for non-medical exemptions to vaccine mandates, although they vary in how they apply.[14] As of 2022, West Virginia, Mississippi, California, New York, Maine and Connecticut only offer medical exemptions (the states are listed in the order in which that happened In 2023, Mississippi, under judge's order, started allowing religious exemptions for childhood vaccinations). Some of the other states—those with non-medical exemptions—only allow religious exemptions and may require proof to substantiate the exemption, while a smaller number of states recognize broader personal exemptions.[15]

15.2.2.1 Religious
States are not, at this point, constitutionally required to offer religious exemptions to vaccine mandates, but most states do.[16] Debates over this non-medical exemption typically center on what limitations can be placed on religious exemptions.[17] For

---

[11] WebMD (2020).

[12] Salmon (2003).

[13] WebMD (2020).

[14] Salmon (2003).

[15] WebMD (2020).

[16] Shen (2019) and Cole and Swendiman (2014).

[17] Salmon (2003).

example, some states require applicants to provide a letter with an explanation for why the individual or child should fall into the religious exemption to the vaccine requirement.

There are two parts to assessing a religious belief. The first question is whether it is religious, and the second part is whether it is sincere. Courts have struggled with both; but while we do not have supreme court guidance on this, several themes emerge from the cases.

First, although not in the school mandate context, federal courts have come up with a test they apply consistently to this issue. It is clear that "religious" here goes beyond belief in an acknowledged religion or even a single deity, but it is limited. The courts use three criteria.

(1) They ask whether the belief addressed the type of subject matter that fits what is usually religion, addressing ultimate questions like the meaning of life and death, man's role in the universe, or a broad moral code.[18]
(2) The belief needs to be part of a comprehensive whole—not just a verse or point adopted in isolation.
(3) Is there support from any "formal, external, or surface signs" like rituals? (these are not required, but would help).

Second, courts and states have struggled with assessing the sincerity of a claim that vaccines conflict with one's religion.[19] As one scholar puts it, "scrutinizing sincerity may not be just and risks public backlash."[20] That said, people can—and do—lie and claim religious beliefs in order to avoid a vaccine mandate.[21] Courts have struggled how to thread this needle. States requiring proof of sincerity do so to balance an individual's right to practice religion with the public health goal of improving vaccination rates.

Generally, courts do not permit limiting religious exemptions to members of organized religions that oppose vaccines, but require the state to "allow all who have sincerely held religious beliefs in opposition to vaccination to qualify."[22] Courts have also upheld exemptions where the believer's views deviated from those of the organized religion—for example, allowing Catholics to claim religious exemptions from vaccines the Pope supported.[23] While the state should not simply enforce the rules of organized religion on believers, this makes it harder for states to police sincerity, because it cannot, for example, use a pastor who knows the person as a gateway.

The difficulties in assessing sincerity—and the fact that misuse of religious exemptions can be widespread—is why some states have removed religious

---

[18] Reiss and DiPaolo (2021), pp. 1–66.
[19] Salmon (2003).
[20] Id.
[21] Reiss (2014), pp. 1568–1570.
[22] Salmon (2003).
[23] Reiss (2014).

exemptions. In 2015, California removed its non-medical exemption (which was broader than just religion), and in 2019 Maine and New York removed their religious exemption, followed by Connecticut in 2021. Given the recent changes in Supreme Court jurisprudence, it is possible that certain state courts may lean towards permitting religious exemptions.

15.2.2.2 Philosophical

There are no clear rules for defining philosophical objections (also known as personal belief exemptions).[24] Sometimes known as conscientious objectors, individuals who are granted philosophical exemptions may oppose vaccination for personal, non-medical, or non-religious reasons. Some conscientious objectors may be concerned with vaccine safety or believe that being unvaccinated makes for a stronger immune system.[25] Others may be vaccine-hesitant for various reasons. For example, many people became vaccine-hesitant after a now-debunked study reported a connection between vaccinations and autism. Although the study has been discredited and retracted, it continues to influence how people view vaccines.

Only 19 states explicitly offer philosophical exemptions to vaccine mandates, although some states define "religious" broadly enough to incorporate many of the same groups (in some states, religious exemptions are "check the box" exemptions, where the state has to accept any claim).[26] States with broadly defined religious exemptions or recognized philosophical exemptions tend to have lower vaccination rates.[27]

15.2.3 Implications for Disease Outbreaks

There are societal and individual risks associated with exemptions to vaccine mandates.[28] Vaccines are not for the sake of the individual alone, but about societal protection and public health goals.[29] Vaccine exemptions decrease the chances of achieving herd immunity, which would protect those who are unable to get vaccinated because they are too young or they have a medical condition that would make vaccines unsafe for them.[30] Pockets of unprotected or susceptible people create a weakness in defense against infectious diseases, and disease is likely to spread to vulnerable people when these weaknesses are exposed.[31]

---

[24] Salmon (2003).

[25] WebMD (2020).

[26] Salmon (2003) and Malone & Hinman.

[27] Malone & Hinman.

[28] Salmon (2003).

[29] Gostin (2021).

[30] WebMD (2020).

[31] Salmon (2003).

States with easy opt-outs and exemption policies have lower vaccination rates, and lower vaccination rates lead to higher transmission rates.[32] Higher transmission rates exacerbate the risk for those who are exempt for medical reasons—who really cannot be safely vaccinated—or those who don't develop a sufficient immunological response to a vaccine.[33] One study found that children with vaccination exemptions were 35 times more likely to contract measles than vaccinated children.[34] This statistic was similar to a study done with whooping cough disease. In recent times, we have seen measles outbreaks in several communities with low vaccination rates, like the Somali community in Minnesota and several Orthodox Jewish communities in New York state.

States have important interests in protecting the population—especially vulnerable people—from vaccine-preventable diseases. Offering exemptions helps states balance public health goals with liberty interests, but areas with higher opt-out statistics have lower vaccination rates and are thus more vulnerable to the spread of disease. Policymakers should consider the risks associated with broad and easily-claimed exemptions.

15.3 Current Landscape

Historically, school mandates have typically only been adopted for long established vaccines. As the pandemic and its aftermath continue to unfold, the COVID-19 vaccines will become an interesting test case. As of 2022, no state has mandated them in practice. California's department of health ordered a mandate, but it will only become operational once the vaccines gain full FDA approval and will have a broad personal belief exemption attached.

Several California districts tried to mandate vaccines, but none of the mandates have become operational, in large part because of strong opposition from parents, as COVID-19 vaccines for children do not have widespread acceptance. This example highlights some of the challenges with school mandates and emphasizes the importance of a high level of support for vaccines to succeed in a population.

15.4 Conclusion

The history of effective school vaccine mandates in all 50 states serves as a powerful example of how state-required vaccines can benefit the public. Vaccine mandates should remain under the role of state governments, backed by the legal protections of police power and *parens patriea*. As new mandates are required, it will be essential for policy makers to carefully evaluate the mandates' exemption policies. Further

---

[32] Gostin (2021) and Salmon (2003).

[33] Salmon (2003).

[34] Salmon et al. (1999), pp. 47–53.

research is needed to identify implications of exemptions and to create clear guidelines for how these exemptions should be qualified. Lastly, states should preserve the balance between public safety and individual choice, with respect to vaccines, to promote a healthy society.

References

Cole JP, Swendiman KS (2014) Mandatory vaccinations: precedent and current laws. Library of Congress. Congressional Research Service, Washington, D.C.

Gostin LO (2021) Vaccine mandates are lawful, effective, and based on rock hard science, Scientific American. https://www.scientificamerican.com/article/vaccine-mandates-are-lawful-effective-and-based-on-rock-solid-science/. Accessed 20 Oct 2022

Malone & Hinman at 271–272

Reiss DR (2014) Thou shalt not take the name of the Lord Thy God in vain: use and abuse of religious exemptions from school immunization requirements. Hast Law J 65:1551, 1568–1570

Reiss DR, DiPaolo J (2021) Covid-19 vaccine mandates for university students. N Y Univ J Legis Public Policy 24:1–66. https://doi.org/10.2139/ssrn.3874159

Reiss DR, Weithorn LA (2015) Responding to the childhood vaccination crisis: legal frameworks and tools in the context of parental vaccine refusal. Buff Law Rev 63:881–910

Salmon DA (2003) Unpublished commentary, mandatory immunization laws and the role of medical, religious and philosophical exemptions

Salmon DA et al (1999) Health consequences of religious and philosophical exemptions from immunization laws individual and societal risk of measles. JAMA 282:47–53. https://doi.org/10.1001/jama.282.1.47

Shen W (2019) Cong. Rsch. Serv., LSB10300, an overview of state and federal authority to impose vaccination requirements

WebMD (2020) What are the rules on vaccine exemptions? https://www.webmd.com/children/vaccines/what-are-the-rules-on-vaccine-exemptions. Accessed 25 Oct 2022

Workplace Vaccine Mandates

16

Abstract

Just like school mandates, workplace mandates have a long history. They have existed since the nineteenth century. Most of these mandates have been imposed by private employers, but during the twentieth century some states trialed government requirements for healthcare workers to be vaccinated against some diseases, including measles, mumps, and rubella (MMR) (Cole and Swendiman, Mandatory vaccinations: precedent and current laws, 2014.). Vaccination mandates for healthcare workers are supported by many medical professional organizations who believe healthcare workers have a professional and ethical responsibility to reduce the spread of vaccine-preventable diseases. Additionally, the Department of Defense (DoD) issued a policy directive requiring civilian healthcare personnel who provide direct patient care in DoD medical facilities to get the flu vaccine.

Despite the potential benefits of workplace mandates, individuals should not be forced to accept disproportionate physical risks for them. Hence, like many of the vaccine requirements for school attendance, private, state, and federal employers allow healthcare workers to opt-out of the vaccine for medical reasons. Some employers will also allow exemptions for non-medical reasons, such as conflict of religion or personal belief. The framework of exemptions in the workplace is somewhat different than that within the school system. All employers—public or private—are subject to several important federal anti-discrimination laws (and potentially to their state equivalents) and may face constraints from collective bargaining laws. Employer mandated vaccination is further complicated by workers' compensation consequences that apply to all employers. But state and federal employers are also subject to potential constitutional and legal constraints.

Here we have separated out the discussion of federal vaccine mandates, which will be discussed in Chap. 17, to focus on employer-enforced vaccination policies. However, in the context of federal employees, when the federal

© The Author(s), under exclusive license to Springer Nature Switzerland AG 2023
Y. T. Yang, D. R. Reiss, *Vaccine Law and Policy*, Law for Professionals,
https://doi.org/10.1007/978-3-031-36989-6_16

government is acting as an employer rather than a governing body, the framework described here applies.

First, there are a few features that must be pointed out that make policy in the workplace unique from government-enforced laws. Employment in the United States (U.S.) is by and large at will. That means that while you have the right to voluntarily resign at any point, your private employer similarly has the right to fire you for any reason that is not expressly prohibited by law (though some states also have a public policy exception to this). If your employer does not like your t-shirt's political slogan, your employer can fire you over it; your first amendment does not protect you against private action. If your employer decides they like another employee's vocal timber better, and that employee will be more liked by customers, they can fire—or demote—you and replace you with an employee that better suits the role. If your employer wants you to wear a blue nose every Tuesday, you can choose to resign or wear the blue nose, but if you ignore the workplace rule, your employer can, legally, fire you, even if you are right to argue that the rule is silly. The essence of the employment relationship is that your employer sets the workplace rules, and you accept following them as part of the agreement of employment.

A private employer, however, also has responsibilities; In the same way that a public government has a duty to provide a safe and habitable society for its citizens, a private employer is ethically expected to provide a safe workplace for its employees, to protect you, your co-workers, and customers (or patients, in the healthcare setting). That means that your employer, in theory, has an ethical duty to put in place workplace safety rules. Beyond moral and ethical responsibility, employers in a capitalist society such as the U.S. are further motivated by their own company gains. This can result in one of two actions: employers may be inclined to enforce strict safety rules to avoid losing trained workers, or they may be tempted to cut safety corners to increase their profits, trusting they won't have to pay if an employee is hurt, disabled, or killed. To guide employers towards more ethical decisions, states and the federal government step in to regulate workplace policy. For example, employers are prohibited from terminating workers on a historical basis of prejudice, or for reasons the state deems unacceptable, by federal and state anti-discrimination laws. To provide equal protection to employees, the government defends an employee's right to collective bargaining through an acknowledged union.

Throughout this chapter, we will explore the duty of an employer to provide a safe workplace and how that applies within the context of mandated vaccination. In general, an employer is legally allowed to require vaccines from their workers, unless explicitly prohibited by state law, a precedent that is powerfully protected under the notion that vaccine mandates fall under health and safety policy in the workplace. Employers defend their right to mandate on the basis of three valid reasons: (1) Vaccination protects the employee on an individual level, (2) Immunity from disease protects the employer from collateral harm of high infection rates, and (3) High rates of immunization reduce the likelihood of employees spreading a disease to each other and to the general population they interact with as a part of employment (i.e., customers and patients). The remainder of this chapter will be spent outlining the legal challenges of enforcing vaccine mandates in the workplace.

16.1   Federal Civil Rights Laws and Employee Vaccination Policies

Federal antidiscrimination statutes can be useful examples to help guide the implementation of vaccination mandates, but conversely, they may also constrain their impact.[1] Two anti-discrimination laws are relevant in this context; The Americans with Disabilities Act (ADA), which protects against discrimination against people with disabilities, and Title VII of the Civil Rights Act of 1964 (Title VII), which prohibits discrimination against several categories of workers ("race, color, religion, sex, or national origin"), of which the most salient one is religion.

The Equal Employment Opportunity Commission (EEOC) issued guidance on COVID-19 and vaccination policies, generally outlining the interpreted applicability of the ADA and Title VII. While the EEOC's interpretation is not authoritative, it is based on the agency's expertise and the existing jurisprudence, and likely reflects the way courts would apply these laws. Therefore, they serve as useful tools to inform employers considering the use of vaccine mandates.

For companies with greater than 15 employees, the ADA and Title VII may require employers to offer reasonable accommodations for individuals who claim medical or religious conflict in opposition to a vaccine mandate. Additionally, most states have their own equivalent statutes to the federal anti-discrimination laws, which will need to be carefully addressed when drafting any vaccine mandate policy.[2] While policies should be careful not to discriminate against groups of workers according to these statutes, concerns about the risk of spreading contagious diseases will weigh heavily in legal challenges to employer-imposed vaccine mandates. Therefore, accommodations must be reasonable, protecting the rights of individuals who have valid opposition to the vaccine while still ensuring a safe and healthy workplace for the employee population.

16.1.1   Reasonable Accommodations for Employees with Disabilities

16.1.1.1   Vaccination Risks and Disability
The ADA and the Rehabilitation Act of 1973 (Rehabilitation Act) require employers to adapt the rules to offer exemptions for some employees with disabilities. These statutes cover "impairment[s] that substantially limit[s] one or more major life

---

[1] Cole and Swendiman (2014).

[2] National Conference of State Legislature (2015).

activities."[3] Some medical conditions make vaccinating unusually dangerous, such as a severe allergic reaction to an ingredient of the vaccine, therefore workers with these conditions may claim a disability that justifies a non-vaccine accommodation. [4] In these cases, the employer can examine the claim, and in some circumstances may deny it, if the claim is proven to be inadequate. If the claim is determined to be a serious impairment, the disability is deemed valid and employers are barred from taking adverse action against a worker. Under these circumstances, the employee is entitled to reasonable accommodation, as long as the burden of accommodation is not so high that it harms the safety of the workplace.

Employees are not necessarily entitled to their preferred option (for example, in this context, an employer does not have to let them work on the same conditions as everyone else, regardless of the risk). When an employee makes an accommodation request due to a disability, the employer must assess available alternatives, possible threats from vaccine exemptions, and whether the employee's disability precludes vaccination. Reasonable accommodations may include reassigning the employees' responsibilities, allowing the employee to work from home, distancing the employee from coworkers or customers, or other reasonable measures. If no reasonable accommodation is possible, or if the burden of accommodation is extreme, the EEOC acknowledges that an employer may not be able to offer alternatives and may bar the employee from the workplace should they remain unable to receive the vaccine.

16.1.1.2 Direct Threat Exception to Reasonable Accommodation

In some circumstances, an employer may refuse to accommodate a disabled worker and claim that the worker poses a direct threat to others. A direct threat means the presence of the employee would create a significant risk of substantial harm to the health or safety of the individual or others that cannot be eliminated or reduced by reasonable accommodation. The EEOC concluded that the direct threat exception applies in the circumstances of a pandemic to allow employers "to keep infected employees out of the workplace."[5] There is speculation, however, that this exception may further apply to unvaccinated employees, even if a disability prevents vaccination.

Before the direct threat exception applies, however, it requires an "individualized, objective assessment of the risk the unvaccinated employee presents."[6] Employers should consider important factors such as the duration of the risk, imminence, the likelihood of harm, and the degree of harm. The EEOC suggests that in the context of a pandemic, a direct threat includes a determination that an unvaccinated individual will expose others to the virus in the workplace.[7]

---

[3] Anderson and Yuengert (2022).

[4] Anderson and Yuengert (2022).

[5] *Id.*

[6] *Id.*

[7] Anderson and Yuengert (2022).

Importantly, this determination is workplace specific. Not all workplaces are designed the same way or require the same types of interactions among employees and customers. The number of vaccinated employees may also be a factor in assessing the degree of risk. The EEOC clarified their guidance in light of COVID-19 countermeasures to state that "the ADA and Rehabilitation Act do not interfere with employers following advice from the Centers for Disease Control and Prevention (CDC) and other public health authorities on appropriate steps to take relating to the workplace."[8]

16.1.1.3 Courts' Assessments of Mandatory Vaccination Under Federal Disability Statutes

We do not yet have much litigation about COVID-19 vaccine mandates and federal disability statutes. However, courts have considered other employer-imposed vaccine requirements in the past. For example, many workplaces follow the CDC issued guidance for health care providers to require the annual flu vaccination. In many cases when employees challenged the mandatory flu vaccination requirements under the civil rights statutes, the employers won. One court ruled in the employer's favor when a worker did not prove she had an alleged allergy and did not seek out available hypoallergenic vaccines as a reasonable alternative. In another case, the court concluded that an employee could not show she had a disability, if she did not prove that her allergy substantially limited a major life activity, as defined by the ADA.

Courts can take different approaches, and some are stricter than others. An employee was allowed to take her case to fact-finding in a Third Circuit case when the court concluded that severe anxiety over injection may qualify as a disability (though note that the court did not, at that stage, rule whether the employee won her case).[9] Importantly, the employee proposed wearing a mask as a reasonable alternative, and the court accepted that she raised a valid ADA claim. Courts look at the evidence of a disability and the availability of alternatives when addressing these challenges.

16.1.2 Religious Accommodations Under Title VII

When an employee's religious beliefs or practice conflicts with a job requirement, Title VII requires employers to consider employees' religious objections to vaccination.[10] When an employee raises a Title VII concern over a religious objection, employers are required to accommodate workers' religious practices unless they impose undue hardship on the conduct of the employers' business. While this statute shares many similarities with the ADA standard we just discussed, there are key

---

[8] *Id.*

[9] Anderson and Yuengert (2022).

[10] *Id.*

differences. The ADA requires a larger burden of accommodation from the employer, within reason, while Title VII places less responsibility on the employer to adapt to the employee's needs. In 2023, the Supreme Court of the United States unanimously held that to deny a sincere religious accommodation request under Title VII, employers must show that the burden of granting it would result in substantial increased costs in relation to the conduct of its particular business. De minimis is a fancy term for "minimal"—in other words, if accommodating an employee imposes on the employer more than minimal costs, the employer does not have to provide the accommodation. The costs involved may include other employees' rights, efficiency, the financial cost to the business, and other considerations. A crucial analysis of these costs is necessary to determine the limits of a reasonable accommodation.

EEOC regulations provide that religious accommodations include beliefs held with "the strength of traditional religious views."[11] That is, individuals are not barred from raising a complaint if they do not belong to an organized religion as long as their beliefs are sincere.[12] The EEOC recommends that employers "should assume that an employee's request for religious accommodations [is] based on a sincerely held religious belief."[13] However, an employer may request additional supporting information from the employee if there is an objective basis for questioning the religious nature or sincerity of a belief. Title VII protections for religious objections are not absolute. If no reasonable accommodation is possible, the EEOC acknowledges that the employer may bar the employee from the workplace in order to protect the safety of their workforce.

Courts have ruled on cases regarding a variety of religious beliefs and possible accommodations. When a Muslim healthcare worker challenged an employer-imposed flu vaccine mandate over concerns of possible pork ingredients in a vaccine, her employer first accommodated the opposition with an alternate vaccine with different ingredients. When the plaintiff expressed a belief that the vaccine was still contaminated, her employer found her a position outside of patient care.[14] The court found that the employer reasonably accommodated the plaintiff by providing alternatives, and that retaining her in her patient care position while unvaccinated would impose an undue hardship.

16.1.3 Vaccination and Pregnant Employees

In addition to protecting individuals with religious objections, Title VII also requires employers to consider the health concerns of pregnant employees. Within Title VII is the Pregnancy Discrimination Act (PDA), which mandates that pregnant women be treated the same as non-pregnant persons who are similar in their ability or inability to work. Therefore, in relation to vaccine mandates, the PDA may prevent employers

[11] *Id.*

[12] Anderson and Yuengert (2022).

[13] *Id.*

[14] Anderson and Yuengert (2022).

from denying exemptions to pregnant women from vaccines contraindicated in pregnancy if they offer exemptions to other workers. However, it should be noted that the PDA does not expressly require accommodations. Not many vaccines are contraindicated in pregnancy, but some (like MMR) are.

In addition to the PDA, pregnant women have other legal protections related to their particular medical concerns.[15] The ADA and the Rehabilitation Act also cover some pregnant women if a pregnancy-related complication leads to a disability. If a pregnant woman's condition is covered by the ADA or Rehabilitation Act, she would be eligible for ADA and Rehabilitation Act protections, including reasonable accommodations.

16.1.4 Medical Examinations or Inquiries Under the ADA and the Rehabilitation Act

Some laws restrict employers from making medical examinations or inquiries. The ADA and the Rehabilitation Act restrict certain medical inquiries for all employees. Any medical examination or inquiry must be "job-related and consistent with business necessity."[16] Further, even with a legitimate inquiry, the employer needs to protect the employee's privacy.

According to EEOC guidance, vaccination itself is not a medical examination, and requiring proof of vaccination is not a disability-related inquiry under the ADA.[17] Employers may generally require vaccinations and ask for documentation of vaccination status, although "courts have yet to evaluate requiring vaccinations in a pandemic setting."[18]

A disability-related inquiry that comes up as part of a pre-vaccination screening question could implicate the ADA and Rehabilitation Act. The EEOC guidance for this situation explains "if the employer administers the vaccine, it must show that such pre-screening questions it asks employees are job-related and consistent with business necessity."[19] The EEOC explains further that to meet the standard, an employer would have to have a reasonable, objective belief that an employee who does not answer questions and, therefore, does not receive a vaccination "will pose a direct threat to the health and safety of her or himself or others."[20]

In addition to the ADA implications of medical inquiries, if pre-vaccination screening questions seek genetic information, it may implicate the Genetic Information Nondiscrimination Act, which was enacted to prohibit genetic discrimination.

---

[15] Anderson and Yuengert (2022).
[16] Id.
[17] Anderson and Yuengert (2022).
[18] Id.
[19] Id.
[20] Id.

According to the Congressional Research Service, "under the current federal framework, a voluntary, employer-administered vaccination requirement would appear to avoid [confidentiality concerns]" since the employees could decline the vaccine and related pre-screening questions.[21] Furthermore, "if a third party... administers a required screening and vaccination, screening questions would not violate the disability laws."[22]

16.2 Considerations Under the Religious Freedom Restoration Act and Other Laws

Public employers may face additional constraints, compared to private employers. First, public employers are subject to the constitutional limits discussed in Chaps. 14 and 15. Further, for federal employees and employees in a significant minority of states, religious freedom restoration acts may add an additional burden.

A private employer may exclude the employee from the workplace if the employer cannot reasonably accommodate a worker's disability or religious practice. However, public employers must also consider other employee protections, like the federal Religious Freedom Restoration Act (RFRA) and its state equivalents, before terminating an unvaccinated worker.

The federal RFRA prohibits the federal government from "substantially burdening a person's exercise of religion with limited exceptions."[23] A person may sue the government if the person's religious practice has been burdened in violation of RFRA. For the government to dispute the challenge, they must show that the burden imposed on the challenger's religious exercise furthers a "compelling government interest" and is "the least restrictive means of furthering that interest."[24] This is a much more rigorous standard than those applied under Title VII's religious accommodations.[25]

When the federal government mandates vaccination for public or private employees, employees with religious objections may have a cause of action against the government. If the law or rule imposes vaccination obligations on private employers (for example, the Occupational Safety and Health Administration (OSHA) COVID-19 vaccine mandate), employers with religious objections may also have an RFRA claim against the government.

An employee challenging a vaccine mandate under RFRA would have to demonstrate that a substantial burden on their religious exercise is not justified by the compelling government interest, or that compulsory vaccination is not the least restrictive means of furthering that interest. A reviewing court would then have to

---

[21] Anderson and Yuengert (2022).

[22] Id.

[23] Id.

[24] Anderson and Yuengert (2022).

[25] Id.

consider the public health interests associated with the vaccine mandate as well as any exemptions or accommodations available to the challenger.

16.3 Unionized Workers

Laws in the U.S. offer some protection to unionized workers against unilateral action from management, though these protections are less aggressive than those that exist in other countries.[26] These protections mean that management may have to bargain with the union before making implementing mandate policies in the workplace.[27] The nature of this challenge will depend on the specific collective bargaining agreement between that union and the management as well as the union's attitude. Some unions have supported vaccine mandates as a tool to protect employees while others opposed them for violating employee's freedoms. Results when a union challenged vaccination policies also tend to vary. If a workforce is unionized, employers may need careful consideration when implementing vaccine mandate policies and should be prepared for feedback from the union in the case of opposition.

16.4 EUA Status

Another question is whether employers can mandate a vaccine that is not fully licensed but rather is only authorized under an emergency use authorization (EUA). We discuss emergency use authorization in Chap. 2, but some discussion of the effect of EUAs on workplace vaccine mandates is relevant here since it came to the front with the COVID-19 vaccine. In the early days of the COVID-19 pandemic, and likely in future pandemics, the question of whether employers can mandate an EUA vaccine was very important—because until August 2021, when the FDA licensed Pfizer's COVID-19 vaccines, the only vaccines available against COVID-19 were under an EUA.[28] While this question is no longer relevant to the now-approved COVID-19 vaccines, it has not been legally settled and will remain a challenge for vaccine mandates in the future.

There are two arguments against allowing mandates of EUA vaccines, one legal and one policy related. The legal argument focuses on the fact that the statute creating the possibility to give an emergency authorization requires the secretary of health and human services to "ensure that individuals to whom the product is administered are informed. . . (III) of the option to accept or refuse administration of the product, of the consequences, if any, of refusing administration of the product, and of the alternatives to the product that are available and of their benefits and

---

[26] Doellgast and Benassi (2020).

[27] Rothstein et al. (2021), pp. 1061–1064.

[28] Reiss and DiPaolo (2021), pp. 1–66.

risks."[29] Mandate opponents draw special attention to the "option to accept or refuse", arguing that if the secretary of health and human services requires an option of refusal, a policy cannot be implemented that mandates administration of the vaccine for all individuals.

Mandate supporters counter by saying the provision in question is directed to inform the secretary which materials must be presented to people. Importantly, the clause informs individuals of their right to refuse the vaccine. It does not, however, limit private employers, who have a long history of mandating vaccines, from exercising their right to reassign responsibilities, or in some cases terminate an individual who chooses to refuse the vaccine. While forcible injection of an individual with a mandated vaccine against their will—physically holding someone and vaccinating—is ethically problematic since it violates bodily autonomy, there are legal grounds for enforcing consequences for those who refuse vaccination in order to protect the general public and ensure a safe workplace. It should not be assumed that the statute was meant to change a long-standing law in silence and remove something that allows employers to make the workplace safer.

Many base the argument against mandating EUA vaccines on the idea that EUAs require a smaller amount of data for authorization than a full license, drawing into question concerns about the safety of such vaccines. Others, however, point out that COVID-19 vaccines, at least, were assessed over millions of administrations to individuals, providing a reliable body of evidence that the immunization is safe and effective for widespread use.[30]

There is no clear legal answer to this. During the COVID-19 pandemic, many cases were brought to the courts—though none won. The only case that explicitly rejected the claim was a federal district court decision in Texas. While federal district court decisions can be persuasive, they are not binding and this case is unlikely to set legal precedent for future claims. [31]

While the debate around the COVID-19 vaccine mandates and their validity under Emergency Use Authorization is temporary, this will hardly be the last time society faces this challenge. It will be important to further evaluate the morality behind such a mandate prior to the next pandemic so that we may be better equipped to enforce regulations for the greater good of the public.

---

[29] 21 U.S.C. § 360bbb-3(e)(1)(A)(ii)(III).

[30] Reiss and Caplan (2021).

[31] Bridges v. Hous. Methodist Hosp., Case 4:21-cv-01774 (S.D. Tex. Jun. 12, 2021); Bridges v. Methodist Hosp., No. 21-20311, (5th Cir. June 13, 2022)(Fifth Circuit upholding the lower court's decision, but without explicit reference to the EUA law).

16.5   Conclusion

By providing information about vaccinations and establishing supportive policies and equitable practices, employers can help increase vaccine uptake among workers. Employers should share clear, complete, and accurate messages, promote confidence in the decision to get vaccinated, and engage employees in plans to address potential barriers to vaccination. The information presented below explains the benefits of employee vaccination and can help employers implement employee vaccination either at the workplace or in the community.

References

Anderson KS, Yuengert AR (2022) To mandate VAX or not, that is the question: federal contractor vaccine mandates before several appellate courts. In: The National Law Review. https://www.natlawreview.com/article/to-mandate-vax-or-not-question-federal-contractor-vaccine-mandates-several-appellate. Accessed 27 Oct 2022

Bridges v. Hous. Methodist Hosp., Case 4:21-cv-01774 (S.D. Tex. Jun. 12, 2021)

Bridges v. Methodist Hosp., No. 21-20311, (5th Cir. June 13, 2022)

Cole JP, Swendiman KS (2014) Mandatory vaccinations: precedent and current laws. Library of Congress. Congressional Research Service, Washington, D.C.

Doellgast V, Benassi C (2020) Collective bargaining. Handbook of Research on Employee Voice 239–258. https://doi.org/10.4337/9781788971188.00022

National Conference of State Legislature (2015) Discrimination - employment laws. https://www.ncsl.org/research/labor-and-employment/discrimination-employment.aspx.   Accessed 25 Oct 2022

Reiss DR, Caplan A (2021) Experimental? It doesn't mean what you think it means. Denver Law Rev. https://doi.org/10.2139/ssrn.3900193

Reiss DR, DiPaolo J (2021) Covid-19 vaccine mandates for university students. N Y Univ J Legis Public Policy 24:1–66. https://doi.org/10.2139/ssrn.3874159

Rothstein MA et al (2021) Employer-mandated vaccination for Covid-19. Am J Public Health 111: 1061–1064. https://doi.org/10.2105/ajph.2020.306166

21 U.S.C. § 360bbb-3(e)(1)(A)(ii)(III)

Federal Vaccine Mandates

17

Abstract

An important feature of democracy in our country is a system of checks and balances that distributes authoritative power between the federal, state, and local governments. Consistent with this notion, the Tenth Amendment of the Constitution serves to prevent the federal government from commandeering the states, or otherwise requiring officers of the states to carry out federal directives, by limiting the federal government to only operate under the powers explicitly granted by the Constitution. As a result, many matters of public health, including laws surrounding vaccination, are generally left to individual state police powers. Consequently, within constitutional constraints, the federal government has traditionally limited its role to promoting, facilitating, and monitoring the manufacturing and use of vaccines. As such, there are currently no federal laws in the United States requiring vaccination for the general population. Despite constitutional limitations, however, the federal government does retain some authority over public health measures and has previously drawn on this power to mandate vaccination of specific populations, such as immigrants and the military, even prior to the COVID-19 pandemic (Shen, Cong. Rsch. Serv., LSB10300, An overview of State and Federal Authority to impose vaccination requirements, 2019).

The federal mandate of immunization on subgroups of the population draws its legal authority by powers of the Constitution, specifically, the Commerce Clause and the Spending Clause. The Commerce Clause grants congressional power to regulate three broad categories of activities: (1) "channels of interstate commerce," like roads and canals; (2) "persons or things in interstate commerce, and (3) activities that substantially affect interstate commerce." (Shen, Cong. Rsch. Serv., LSB10300, An overview of State and Federal Authority to impose vaccination requirements, 2019). While the Commerce Clause highlights a specific area that the federal government is allowed to regulate, the Spending Clause classifies the ways in which the federal government may impose taxes and spend

© The Author(s), under exclusive license to Springer Nature Switzerland AG 2023
Y. T. Yang, D. R. Reiss, *Vaccine Law and Policy*, Law for Professionals,
https://doi.org/10.1007/978-3-031-36989-6_17

such revenue. Within this power, Congress may impose conditions on the use of federal funds granted to nonfederal entities. This power is broad, but is subject to certain limitations, including that "[funding conditions] must be germane to the federal interest in the particular national projects or programs to which the money is directed." (Shen, Cong. Rsch. Serv., LSB10300, An overview of State and Federal Authority to impose vaccination requirements, 2019).

While both the Commerce Clause and the Spending Clause have been interpreted to allow for federal regulation of vaccine mandates in past contexts, the experimentation with several new vaccine programs during the COVID-19 pandemic were largely halted by the courts amid a national debate surrounding federal powers. In this chapter, we will explore the applicability of enumerated powers of the Constitution, specifically the Commerce Clause and the Spending Clause, and how the federal government may or may not derive its authority to regulate the space of public health.

17.1 Executive Branch Authority to Mandate Vaccination

The Commerce Clause does not directly mention vaccines or the public health, but the power to regulate interstate commerce has been used for broad programs of various types in the past. In 1944 Congress recognized the need for federally coordinated approach to regulating the spread of infectious disease and thereby, under authority bestowed by the Commerce Clause, drafted the Public Health Service Act (PHSA). As part of this act, Congress passed legislation granting "broad, flexible powers to federal health authorities who must use their judgment in attempting to protect the public against the spread of communicable disease". This allows the Centers for Disease Control and Prevention (CDC) to "make and enforce regulations necessary" to prevent the spread of disease among the states.[1] The CDC is unlikely to use this power to order a general vaccine mandate; Rather, it may be used to impose a vaccine mandate in more limited contexts, such as on interstate or international travel.

Recently, the strain of the COVID-19 pandemic put the boundaries of executive authority to the test, and the federal government acted in a variety of ways in an attempt to mitigate the harms of a rapidly spreading virus. In September 2021, President Joe Biden, as part of the White House's COVID-19 plan, announced an intent to require vaccination—or at least impose consequences on the unvaccinated—through several federal agencies. Recognizing the heightened tensions of the political climate, and the debate around the legitimacy of a widespread federally imposed mandate, initial policies were trialed in more limited settings in which the federal government has previously used its powers in other ways. Most far reaching, the President instructed the Occupational Safety and Health administration (OSHA) to create an emergency temporary standard requiring

---

[1] Shen (2019).

employers with over one hundred workers to adopt plans that would require unvaccinated workers to mask and test routinely.[2] In addition, the President called on the Centers for Medicare and Medicaid to require the facilities they funded to mandate vaccination for healthcare workers, except in the case of a valid exemption. He also required all federal executive employees and contractors to vaccinate, with exemptions, as well as Head Start educators and staff.

These mandates—and the subsequent litigation—provided an opportunity to examine the limits of authority granted by the Commerce Act and the PHSA to allow federal executive power over public health regulations. Some matters have been resolved in favor of the federal government—for example, the Supreme Court approved of Medicare and Medicaid funding being conditional on vaccine mandates. Other issues—like the OSHA emergency temporary standard—have not fared well. While some issues are still making their way through the court system, and while we have yet to see the fallout, it has already become evident that the courts are seemingly reluctant to grant the federal government power to require vaccines.

17.1.1 OSHA's Vaccine Program

The broadest program in President Biden's COVID-19 plan was the OSHA emergency temporary standard we mentioned above. In his directive President Biden charged OSHA with developing an emergency temporary standard (ETS) requiring all employers with 100 or more employees to require their workers to be fully vaccinated or to show proof of a negative virus test at least once per week before coming to work.[3] Note that this is not a traditional mandate: employers are not required to dismiss unvaccinated employees, rather an alternative option of testing and masking may be provided for those who cannot, or will not, vaccinate. As such, the vaccine policy under OSHA is referred to as a "vaccine program" to highlight its contrasts with the typical definition of a mandate. In addition—and separate from— the requirement aimed to increase vaccination, President asked OSHA to require businesses subject to the rule to give workers paid time off to get vaccinated and recover from potential side effects.

As with any change in policy, and especially one that results in increased regulation, the vaccine requirements under OSHA were likely to face anticipated opposition. Nonetheless, OSHA created the rule, and would be responsible for enforcing it; fines for noncomplying businesses could cost up to $14,000 per violation.

To examine the power of OSHA to regulate vaccines in the workforce, we turn first to the very broad notion of health and safety. The Occupational Safety and Health Act (OSH Act) gives the Department of Labor (DOL) broad authority to protect workers' health and safety. The statute authorizes the Secretary of Labor "to

---

[2] The White House (2021).

[3] Scalia et al. (2021).

set mandatory occupational safety and health standards applicable to businesses affecting interstate commerce" and "providing medical criteria which will assure insofar as practicable that no employee will suffer diminished health, functional capacity, or life expectancy as a result of his work experience." A majority of OSHA mandates typically focus on work conditions at the property of the company, but at least some argue that OSHA plays a public health role where the spread of disease is a workplace concern.

When debating the legitimacy of the OSHA enacted vaccine program and its impact, it becomes important to understand the implications of an ETS. Under normal circumstances, OSHA rules can take months to promulgate. In instances such as a global pandemic, under the declaration of a national emergency, policies can be enacted in a more immediate fashion via an ETS. Unlike the standard rulemaking process which can take months or years, an ETS undergoes an expedited review process before taking effect and bypasses the process of notice and comment.

The OSH Act authorizes the Secretary of Labor to enact an ETS when it is determined (1) "that employees are exposed to grave danger from exposure to substances or agents determined to be toxic or physically harmful or from new hazards," and (2) "that such emergency standard is necessary to protect employees from such danger."[4] An ETS may be in effect for up to 6 months, at which time OSHA is expected to issue a permanent standard that has been adopted through the standard rulemaking process.[5]

Pre-pandemic, the last time OSHA attempted to issue an emergency standard was under President Reagan in 1983. The Reagan administration tried to reduce the number of asbestos workers could be exposed to by 75%, but the rule was struck down by the 5th Circuit. Despite its failure, the rule was thwarted on narrow grounds and the court suggested OSHA has a significant amount of discretion to decide when an emergency standard is warranted. Notably, the court said "Gravity of danger is a policy decision committed to OSHA, not to the courts."[6] Given this, some observers might have expected a high level of deference to OSHA. Following a growing trend of actively scrutinizing and limiting federal agency powers, the Court took a different track.

On January 7, 2022 the Supreme Court had a lengthy oral hearing on the ETS, and on January 13, 2022 it concluded that the ETS was outside OSHA's powers. In a decision joined by six justices, the Court ruled the Occupational Health and Safety Act did not allow OSHA to regulate against a danger that is not specific to the workplace, but generally present in the population. The court found that for matters not explicitly deemed a regular exercise of federal power, that Congress must clearly authorize an agency to use powers of great economic significance, such as this one, which it was decided that Congress had not done so and therefore, OSHA lacks the

---

[4] 29 U.S.C. § 655(c)(1).

[5] Scalia et al. (2021).

[6] National Federation of Independent Business v. Biden, 595 U. S. ____ (2022).

authorized power to enforce the ETS.[7] The majority decision left open the option of a far more narrow vaccine program, one that is limited to places where workers face a risk beyond the general COVID-19 risk of the population, withstanding judicial review. The three dissenting justices believed, and reminded the majority, that the OSH Act does not specify that the danger must be specific to the workplace, and therefore should have the ability to uphold the program.

After the decision, OSHA withdrew the ETS, and at present, there is no general federal workplace program. The ruling made it clear that the Supreme Court would not let OSHA impose broad vaccine requirements without explicit Congressional authorization.

17.1.2 The Centers for Medicare and Medicaid Healthcare Workers Requirement

Following the direction of President Biden, the Centers for Medicare and Medicaid (CMS) created a rule requiring 14 categories of healthcare facilities to impose a vaccine mandate (with medical and religious exemptions) on healthcare workers, in order to receive funding from CMS.[8] The rule was challenged in multiple courts around the country, and by the time the Supreme Court took up the case, it had been stayed in 25 states. In contrast to its ruling on the OSHA's vaccine program, the Supreme court found, in a 5:4 decision, that the rule challenged CMS' authority. In this case, the majority found that different statutory provisions applied to CMS, and as such, they had the authority to impose additional safety conditions on the facilities they fund. It was deemed appropriate, and reasonable, for CMS to require vaccines for healthcare workers on this basis of safety conditions.[9] To back up their decision, the majority pointed to the already extensive body of requirements CMS imposes. The dissenting justices argued along the same reasons outlined in their decision against the OSHA COVID-19 program, finding no clear authorization and making it clear that they would have required an explicit authorization from Congress to allow the rule.

While the two opposite rulings of the Supreme Court may seem contradictory, it's important to remember that each of them interpreted a different statute, and that the Court can read different statutes differently. In addition, another difference may explain the inconsistency. OSHA is a regulatory agency; it issues top-down commands. In contrast, CMS gives federal money. Traditionally, the courts gave the federal government broad (though not unlimited) leeway to attach conditions when it gives money to state or private actors, and the ruling on the CMS vaccine mandate for healthcare workers is in line with that history.

---

[7] National Federation of Independent Business v. Biden, 595 U. S. ____ (2022).

[8] Medicare and Medicaid Programs (2021).

[9] Biden v. Missouri, 595 U. S. ____ (2022).

17.1.3 Federal Employees mandate

When the federal government acts as an employer, it should have the same authority over its employees as other public employers. In this context, the federal government would have to follow the laws that apply to all employers (as described in Chap. 16, workplace mandates) and respect employees' constitutional rights to the same degree that is expected of other public employers. Within these boundaries, the government would also have the authority to impose workplace conditions over its employees.

Further, over the last years, the Supreme Court has strengthened the control of the President over other federal employees, on the basis of the President's special role as the head of the executive branch.[10] In spite of this, some lower courts have stayed the federal order requiring federal employees to vaccinate unless they qualify for a medical or religious exemption.[11]

We believe this is in error, and that the Supreme Court will uphold the President's authority to impose workplace conditions—including a vaccine mandate—on employees, but readers should be aware that not all courts agree.

17.1.4 Federal Contractors Mandate

Under the Federal Property and Administrative Services Act of 1949 (Procurement Act), the President can prescribe conditions for federal contracting. Historically, that power has been interpreted broadly, and the courts have generally determined that the federal government has the right to set the conditions in which it will contract with others.[12] However, in the context of vaccine mandates the courts' approach was different. In an executive order, President Biden ordered federal contracts to include a vaccine mandate when new conditions were added.[13] In spite of the previous broad interpretation of the Procurement Act, several lower courts concluded that the vaccine mandate goes beyond the President's power.[14] The courts that stayed the mandate were of the view that the provisions of the act did not authorize the President to issue such an order. At this point, the Supreme Court has not yet addressed the issue, and it is unclear how it would rule if the question came before it.

[10] Selia Law LLC v. CFPB, 591 U.S. ___ (2020); Collins v. Yellen, 594 U.S. ___ (2021).
[11] Feds for Medical Freedom v. Biden, No. 3:21-CV-356 (S.D. Tex. Jan. 21, 2022).
[12] Burrows and Manuel (2012).
[13] Executive Order (EO) (2021).
[14] Kentucky v. Biden, No. 21-6147 (6th Cir. 2022); Louisiana v. Biden, No. 21-cv-3867 (W.D. La. Dec. 16, 2021); Anderson and Yuengert (2022).

17.1.5 Head Start Mandate

Included in Biden's COVID-19 plan outlined above, the President has ordered for workers in the Head Start program to be vaccinated. In a preliminary injunction decision, a federal judge called the mandate "lawless."[15] The judge found the mandate to be an exercise of broad power with major "economic, social, and political significance" that triggers the major questions doctrine. Under the major questions doctrine, judges only allow agencies to exercise such broad powers if Congress expressly authorized it, which Congress has yet to do. While Congress has not issued such an authorization, the judge also expressed doubt on whether Congress has the power to delegate such power to the federal government at all.

17.2 Congress's Authority to Mandate Vaccination

Congress's power to mandate vaccination is limited to the enumerated powers.[16] Under these Constitutional limitations, any federally mandated program applicable to the general public would likely be limited to areas of existing federal jurisdiction. The restrictions on federal authority to regulate the public health acknowledges the principles that states have the primary responsibility for protecting the public health, but that "under certain circumstances, federal intervention may be necessary."[17]

If Congress were to impose a vaccine mandate under the Commerce Clause authority, the mandate would have to be specifically tied to regulating the recognized categories of interstate commerce.[18] If Congress used the Spending Clause to offer federal funds to prescribe mandatory vaccinations as a condition for states to receive and use funds, the conditions must fall within the limitations of the Spending Clause.

A Congressional vaccine mandate through the Commerce Clause or Spending Clause would likely be challenged as an overstep of Congressional authority, and the inherent limitations on federal jurisdiction to regulate the public health may—depending on the circumstances—make a Congressionally-imposed vaccine mandate legally dubious. To withstand a Constitutional challenge, Congress would have to narrowly tailor a mandate or the conditional funding to fit within the enumerated powers.

---

[15] Complaint, Louisiana v. Becerra, 577 F. Supp. 3d 483 (W.D. La. 2022), https://law.alaska.gov/pdf/press/211221-Complaint.pdf.

[16] Cole and Swendiman (2015).

[17] Id.

[18] Shen (2019).

17.3 Conclusion

During the COVID-19 pandemic, the federal government has experimented with a range of tools to try and mandate vaccines, using interpretations of existing federal powers to do so. With the exception of a mandate for healthcare workers, federal courts were reluctant to allow application of existing federal powers in this context. Federal courts see vaccine mandates as a significant exercise of federal power that required, in their view, explicit Congressional authorization. This is likely to make it hard or impossible for the federal government to mandate vaccines, outside a carefully and specifically defined specific context (like for healthcare workers), going forward without Congressional authorization.

References

29 U.S.C. § 655(c)(1)

Anderson KS, Yuengert AR (2022) To mandate VAX or not, that is the question: Federal Contractor vaccine mandates before several appellate courts. The National Law Review. https://www.natlawreview.com/article/to-mandate-vax-or-not-question-federal-contractor-vaccine-mandates-several-appellate. Accessed 27 Oct 2022

Biden v. Missouri, 595 U.S. (2022)

Burrows VK, Manuel KM (2012) Presidential authority to impose requirements on federal contractors. UNT Digital Library. https://digital.library.unt.edu/ark:/67531/metadc87183/. Accessed 27 Oct 2022

Cole JP, Swendiman KS (2015) Mandatory vaccinations: precedent and current laws. Curr Polit Econ 17:255

Collins v. Yellen, 594 U.S. (2021)

Complaint, Louisiana v. Becerra, 577 F. Supp. 3d 483 (W.D. La. 2022). https://law.alaska.gov/pdf/press/211221-Complaint.pdf

Executive Order (EO) (2021) 14042. https://www.employmentlawinsights.com/wp-content/uploads/sites/36/2022/05/86FedReg5-1.pdf Accessed 27 Oct 2022

Feds for Medical Freedom v. Biden, No. 3:21-CV-356 (S.D. Tex. Jan. 21, 2022)

Kentucky v. Biden, No. 21-6147 (6th Cir. 2022)

Louisiana v. Biden, No. 21-cv-3867 (W.D. La. Dec. 16, 2021)

Medicare and Medicaid Programs (2021) Omnibus COVID-19 health care staff vaccination. Federal Register. https://www.federalregister.gov/documents/2021/11/05/2021-23831/medicare-and-medicaid-programs-omnibus-covid-19-health-care-staff-vaccination. Accessed 27 Oct 2022

National Federation of Independent Business v. Biden, 595 U.S. (2022)

Scalia E et al (2021) President Biden announces COVID-19 vaccine mandates, with legal challenges likely to follow. Gibson Dunn. https://www.gibsondunn.com/president-biden-announces-covid-19-vaccine-mandates-with-legal-challenges-likely-to-follow/. Accessed 27 Oct 2022

Selia Law LLC v. CFPB, 591 U.S. (2020)

Shen W (2019) Cong. Rsch. Serv., LSB10300, An overview of State and Federal Authority to impose vaccination requirements

The White House (2021) Press briefing by White House COVID-19 response team and public

Vaccine Mandates in Global Comparison 18

Abstract

Few public health measures have had as remarkable of an impact on population health and safety as the invention of vaccinations. The World Health Organization (WHO) reports that vaccines prevent an estimated four to five million deaths each year from vaccine-preventable illnesses. In recent modern advances, the scope of vaccination has expanded beyond infectious diseases, with researchers making miraculous progress in the advent of immunizations against cancers and other chronic illnesses. A vaccine, however, is only as effective as its widespread uptake and implementation. Low vaccination rates have prompted nations to impose a variety of vaccine mandate strategies, enforcing consequences on individuals who choose to forego vaccination despite threats to public health and safety. General hesitation and opposition to vaccinations is hardly a new issue, but to date, there is no coordinated global strategy to implement a schematic mandate. As public outcry increases and the effects of anti-vaccine rhetoric become more immediately apparent in the context of the COVID-19 pandemic, it is crucial that researchers and public health officials focus significant effort on evaluating vaccination strategies worldwide.

18.1 Background

A popular approach to increasing vaccine uptake dates all the way back to the 1800s, when the State of Massachusetts implemented the first-ever vaccine mandate in 1809, just 13 years after the invention of the smallpox vaccine.[1] Other nations began experimenting with mandates in the years to follow, with a broad Compulsory

---

[1] Chemerinsky and Goodwin (2016), p. 110.

© The Author(s), under exclusive license to Springer Nature Switzerland AG 2023
Y. T. Yang, D. R. Reiss, *Vaccine Law and Policy*, Law for Professionals,
https://doi.org/10.1007/978-3-031-36989-6_18

Vaccination Act in England in 1853,[2] and Germany adopting its own mandate in 1874.[3] Smallpox vaccine requirements spread to the African continent and when the Belgian Congo implemented a mandate in 1894, the British colony of the Gold Coast followed suit in 1920. As lack of public acceptance of vaccinations challenged infection control efforts, the use of mandates exploded across the globe in the twentieth century. Many countries, such as Belize, Bulgaria, Jamaica, Kosovo, and Mongolia, even enforced criminal sanctions on those who chose not to vaccinate their children, in an attempt to increase compliance. But with increased regulation often comes increased opposition and policies regarding mandatory vaccination as no exception. Much of vaccine opposition is rooted in religious conflict, battles against a colonial regime, mistrust in the government, and, more recently, misinformation regarding the safety of the vaccine itself. Vaccination mandate strategies have had to adapt and evolve in response to changing public opposition. More importantly, experts in the field have acknowledged a growing need for effective tools to measure the impact of mandate policies to better inform policymakers moving forward.

In previous chapters, we closely examined the law around vaccine mandates in the United States (U.S.). Here we look at the current political landscape of vaccine mandates and make a global comparison of the types of mandates, the severity of non-compliance consequences, the efficacy of policies, and the potential unintended consequences of mandates on public safety and productivity.

18.2 Global Vaccine Policy

A global assessment of vaccine mandate policies in 2020, prior to the COVID-19 pandemic, detected 105 countries across the world which had at least one vaccination mandate policy at the national level. Some type of mandate exists in countries in every continent—from Africa (E.g. Albania, Egypt, Macedonia and Uganda) through America (E.g. Argentina, Paraguay and the U.S.), to Asia (E.g. Republic of Korea, Kuwait, Nepal), Australia, and Europe (E.g. Bulgaria, Czech Republic, Latvia).[4] There is, however, no global scheme of mandates, or a consistent approach.

When the COVID-19 virus spread from nation to nation, additional countries were prompted to experiment with vaccine mandates. The term mandate is loosely defined by us, and these policies can come in many different forms. The effectiveness of each can vary, not only based on how the mandate is imposed, but also by factors such as the public view of and trust in vaccination in the region the mandate is imposed, the strength and value of the consequence posed for not getting vaccinated, a range of fears regarding the disease, and desire to avoid infection. To evaluate which parameters have the strongest influence on the efficacy of a vaccine mandate,

---

[2] Durbach (2005).

[3] Batniji (2021), p. 791.

[4] Attwell et al. (2019), pp. 2843–2848.

we must first identify the types of mandates that exist, the countries which impose them, and the details surrounding their approach.

18.3   Approaches

For at least some childhood diseases (i.e. measles, mumps, rubella, diphtheria, tetanus, pertussis, polio, rabies, hepatitis B, rotavirus, haemophilus influenzae type B, and tuberculosis), a common approach is to require that children be vaccinated to attend school, like the state-level school immunization mandates imposed in the U.S. Not only does this reduce the likelihood of the disease spreading in a high-risk environment, such as classrooms, but it also creates immunity from an early age, reducing the lifetime likelihood of contracting vaccine-preventable diseases. The school vaccination mandate approach has been adopted by several countries.

For emerging diseases, this strategy may be less effective, since large segments of, especially, the adult population are out of the public education system. One option is for government to impose requirements on specific professions or segments of workers. For example, Germany Italy, France, and Greece require healthcare employees to get COVID-19 vaccine.[5] In a range of countries, like in much of Europe, private employers are prohibited from requiring vaccines without specific legal authorization from the state—in contrast to the U.S. approach.[6] Labor laws may also limit the ability to impose workplace requirements.

During the COVID-19 pandemic, countries like Lithuania, France, and Ecuador chose to implement vaccine passport requirements for public spaces. A passport or certificate-based policy grants individuals access to public venues on the contingency of providing proof of immunization. By placing the consequences of foregoing vaccination on less crucial parts of living, this approach poses less of an imposition on an individual's freedom of choice. However, depending on the value that citizens place on their freedom of enjoying public services and public entertainment, the preservation of freedom of choice may come at a cost to the efficacy of such a mandate. The fallout of vaccine passport policies ranged significantly depending on the country it was implemented in, offering an interesting opportunity to evaluate the characteristics of populations that may lead to success with certificate-based policies.

Rather than tie vaccination status to access to public services or employment, other countries have imposed mandates with financial consequences. In Australia, for example, vaccination was encouraged from 1998–2012 by giving a Maternity Immunization Allowance to parents who vaccinated their children. In 2012, this model was replaced when the federal government linked a means-tested payment to vaccination status. The payment was made available to the middle class and below,

---

[5]DW (2022) and Förster et al. (2021).
[6]Jones Day (2021).

removing all exemptions other than for medical purposes, thereby linking childhood subsidies to vaccination.

Australia is not the only country to have imposed financial consequences on the unvaccinated. Singapore took a unique approach to encourage vaccines by requiring unvaccinated individuals to pay for their health care expenses related to COVID-19 infections. While this doesn't impose a direct mandate or immediate consequence on unvaccinated individuals, it does offer a personal incentive to get vaccinated. Additionally, in the event individuals still chose to forego the immunization, it shifts the burden of health care costs directly onto those who refuse to take efforts to prevent infection.

18.4 Efficacy, Challenges, and Opposition

Studies found that mandates prevented thousands of deaths in several countries. But, to determine the best approach to a vaccine mandate, it is important to outline the intended goals of the policy and determine parameters to measure its success. While some governments may see increasing vaccination rates as successful, others may find societal productivity to be a better measure. If the ultimate goal of increasing vaccination rates is to preserve economic productivity by reducing illnesses, we need to consider whether a mandate may decrease productivity if it causes employees to resign, and if that creates staff challenges. In a study comparing six countries that adopted COVID-19 vaccine certificates—certificates of vaccination are required before people could access services like restaurants, hotels, etc.—to 19 countries that did not, researchers found that the rate of vaccination increased dramatically even before the certificate program became operational. That sounds like success, but the study did not look at rates of resignation by employees because of the mandate, so it may not paint a complete picture.

Similarly, a 2022 article in Nature found strong evidence that vaccine requirements increase vaccination rates. The study showed large effects of the requirements in France, Lithuania, Canada, and elsewhere. This study, too, did not completely look at staff attrition, but it did mention a reduction in care-home staff in the United Kingdom (UK) between announcing the policy and its planned implementation. If staff resign, the effect on economic productivity may be less. Of course, for care-homes, economic productivity may be secondary to residents' safety, which the vaccines may increase—but this highlights the importance of clearly identifying the goals of the mandate, which the policies often do not do.

Not all vaccine mandate strategies have the same effect in different geopolitical locations. While Germany found success in involving major German-brand companies in their vaccination efforts, attempts to incorporate a vaccine passport, or certificate-based policy were found to have no significant increase in vaccination rates. These certificates did, however, prove successful in countries like France and Canada increasing vaccination rates by an average of 66%. The range of efficacy varied from region to region quite remarkably, hinting that certain characteristics may facilitate the greater success of a vaccine passport in some populations compared to others.

Measuring solely the benefits of a mandate, however, fails to capture the whole picture. Vaccine mandates come at a notable cost to individual freedom, and therefore must be used only when the added benefits outweigh the possible harms. One study found that opposition to vaccination actually increased from 3% to 16% when a mandate was imposed, presumably provoked by the infringement upon freedom of choice. Careful deliberation must be made when policymakers are considering the use of a mandate to increase vaccination rates in their jurisdiction.

As mandates are implicated across nations, there will inevitably be an increased number of court cases regarding legal disagreements surrounding the mandates. This has been observed historically. For example, France saw a case in which non-vaccinating parents were fined in 2015. In an even more recent case, the European Court of Human Rights examined the Czech's Republic childhood vaccination mandate. The Court, in that case, upheld the mandate, but made it clear that vaccine mandates need to meet requirements of reasonableness and proportionality.

Some opposition to vaccination is rooted in concerns around the safety of vaccination. The majority of individuals receiving vaccinations will experience little to no side effects from the inoculation. However, in the rare cases that an individual suffers unintended health consequences as a result of vaccination, it is reasonable for them to expect quick, generous, no-fault compensation. One mind of thought on this matter is that since the mandates are imposed for the general good, those who suffer harm from them should be compensated. In one study evaluating vaccine mandates globally, only 7 of 62 countries with vaccine requirements have a no-fault compensation scheme. If countries are going to increase the use of immunization mandates, stronger policies must be included to ensure compensation for any individual that suffers harm.

18.5   Conclusion

It is no doubt that increased vaccination rates can provide great benefits to the protection of public health and safety. However, it is imperative that we achieve these benefits at minimal cost to freedom, public trust, and individual safety. Not all countries respond to vaccine mandates in the same way; Mandates have a long history globally and policymakers should carefully evaluate the impact of previously implemented mandates across different geographical locations prior to drafting a policy in their own nation. Smallpox and measles outbreaks led to waves of government-mandated vaccine requirements that served as examples for the public to learn from when the COVID-19 pandemic prompted similar action. Experts should now conduct a broad, coordinated study of the efficacy of COVID-19 vaccine policies in order to provide evidence to inform policy when the next outbreak emerges.

References

Attwell K et al (2019) Mandatory vaccination and no fault vaccine injury compensation schemes: an identification of country-level policies. Vaccine 37:2843–2848. https://doi.org/10.1016/j.vaccine.2019.03.065

Batniji R (2021) Historical evidence to inform covid-19 vaccine mandates. The Lancet 397:791. https://doi.org/10.1016/s0140-6736(21)00267-1

Chemerinsky E, Goodwin M (2016) Compulsory vaccination laws are constitutional. Nw Univ Law Rev 110

Durbach N (2005) Bodily matters: the anti-vaccination movement in England, 1853–1907. Duke University Press, Durham

DW (2022) Covid: vaccine mandate for German health workers approved. https://www.dw.com/en/covid-digest-german-court-approves-vaccine-mandate-for-health-workers/a-61847549. Accessed 27 Oct 2022

Förster J et al (2021) EU and beyond: workplace COVID-19 testing and vaccination protocols. SHRM. https://www.shrm.org/resourcesandtools/hr-topics/global-hr/pages/coronavirus-eu-covid-19-testing-vaccination-protocols.aspx. Accessed 27 Oct 2022

Jones Day (2021) Covid-19 vaccinations and European employers. https://www.jonesday.com/en/insights/2021/03/covid19-vaccinations-and-considerations-for-european-employers. Accessed 27 Oct 2022

WHO (2019) Immunization. World Health Organization. https://www.who.int/news-room/facts-in-pictures/detail/immunization. Accessed 27 Oct 2022

Vaccine Passports for Travel

19

Abstract

In response to an extreme pandemic like COVID-19, significant air travel restrictions were put in place to prevent the spread of the virus (Schlagenhauf, Travel Med Infect Dis, https://doi.org/10.1016/j.tmaid.2021.101996, 2021). Policymakers are searching for options to rework lockdown restrictions while preventing further spread of COVID-19 (Rouw et al., 2021, Key questions about COVID-19 vaccine passports and the U.S. KFF. https://www.kff.org/coronavirus-covid-19/issue-brief/key-questions-about-covid-19-vaccine-passports-and-the-u-s/. Accessed 28 Oct 2022). One strategy for resuming travel is implementing vaccine passports. Travel passports are not new, but are reemerging as a focus of debate because of COVID-19. Requiring vaccine passports would allow individuals who can prove they are vaccinated against COVID-19 to resume unrestricted travel. Vaccine passports are different than government-imposed vaccine mandates, but some of the same concerns apply. Legal, ethical, and practical considerations should be taken into account by policymakers before implementing a vaccine passport system.

19.1 What Are Vaccine Passports and Where Are Vaccine Passports Being Used Now?

During the pandemic, travel restrictions have had detrimental economic and societal effects, including tourism crises and massive job losses.[1] Vaccine passports are "certifications of vaccination that reduce public health restrictions for their bearers."[2] In other words, vaccine passports would enable international travel to continue while

---

[1] Nalubola (2021).

[2] Hall and Studdert (2021).

© The Author(s), under exclusive license to Springer Nature Switzerland AG 2023
Y. T. Yang, D. R. Reiss, *Vaccine Law and Policy*, Law for Professionals,
https://doi.org/10.1007/978-3-031-36989-6_19

decreasing the risk of contracting COVID-19 while traveling.[3] Vaccine passport policies have been under consideration or implemented in different parts of the world.[4] Vaccine passports are intended to balance public health risks with limitations on freedom by simultaneously relaxing restrictions for vaccinated people and reducing the risk of spreading COVID-19.

19.1.1 COVID-19 Vaccine Passports

Before the development and widespread availability of COVID-19 vaccines, some countries considered the use of "immunity passports," which would indicate whether a person had natural immunity after recovering from COVID-19.[5] However, the fast introduction of COVID-19 vaccines kept immunity passports from being imposed. Once vaccines were widely available, policymakers considered vaccine passports as a system to tailor travel restrictions for vaccinated people to limit their impact on "socially valuable activities" like flying.[6] The concept of requiring vaccination certificates for travel to certain parts of the world is not new.[7] For example, select countries in Africa and South America have long required visitors to be vaccinated against yellow fever, and the World Health Organization (WHO) recommends travelers be vaccinated against certain diseases if their destination country is experiencing an outbreak of a vaccine-preventable disease.

Supporters of vaccine passports say that if vaccine passports allow those with proof of vaccination to travel freely, this would "facilitate the reopening of air travel and assist in reviving national economies."[8] In addition, vaccine passports would also incentivize getting vaccinated so individuals could return to pre-pandemic travel activities.[9] The anticipated benefits of a vaccine passport system have made it a viable policy option moving forward.

19.1.2 Where Are COVID-19 Vaccination Passports Required?

The United States (U.S.) has required non-immigrants or non-citizens to have vaccines for travel since November 2021. Furthermore, the U.S. has not implemented a state or federal vaccine passport system yet, but other countries and local jurisdictions have passport systems.[10] Israel began issuing "green passes" to

---

[3] Nalubola (2021).
[4] Hall and Studdert (2021).
[5] Nalubola (2021).
[6] Hall and Studdert (2021).
[7] Wiley (2021).
[8] Schlagenhauf et al. (2021).
[9] Nalubola (2021).
[10] The White House (2021) and Hall and Studdert (2021).

vaccinated residents for travel and other everyday activities, and China and Bahrain are using digital vaccine passports to allow vaccinated citizens to travel internationally.[11] Additionally, Georgia, Estonia, Poland, and Seychelles allow travelers to avoid certain travel restrictions like quarantining or testing if proof of COVID-19 vaccination is provided.

Other countries have also began to record vaccination status but have not implemented any restrictions. For example, in Manitoba and Quebec, Canada, the local governments have begun digital records of vaccination that can be scanned to verify vaccination status. However, neither province has issued information yet to explain how the systems will be used nor whether proof of vaccination will be required for travel.[12] Several local governments in the U.S. also adopted such requirements.

19.2   Vaccine Passports and the U.S.

The Biden Administration has started to consider requiring a vaccine passport for international travel.[13] However, the administration said it will not impose a federal vaccine passport requirement for domestic travel. Vaccination passports are different than vaccine mandates.[14] Vaccine mandates require vaccination as a condition to participate in essential activities like work or school, but vaccination passports would be used for non-essential (but economically and socially valuable) activities, like international travel or restaurant dining.

In the U.S., federal and state governments have authority to impose public health measures, like travel restrictions, on people who cross state or international borders. This authority has been used for measures such as requiring individuals traveling from certain parts of the world to quarantine. During the pandemic, many nations require international travelers to quarantine for days or weeks when they enter their countries.[15] One possible use of vaccine passports would be to exempt vaccinated travelers from such quarantine or testing requirements.

While the conversation around vaccine passports focuses on travel regulations, there may be greater implications from their use. For example, Israel's "green pass" allows entry to hotels, gyms, restaurants, theaters, and other public places, and New York City's "Excelsior Pass" for vaccinated individuals permits entry to theaters, large gatherings, and other public venues. These passport systems can restrict an individual's participation in non-essential activities. Therefore, there are legal, ethical, and practical considerations to take into account before creating a passport system.

---

[11] Rouw et al. (2021).

[12] Thomas (2021).

[13] Rouw et al. (2021).

[14] Hall and Studdert (2021).

[15] Hall and Studdert (2021).

19.3   Key Considerations

19.3.1 Legal Considerations

Vaccine passports raise questions about how regulators will require individuals to display and verify vaccination status.[16] These decisions could have serious legal implications for effectiveness, privacy, and security. When developing a vaccine passport system, regulators will have to consider the diverse vaccine authorization and approval landscape, the method of requiring proof, privacy, security concerns, and international and interjurisdictional standards for recognition.

With multiple COVID-19 vaccinations available, there are several concerns that could influence the regulation of vaccine passports. One concern is whether all COVID-19 vaccines are equal. Policymakers considering requiring vaccine passports will have to address which vaccines will satisfy the requirement, and whether a person who received a vaccine that is not currently licensed in the destination country will be permitted to travel there. Different countries have authorized and approved different combinations of vaccines.[17] The U.S. will have to decide how to certify different vaccines that may not be approved domestically. For example, Iceland has a policy that only vaccines approved for use by the European Medicines Agency or the WHO will be recognized.

Once regulators determine what the vaccination standards are, they will need to decide the method of requiring proof, and what personal information must be included in the proof. Vaccine passports could be issued as a physical document (like a vaccination card) or a digital record (like a QR code on a Smartphone).[18] Each method of proof has trade-offs. Paper-based proof has a high risk of falsified certificates, but digital proof is more susceptible to violations of privacy, and may increase barriers to access.[19]

Electronic devices collecting personal medical information such as vaccination status creates a risk that the user's personal information will be tracked and collected.[20] To address privacy concerns, some scholars suggest a vaccine passport system that includes vaccination status without including other identifying information.[21] However, the scholars acknowledge that this method could increase the likelihood of fraud and abuse. For example, the person or system checking the method of proof can only see vaccination status without other identifying information, reducing verification quality. Policymakers would have to weigh the privacy concerns against the public health benefits when deciding what information to require in a vaccine passport.

---

[16] Schlagenhauf et al. (2021).

[17] Rouw et al. (2021).

[18] Thomas (2021).

[19] Schlagenhauf et al. (2021).

[20] Nalubola (2021).

[21] Thomas (2021).

Currently, there is no consensus approach to accurately certify vaccination.[22] If countries want a truly effective system, they will need to work together to effectively implement vaccine passports, including establishing standards for reliable documentation of vaccination. Mutual recognition of passports will be essential to have an effective global vaccine passport system.[23] The current fragmented approach will cause problems as different jurisdictions take different approaches and enforce different standards.

In addition to the legal considerations regarding method of proof, some people may also see vaccine passports as a means of mandating vaccines, since unvaccinated people would be deprived of liberty rights,[24] including freedom to travel.[25] However, the right to freedom of movement can legally be restricted to prevent the spread of infectious diseases. Courts balance important government interests, like the spread of infectious diseases, against the rights of individuals. If the government can show that the vaccination passport is necessary to further the compelling government interest of reducing the spread of COVID-19, a legal challenge on these grounds is unlikely to succeed.

19.3.2 Ethical Considerations

Currently, the WHO does not endorse vaccine passports because of ethical issues surrounding these systems.[26] The WHO cautioned countries against the use of requiring COVID-19 passports for international travel because vaccination should not exempt individuals from other risk-reduction measures while traveling. Additionally, the WHO noted that vaccination as a requirement to travel may inequitably impact low income countries who have substantially less access to vaccines, and groups without access to vaccines, including racial minorities. These ethical considerations should be taken into account when making decisions about imposing a vaccination passport system.

Without unfettered universal access to the vaccine, vaccine passports are associated with equity issues.[27] Vaccine passports give certain privileges to those who have been able to access the vaccine, but this may be discriminatory against groups who tend to have lower rates of vaccination,[28] thereby limiting freedom and disadvantaging poor nations and populations where vaccine rollout is slower.[29] In

---

[22] Hall and Studdert (2021).

[23] Rouw et al. (2021).

[24] Thomas (2021).

[25] Schlagenhauf et al. (2021).

[26] Rouw et al. (2021).

[27] Schlagenhauf et al. (2021).

[28] Hall and Studdert (2021).

[29] Schlagenhauf et al. (2021).

relation to COVID-19 vaccines, there are substantial inequalities in access to the vaccine among countries.

One inequality in access involves supply constraints. Supply constraints, where less of the vaccine is available, directly affect population groups who do not fit into priority groups to be vaccinated.[30] Moreover, there is uncertainty of the duration of immunity provided by vaccines.[31] In addition to the existing supply constraints, the potential need for boosters may add to the existing inequity among wealthy and poor countries. Some countries may be able to offer boosters before poorer more vulnerable populations have had the chance to receive even a first round of vaccines.

Another point of inequality is access to technology. Digital records could disadvantage low-income groups if they require a smartphone or other costly technology to display the record.[32] If a vaccine passport policy were implemented, it should not be designed to exclude those who may not be able to afford the essential tools to enjoy the privileges conferred by the passport.

Other ethical considerations include possible exemptions from the vaccine passport. Medical exemptions may be necessary to avoid discriminating against those who are unable to be vaccinated due to health problems by excluding them from public places and activities. Additionally, people with lawful religious or philosophical objections to vaccination would be penalized by vaccine passport policies, either by losing their privilege to travel freely or by sacrificing their beliefs to get the vaccine.[33] Regulators could consider incorporating lawful religious or philosophical belief exemptions to vaccine passport requirements, similar to those used for other vaccine mandate laws to prevent infringing on sincerely held beliefs.[34]

Policymakers considering implementing vaccine passports requirements should ensure that certain groups are not disadvantaged or overburdened by them.[35]

19.3.3 Practical

There are several practical considerations for the introduction of vaccine passports. First, scientific uncertainty surrounding the "nature and degree of immunity that vaccination confers" may affect the effectiveness of vaccine passports in preventing disease.[36] Second, a lack of standardized guidance for COVID-19 passports could lead to various complications when implementing a vaccine passport system.[37] A

---

[30] Hall and Studdert (2021).

[31] Schlagenhauf et al. (2021).

[32] Thomas (2021).

[33] Hall and Studdert (2021).

[34] Thomas (2021).

[35] Nalubola (2021).

[36] Hall and Studdert (2021).

[37] Rouw et al. (2021).

vaccine passport system should be scientifically justified and easily operable across jurisdictions to be effective.

Vaccine effectiveness suffers from scientific uncertainty. If vaccination against COVID-19 does not actually reduce the risk of transmission to unvaccinated individuals, it may not make sense to implement the policy.[38] Currently, scientists have limited data on the length that immunity lasts for and the risk of vaccinated people transmitting the virus to infect others.[39] Additionally, COVID-19 variants have different levels of transmissibility, severity, and detectability which effects their susceptibility to treatment and "natural or vaccine-induced immunity."[40] Vaccine passports are proposed "as a means of controlling the risk of unvaccinated people . . . where they might contract the disease."[41] If immunity wears off, is ineffective against variants, or if vaccinated people can easily transmit the virus to unvaccinated people, then vaccine passports may not serve a useful purpose in preventing the spread of COVID-19.[42]

Another practical concern is that there is no standardized guidance related to the design of COVID-19 vaccine passports, including any standards for issues such as data privacy or interoperability. Using different standards of proof of vaccination in different countries could lead to confusion if people are required to have multiple forms of certification. Beyond the international complications from these varying standards, the U.S. faces a potential domestic difficulty with different states and jurisdictions implementing different forms of vaccine passport standards. In addition, U.S. states like Florida and Texas have preemptively banned the use of vaccine passports. Some scholars suggest implementing reciprocal recognition agreements or having uniform standards for vaccine passports to reduce confusion. In the meantime, as more countries and states develop unique standards and methods of proof for vaccine passports—and bans of such passports—this increases the likelihood of logistical complications.

These practical considerations are important to take into account *before* vaccine passport systems are created to ensure the system will be effective in achieving the goal of allowing unrestricted travel for vaccinated people.

19.4 Conclusion

Vaccination passports are a strategy for reducing travel restrictions while COVID-19 continues to pose a public health risk. As the government considers implementing a vaccine passport system to allow vaccinated people to enjoy unrestricted travel, policymakers should take the legal, ethical, and practical considerations into account

---

[38] Wiley (2021).
[39] Nalubola (2021).
[40] Schlagenhauf et al. (2021).
[41] Thomas (2021).
[42] Nalubola (2021).

to ensure the system protects individual interests while effectively achieving its goals.

References

Hall MA, Studdert DM (2021) "Vaccine passport" certification — policy and ethical considerations. N Engl J Med. https://doi.org/10.1056/nejmp2104289

Nalubola S (2021) Vaccine passports and COVID-19: ethical, scientific, and practical considerations. Roundtable J Health Policy

Rouw A et al (2021) Key questions about COVID-19 vaccine passports and the U.S. KFF. https://www.kff.org/coronavirus-covid-19/issue-brief/key-questions-about-covid-19-vaccine-passports-and-the-u-s/. Accessed 28 Oct 2022

Schlagenhauf P et al (2021) Variants, vaccines and vaccination passports: challenges and chances for travel medicine in 2021. Travel Med Infect Dis. https://doi.org/10.1016/j.tmaid.2021.101996

The White House (2021) Fact sheet: Biden administration releases additional detail for implementing a safer, more stringent international air travel system. https://www.whitehouse.gov/briefing-room/statements-releases/2021/10/25/fact-sheet-biden-administration-releases-additional-detail-for-implementing-a-safer-more-stringent-international-air-travel-system/. Accessed 28 Oct 2022

Thomas B (2021) Vaccine ins and outs: an exploration of the legal issues raised by vaccine passports. C.D. Howe. Inst. https://www.cdhowe.org/sites/default/files/attachments/research_papers/mixed/Working%20Paper%202021-07-13.pdf. Accessed 28 Oct 2022

Wiley M (2021) Vaccine passports are a hot-button issue, but travelers already need vaccines to enter certain countries around the world. Insider. https://www.insider.com/proof-of-vaccination-requirements-passports-travel-world-health-yellow-fever-2021-4. Accessed 28 Oct 2022

Part V

Special Contexts

This part explores special issues related to vaccines that don't fit under the other headings. The common thread between these chapters is the exploration of specific contexts related to vaccines. Chapter 20 focuses on vaccines in the U.S. military, including the history of vaccination requirements and their implications for service members. Chapter 21 discusses vaccines in times of emergency, including the regulatory frameworks that govern vaccine development and distribution during crises. Chapter 22 delves into the issue of vaccine misinformation online, including the spread of false information, its impact on vaccine hesitancy, and potential legal responses to combat it. Collectively, these chapters offer unique perspectives on vaccine-related issues, highlighting the diverse contexts in which vaccines are used and the challenges that arise in these contexts.

Military Vaccinations

20

Abstract

Mandatory inoculation of American soldiers predates the creation of the United States (U.S.) and our independence from Great Britain. In 1775, British forces expelled Bostonian citizens infected with smallpox. At the same time, a Continental Army force of 10,000 soldiers was advancing on Quebec, Canada. Infected citizens interacted with healthy soldiers, resulting in 5500 smallpox casualties suffered by the Continental Army (Grabenstein, Epidemiol Rev 28:5, 2006). As John Adams noted, "[t]he smallpox is ten times more terrible than the British, Canadians, and Indians together. This was the cause of our precipitate retreat from Quebec." In 1777, General George Washington ordered a mandatory inoculation program for soldiers who had not survived a smallpox infection earlier in their lives. General Washington's order made the Continental Army the first entity in the world with an organized program to prevent smallpox. Some argue that an earlier mandate would have prevented the disastrous smallpox outbreak and sped up the conclusion of the Revolutionary War. Since the country's founding, the military and Department of Defense (DoD) have mandated vaccines for servicemembers. This chapter discusses the various vaccines—both historically and currently—servicemembers were and are required to take. It discusses the various DoD policies surrounding vaccine requirements, the various legal considerations, and policy and social issues like vaccine hesitancy.

20.1 The Department of Defense and Vaccines

Military servicemembers live, operate, and work in conditions vastly different from their civilian counterparts. In general, every servicemember goes through some form of basic training, which involves long hours outside, exposure to various elements, and unsanitary conditions. Additionally, a servicemember may deploy to geographic

© The Author(s), under exclusive license to Springer Nature Switzerland AG 2023
Y. T. Yang, D. R. Reiss, *Vaccine Law and Policy*, Law for Professionals,
https://doi.org/10.1007/978-3-031-36989-6_20

areas home to diseases not generally found in the U.S. Further, there is a higher risk of attacks with bioweapons towards military targets. For these reasons, military immunization requirements often exceed those of civilian adults. A robust immunization program "protects the personal health of US military personnel and maintains their ability to accomplish missions."[1]

As the government agency overseeing the military, the DoD has an enormous interest in the health of military personnel and their ability to accomplish missions. To further that interest, the DoD administers a variety of force health protection (FHP) measures, including vaccination programs.[2] DoD Instruction 6205.02 establishes the DoD Immunization Program which gives general directions to combatant commands and military departments (MILDEPs) to identify and define "mandatory immunization requirements for servicemembers."[3] The DoD's vaccination requirements usually follow the recommendations from the Advisory Committee on Immunization Practices (ACIP)—a federal expert advisory committee advising the Centers for Disease Control and Prevention (CDC) (for more discussion of ACIP, see Chap. 3).

The Defense Health Agency (DHA) manages the DoD Immunization Program. The DHA coordinates the administration of vaccines to servicemembers and other DoD beneficiaries, based on the MILDEPs' and combatant commands' vaccination requirements. Vaccinations are typically available in military treatment facilities, certain military settings (e.g., basic training), or through participating TRICARE (the healthcare program for servicemembers and beneficiaries) providers. The DHA is also responsible for safety oversight and procurement of vaccines.

Some vaccines are required for all servicemembers. Regardless of occupation, all servicemembers receive the following vaccines: (1) Adenovirus; (2) Hepatitis A & B; (3) Influenza; (4) Measles/Mumps/Rubella (MMR); (5) Meningococcal; (6) Poliovirus; (7) Tetanus-Diphtheria; and (8) Varicella.[4] In addition to these vaccines, combatant commands may require other vaccines for servicemembers (and family members) based on specific health threats in a geographic region.

20.2   Issues with Military Vaccine Mandates

Another difference between the military and civilian worlds interjects itself into vaccination requirements—the chain of command. It is hard to think of a civilian position in which disobeying a supervisor's order can result in criminal punishment for an otherwise lawful act. But the Uniform Code of Military Justice (UCMJ) authorizes criminal punishment for servicemembers who disobey lawful commands

---

[1] Grabenstein et al. (2006).

[2] Mendez Bryce (2021a).

[3] *Id.*

[4] Mendez Bryce (2021a).

by superior officers or disobey lawful general orders or regulations.[5] The chain of command is so sacrosanct that failure to obey an order from a superior officer during a time of war is punishable *by death*.[6]

So, what if a servicemember does not want to take a required vaccine? This part describes two answers to that question. The first answer is an administratively prescribed way for a servicemember to try and avoid the vaccine. The second answer is messier, and dredges up significant policy issues.

20.2.1 Vaccination Opt-Outs

When a vaccine is mandated, a servicemember can request to opt out of the mandate. Upon a servicemember's request, the DoD can authorize a *medical* or *administrative* exemption. DoD healthcare providers (HCPs) can authorize a medical exemption when a servicemember has an underlying health condition or known adverse reaction related to a certain vaccine. The DoD's medical exemption can either be temporary or permanent, based on the servicemember's medical need.

Alternatively, an administrative exemption can be granted by a unit commander. An administrative exemption can be granted in three situations: (1) a servicemember is within 180 days from separating or retiring from the military; (2) a servicemember is within 30 days of departing a permanent assignment location; or (3) religious reasons. To grant an administrative exemption based on religious reasons, the unit commander must first seek input from medical, legal, and chaplain representatives. The unit commander then has to counsel the servicemember on the opt-out's potential adverse impact to "deployability, assignment, or international travel." Finally, a military physician must counsel the servicemember on the benefits and risks of foregoing a required vaccination. If a religion-based administrative exemption is granted, the unit commander can revoke the exemption "if the individual and/or unit are at imminent risk of exposure to a disease for which an immunization is available."[7]

20.2.2 Vaccine Hesitancy

But what if a servicemember is not granted a medical or administrative exemption, yet will not take a required vaccine out of concern for safety? In May 1998, then-Secretary of Defense William Cohen mandated anthrax vaccinations for the entire military. The mandate was highly criticized by the media and Congress, but was implemented nonetheless. A number of servicemembers refused to take the vaccine because they believed it was unsafe, harmful, and ineffective. Some of those

---

[5] 10 U.S.C. §§ 890, 892 (U.C.M.J. Arts. 90, 92).

[6] 10 U.S.C. § 890(1) (U.C.M.J. Art. 90(1)).

[7] Mendez Bryce (2021a).

servicemembers were discharged from the military and lost pension and retirement benefits.[8]

Even if a vaccine has not received Food and Drug Administration (FDA) licensure, the DoD can still administer it to servicemembers. The DoD's preference is to administer fully-approved vaccines, but non-approved vaccines can be administered for FHP purposes.[9] If a vaccine has not received full FDA approval, but is to be used as an FHP measure, certain informed consent procedures are to be followed. A federal statute (10 U.S.C. § 1107), and Executive Order (E.O.) 13,139 require the Secretary of Defense to provide notice when a servicemember receives "an investigational new drug or a drug unapproved for its applied use."[10] Among other things, a service member needs to be informed of the option to accept or refuse a vaccine.[11]

The informed consent process sounds like sufficient protection for servicemembers who are uncomfortable taking a vaccine not yet approved by the FDA. However, this process is not always guaranteed. In fact, the DoD may request from the President a waiver of notice and consent requirements for servicemembers "if the President determines, in writing, that complying with such requirement is not in the interests of national security."[12] If a waiver is granted, the DoD is required—prior to administering the vaccine—to inform servicemembers that a non-FDA approved vaccine is being administered. The DoD is also required to disclose why the vaccine is being administered, information on known side effects, and "other information that the 'Secretary of Health and Human Services may require to be disclosed.'"[13] In other words, information is required but consent may not be. Fortunately for servicemembers—especially for those prone to vaccine hesitancy—E.O. 13,139 limits presidential waivers considerably and allows them only when they are "absolutely necessary."[14]

20.3   The Military's COVID-19 Vaccination Mandate

On August 9, 2021, Secretary of Defense Lloyd Austin notified servicemembers that he intended to mandate COVID-19 vaccinations by mid-September—or earlier, based upon FDA licensure. On August 23, 2021, the FDA approved the licensing application for the Pfizer-BioNTech COVID-19 vaccine for individuals aged 16 years and older. The next day, Secretary Austin issued a memo to all MILDEP Secretaries directing the "full vaccination of all members of the Armed Forces under DoD authority . . . who are not fully vaccinated against COVID-19."[15]

---

[8] Katz (2000), pp. 1835–1863.

[9] Mendez Bryce (2021a).

[10] Katz (quoting 10 U.S.C. § 1107(a)).

[11] 10 U.S.C. § 1107a(a)(1).

[12] *Id.*

[13] *Id.*

[14] Katz (quoting Executive Order. 13,139).

[15] Mendez Bryce (2021b).

At that time, the Pfizer COVID 19 vaccine was the only vaccine that had received full licensure. Therefore, it was the only vaccine that could be mandated. However, servicemembers could voluntarily receive another COVID-19 vaccine and meet Secretary Austin's requirement. The DoD defined "fully vaccinated" status as starting "two weeks after completing" the dosing regiments of the Pfizer vaccine, a COVID-19 vaccine subject to an FDA emergency use authorization (e.g., Moderna or Johnson & Johnson), or a COVID-19 vaccine approved on the World Health Organization's Emergency Use Listing. The U.S. Coast Guard—which falls under the Department of Homeland Security—issued a similar mandate for members on August 26, 2021.

Like all previously mandated vaccines, servicemembers can seek medical or administrative exemptions. The Archbishop for the Military Services recently stated that "[n]o one should be forced to receive a COVID-19 vaccine if it would violate the sanctity of his or her conscience." The Archbishop recognized that the Catholic Church, including Pope Francis, has declared the administration of a COVID-19 vaccine as "not sinful." While various COVID-19 vaccines were tested using abortion-derived cell lines, the Catholic Church determined that receiving the vaccines "does not constitute formal cooperation with abortion."

Nonetheless, the Archbishop's recent statement focused on the "sanctity of conscience," stating that "[t]he denial of religious accommodations, or punitive or adverse personnel actions taken against those who raise earnest, conscience-based objections, would be contrary to federal law and morally reprehensible."[16] Both DoD and MILDEP spokespeople and officials have acknowledged that the process for granting a religious exemption from a vaccine mandate applies to the current COVID-19 mandate.

Each military branch implemented slightly different deadlines that servicemembers must be vaccinated for COVID-19. Overall, the military's vaccination rate has increased since Secretary Austin's August memo, but as some deadlines approached "[h]undreds of thousands" of servicemembers remained unvaccinated.[17] For example, as of mid-October 2021, about 81% of the Air Force is reportedly fully vaccinated. This left about 60,000 personnel with only 3 weeks to be fully vaccinated before the November 2nd deadline. So, what happens—or what can happen—to servicemembers who do not comply with the requirement?

According to Army guidelines, soldiers who refuse to comply can face "administrative or non-judicial punishment . . . *to include relief of duties or discharge. . . .*"[18] Each MILDEP has authorized unit commanders to counsel and take action against noncompliant servicemembers who have not requested or received an exemption, as those servicemembers will be considered in violation of UCMJ Article 92 (Failure to Obey an Order or Regulation).[19]

---

[16] Howe (2021).

[17] Altman-Devilbiss (2021).

[18] Beynon (2021).

[19] Mendez Bryce (2021b).

The Army has recently established guidelines for dealing with noncompliant soldiers. First, noncompliant soldiers must be formally counseled, "effectively creating a paper trail for leaders to show they discussed a topic with a soldier." Then, the soldier must watch an educational video from the CDC explaining the science behind the vaccines. Upon continued refusal, a noncompliant soldier will meet with a medical professional to discuss vaccination benefits and the soldier's concerns. If a soldier still refuses to comply, and has not been granted an exemption, "[c]ommanders will initiate mandatory separation of soldiers who refuse the vaccine. . . ."[20] In 2023, Secretary Austin rescinded the 2021 memorandum mandating that members of the Armed Forces under DoD authority be vaccinated against COVID-19, and the memorandum of Nov. 30, 2021, pertaining to the vaccination of National Guard and Reserve personnel.

20.4 Conclusion

The military differs from its civilian counterparts in countless ways. Those differences include the geographic regions and elements—including diseases—that servicemembers may be exposed to. Additionally, being a part of a warfighting unit requires a level of cohesion and dependency largely unmatched in the civilian world. Thus, it makes sense that servicemembers may need to be vaccinated against diseases civilians otherwise would not be exposed to. And the need to keep all servicemembers as healthy and ready as possible makes vaccine mandates desirable.

Since this country's founding, military servicemembers have been subject to vaccine requirements. But those requirements can cause significant issues when they involve vaccines that have not been fully licensed by the FDA. While servicemembers are afforded some protections in those circumstances, the protections can be waived by the President. And a refusal to take a required vaccine can result in a servicemember's discharge—along with the loss of significant benefits.

References

10 U.S.C. § 1107a(a)(1)
10 U.S.C. § 890(1) (U.C.M.J. Art. 90(1))
10 U.S.C. §§ 890, 892 (U.C.M.J. Arts. 90, 92)
Altman-Devilbiss A (2021) Report: many troops have not complied with COVID-19 vaccine mandate. ABC 15 News. https://wpde.com/news/nation-world/report-many-troops-have-no-complied-with-covid-19-vaccine-mandate. Accessed 26 Oct 2022
Beynon S (2021) What happens to soldiers who refuse the COVID vaccine? Military.com. https://www.military.com/daily-news/2021/09/15/what-happens-soldiers-who-refuse-covid-vaccine.html. Accessed 26 Oct 2022

---

[20]Beynon (2021).

Grabenstein J et al (2006) Immunization to protect the US armed forces: heritage, current practice, and prospects. Epidemiol Rev 28:5. https://doi.org/10.1093/epirev/mxj003

Howe E (2021) Catholic troops can refuse COVID vaccine, Archbishop declares. Defense One. https://www.defenseone.com/policy/2021/10/catholic-troops-can-refuse-covid-vaccine-archbishop-declares/186056/. Accessed 26 Oct 2022

Katz R (2000) Friendly fire: the mandatory military anthrax vaccination program. Duke Law J 50: 1835–1863

Mendez Bryce PH (2021a) Congressional Research Service, IF11816, Defense Health Primer: Military Vaccinations 1. https://crsreports.congress.gov/product/pdf/IF/IF11816/2. Accessed 25 Oct 2022

Mendez Bryce PH (2021b) Congressional Research Service, IN11764, The Military's COVID-19 Vaccination Mandate 1. https://crsreports.congress.gov/product/details?prodcode=IN11764. Accessed 25 Oct 2022

Vaccine Policy in Emergency Situations

21

Abstract

The Public Readiness and Emergency Preparedness Act of 2005 (PREP Act) "authorizes the Secretary of the Department of Health and Human Services (HHS) to issue a declaration that provides immunity from tort liability for claims of loss caused by countermeasures (e.g., vaccines, drugs, products) against diseases or other threats of public health emergencies." (Association of State and Territorial Health Officials, 2012, Public Readiness & Emergency Preparedness Act–fact sheet, legal preparedness series: emergency use authorization toolkit 1. https://legacy.astho.org/uploadedFiles/Programs/Preparedness/Public_Health_Emergency_Law/Emergency_Authority_and_Immunity_Legal_Toolkit/07-EUA%20PREP%20Act%20FS%204-12%20final(1).pdf. Accessed 26 Oct 2022). The liability protection is intended to encourage the development and administration of countermeasures. Without having to worry about legal exposure, individuals and entities covered by PREP Act immunity can engage in rapid response efforts to the declared emergency (Lazzarotti, 2021, PREP Act and COVID-19 vaccinations: health and human services dep't clears way to assist. Jackson Lewis. https://www.jacksonlewis.com/publication/prep-act-and-covid-19-vaccinations-health-and-human-services-department-clears-way-assist. Accessed 26 Oct 2022). The scope of immunity from PREP Act protections is broad, leaving parties injured by covered countermeasures with limited options for recourse and compensation in the event of serious injury (Hickey, 2021, The PREP Act and COVID-19: limiting liability for medical countermeasures, 3. Congressional Research Service, LSB10443. https://crsreports.congress.gov/product/pdf/LSB/LSB10443). This chapter provides an overview of the functions and scope of the PREP Act.

Note that another law that applies to vaccines in an emergency are the provisions of the Food, Drugs and Cosmetics Act that allow the HHS to give emergency use authorization to vaccines in an emergency. We address those in Chap. 2, as part of our discussion of the paths to getting vaccines on the market.

© The Author(s), under exclusive license to Springer Nature Switzerland AG 2023
Y. T. Yang, D. R. Reiss, *Vaccine Law and Policy*, Law for Professionals,
https://doi.org/10.1007/978-3-031-36989-6_21

21.1   Function of the PREP Act

The PREP Act provides immunity from liability to covered persons for certain activities related to covered countermeasures. [1] Without PREP Act immunity, individuals and organizations who may want to develop, manufacture, or administer countermeasures may be concerned about legal liability from injuries caused by their contributions to countermeasure efforts. [2] The PREP Act protections apply to the development, manufacture, testing, distribution, administration, and use of covered countermeasures.[3] "Covered countermeasures" under the PREP Act include vaccines, drugs, or medical devices to be used against chemical, biological, radiological, and nuclear agents of terrorism, epidemics, and pandemics.

PREP Act declarations may provide protections related to products authorized through Emergency Use Authorization (EUA), which "allow for the use of unapproved medical product[s] . . . and devices . . . or an unapproved use of an approved medical product, during a declared emergency."[4] Immunity from liability means that covered entities cannot be sued for monetary damages in court for injuries related to the administration or use of covered countermeasures, with narrow exceptions defined in the act. [5]

Since the enactment of the PREP Act in 2005, there have been 10 PREP Act declarations issued.[6] Past declarations applied to the H1N1 vaccine in 2009 and the Ebola vaccine in 2018. More recently, PREP Act declarations were issued to cover countermeasures for the COVID-19 pandemic.

21.1.1 Scope of Immunity from Liability

The immunity conferred by the PREP Act covers damages including death, disability, and physical, mental, or emotional injury as well as the fear of these conditions.[7] In addition, liability protections "extend to claims made for medical monitoring as well as loss or damage to property, including business interruption."[8] The HHS Secretary also has the authority to extend protection to claims that have a causal relationship to the development, distribution, administration, or use of the covered countermeasure.

Claims within the scope of the Secretary's declaration immunizes a covered person from liability for all claims of loss relating to the administration or use of a

---

[1] Association of State and Territorial Health Officials (2012).

[2] Lazzarotti (2021).

[3] Association of State and Territorial Health Officials (2012).

[4] *Id.*

[5] Hickey (2021).

[6] Administration for Strategic Preparedness and Response (n.d.).

[7] Association of State and Territorial Health Officials (2012).

[8] *Id.*

covered countermeasure. [9] The Congressional Research Service breaks the PREP Act immunity into four elements: "(1) the individual entity must be a "covered person"; (2) the legal claim must be for a "loss"; (3) the loss must have a causal relationship with the administration or use of a covered countermeasure; and (4) the medical product that caused the loss must be a "covered countermeasure."" [10] Covered persons and entities include the government, manufacturers, and distributors of covered countermeasures. Covered persons also include "program planners" that dispense, distribute, administer, or provide guidance and facilities for the use of covered countermeasures, and qualified persons who prescribe, administer, or dispense covered countermeasures. We are going to use the term "covered entity" to address people and organizations covered, to signal that it does not have to be a person. Courts have characterized the PREP Act immunity as "sweeping," because it applies to all types of legal claims under state and federal law.

The broad immunity conferred by the PREP Act reaches "all claims for loss" under federal and state law. [11] In other words, covered entities are immunized from most tort, medical malpractice, and wrongful death claims.

Courts interpret PREP Act immunity broadly, and often favorably toward covered entities. [12] For example, in *Garcia v. Welltower OpCo Grp. LLC*, where a nursing home resident tested positive and died of COVID-19, his family sued the living facility. The family argued that the home's relaxed policies during the COVID-19 state of emergency led to their family member's death and they alleged elder abuse, wrongful death, and intentional infliction of emotional distress. The Court found that the PREP Act (1) preempted the plaintiff's state law claims and (2) immunized the senior living facility from liability. The court reasoned that the senior living facility "attempt[ed] to comply with federal guidelines," relating to COVID-19 and that it is only when a covered person *fails* to make any decisions whatsoever in response to the PREP Act declaration that immunity would not apply. In this case, although the nursing home's COVID-19 prevention policies were relaxed to the point of creating risk for the nursing home residents, the fact that the nursing home (a covered entity) maintained some COVID-related policies and procedures was enough to extend PREP Act liability protections to the home. Note that this case is not related to vaccines, and is brought here just to demonstrate that courts apply the liability protections broadly.

The *Garcia* case illustrates the sweeping protections conferred by the PREP Act. Courts are hesitant to hold covered entities liable where PREP Act declarations are in effect because the statute includes limited exceptions to the liability protections.

---

[9] Hickey (2021).

[10] *Id.*

[11] Hickey (2021).

[12] O'Shea and White (2021) (Discussing Garcia v. Welltower).

21.1.2 The "Willful Misconduct" Exception

One exception to PREP Act immunity from tort liability is for "willful misconduct."[13] The willful misconduct exception applies when a covered entity proximately causes death or serious physical injury to another person through willful misconduct. There are two key elements for determining if the exception applies: (1) whether a serious physical injury occurred, and (2) whether the covered person's actions constituted willful misconduct. A serious physical injury must be life threatening, permanently impair a body function, permanently damage a body structure, or require medical intervention to avoid such permanent impairment or damage. Willful misconduct *requires* that a covered entity acted (1) intentionally to achieve a wrongful purpose; (2) knowingly without legal or factual justification; *and* (3) in disregard of a known or obvious risk that is so great as to make it highly probably that the harm will outweigh the benefit. This is a very demanding standard—the person causing the harm must have been very culpable. Even being reckless would not be enough.

To prove willful misconduct, injured persons or their representatives must first seek compensation through the Countermeasures Injury Compensation Program (discussed in more detail below). Furthermore, they cannot sue if they elect to receive that compensation. If they decline compensation through the Countermeasures Injury Compensation Program and file a lawsuit, then patients must sue in the U.S District Court for the District of Columbia.[14] The legal process is limited for plaintiffs, and the court procedure in these lawsuits is more favorable to defendants. Willful misconduct must be proven by the clear and convincing evidence standard. As the Congressional Research Service observes, this standard is higher than the standard in a typical civil case. During a civil case you only have to demonstrate that there was an increased chance you were harmed—with a probability greater than 50%.[15] To demonstrate willful misconduct, plaintiffs need clear and convincing evidence, which is not quite as high a standard as the "beyond reasonable doubt" standard used in criminal law. However, it is still a high threshold, requiring very strong evidence. Moreover, the statute limits economic recovery from successful challenges.

The PREP Act also contains two statutory defenses to willful misconduct: covered persons cannot be found to have engaged in willful misconduct if they "acted consistent with applicable directions, guidelines, or recommendations by the Secretary regarding the administration or use of a covered countermeasure;" and countermeasure manufacturers and distributors may rely on regulatory compliance as a defense to a willful misconduct allegation.

In one case, a court found that covered entities who fail to administer a countermeasure may not be guilty of willful misconduct, and may still be immune from

---

[13] Hickey (2021).
[14] Hickey (2021).
[15] *Id.*

liability under the PREP Act.[16] In *Goldblatt v. HCP Prairie Village*, the court found that failure to administer a countermeasure should fall within PREP Act immunity if "coupled closely with an act of administration to another." [17] However, the Court found that a close causal connection is required, and in that case, there was no such causal connection; and therefore it allowed the plaintiff's inaction claims to go forward. In other words, although some inaction claims would be covered by PREP Act immunity, they have to be closely connected to administering a vaccine to someone else, and failure to vaccinate by itself—without such causal connection—is not protected from liability.

21.1.3 The CICP

The PREP Act authorizes the Countermeasures Injury Compensation Program (CICP), an emergency fund to provide compensation for injuries directly caused by administration or use of a covered countermeasure. [18] Individuals may recover for serious injuries or death directly caused by the administration of covered countermeasures through the CICP. [19] Eligible individuals who suffer from serious physical injury or death directly caused by the administration of a covered counter-measure may be reimbursed for medical expenses, loss of employment income, or survivor benefits. "Serious physical injuries" are limited to those that warrant hospitalization or a significant loss of function or disability.

Claims to the CICP must be filed within 1 year of administration or use of a covered countermeasure.[20] Unlike other federal vaccine injury compensation programs, like the National Vaccine Injury Compensation Program (VICP), the CICP does not allow compensation for attorney's fees and pain and suffering.[21] Additionally, the law does not allow for judicial review of the CICP determinations.

Congress funds the CICP through appropriations to the Covered Countermeasures Process Fund. During COVID-19, the PREP Act declaration covering COVID-19 vaccines required persons injured through the vaccine to seek compensation through the CICP. Accordingly, the federal government appropriated approximately $30 billion to COVID-19 response efforts, and the HHS Secretary is authorized to transfer funds from the response efforts to the fund.

While the CICP creates a compensation scheme for persons injured by covered countermeasures, the CICP limits compensation and recovery options.

---

[16] O'Shea and White (2021).

[17] *Id.*

[18] Association of State and Territorial Health Officials (2012).

[19] Hickey (2021).

[20] Association of State and Territorial Health Officials (2012).

[21] Hickey (2021).

21.2   How the Law Works

For the PREP Act to take effect, the HHS Secretary must determine that a threat to health, such as a disease, constitutes a public health emergency or a credible risk of a future public health emergency.[22] Then, the Secretary must find that the development of a countermeasure is desirable. The Secretary may then issue a PREP Act declaration specifying: the covered countermeasures; the category of "diseases, health conditions, or health threats determined to constitute a present or credible risk for which the administration and use of the countermeasure[s] is recommended"; the effective time period of the declaration; the population of individuals receiving the countermeasure; limitations on the geographic area for which immunity is in effect; limitations on the means of distribution of the counter-measure; any additional persons identified by the secretary as qualified to prescribe, dispense, or administer the countermeasures.

The PREP Act declaration is distinct and independent from other emergency declarations, and a separate public health emergency determination is not required to enable the PREP Act or for its immunities to take effect. The PREP Act *only* provides immunity from liability for the covered entities, activities, and countermeasures specified in the declaration. In other words, the PREP Act does not automatically protect everyone involved in any kind of medical response to an emergency. In addition to the willful misconduct exception to PREP Act protections, the Act does not protect individuals who "violate a person's civil rights or who violate the Americans with Disabilities Act."[23]

Because of the rapidly evolving status of public health emergencies like the COVID-19 pandemic, the PREP Act gives HHS the authority to act quickly through declarations, amendments, and guidance documents. For example, in March 2020, the HHS Secretary issued a PREP Act declaration for COVID-19.[24] The PREP Act immunity covered manufacturing, testing, development, distribution, administration, and use of covered countermeasures such as antivirals, drugs, biologic, diagnostic, medical devices, and vaccines used to treat, diagnose, cure, prevent, or mitigate COVID-19. The HHS Declaration has been amended several times to broaden the scope of PREP Act immunity, and the General Counsel of HHS has issued advisory opinions to inform interpretation of the PREP Act declarations. The flexibility for amending and clarifying PREP Act declarations allows HHS to adapt to changing circumstances in a public health emergency.

---

[22] Association of State and Territorial Health Officials (2012).

[23] Association of State and Territorial Health Officials (2012).

[24] Hickey (2021).

21.3 How the Law Affects States

The PREP Act has a direct impact on states because it provides a source of liability protection for governmental and private sector entities and individuals developing and administering approved countermeasures during a public health emergency.[25] The PREP Act preempts state law in many contexts.[26] Congress specifically created the PREP Act to displace state law to protect certain entities from liability and ensure that potentially life-saving countermeasures would be developed, deployed, and administered. The federal preemption in the PREP Act is intended to enable states to quickly respond to a public health crisis in situations where state or local requirements might otherwise inhibit a response. [27]

State and local territories may need to rapidly expand their workforce to respond to a public health emergency. The PREP Act helps enable a quick response by providing a pathway for qualified persons to fill roles where needed (such as expanding the vaccination workforce).[28] For example, during the H1N1 outbreak in 2009, PREP Act declarations were issued for H1N1 vaccines, antivirals, and personal protective equipment.[29] The declaration was designed to provide legal immunity to countermeasure manufacturers to increase supply and distribution of countermeasures in the states. Similarly, during COVID-19, the PREP Act declaration helped support the healthcare workforce with widespread distribution of countermeasures. This included vaccines, where immunity from state tort liability was provided to covered entities contributing to development, distribution, and administration. With PREP Act declarations in place, covered entities were able to contribute to the H1N1 and COVID-19 response efforts without concerns about liability under state tort law.

21.4 Conclusion

The PREP Act insulates covered persons from most legal liability for claims of loss caused by a covered countermeasure. The PREP Act's protections are intended to encourage the development, distribution, and administration of countermeasures. Previous PREP Act declarations such as the H1N1 and COVID-19 declaration supported the rapid development and distribution of countermeasures such as vaccines while immunizing covered entities from state tort liability.

Looking forward, the PREP Act's far-reaching liability protections will likely continue to support countermeasure efforts in public health emergencies by protecting covered entities from legal liability for injuries caused by

---

[25] Association of State and Territorial Health Officials (2012).

[26] Hickey (2021).

[27] Boufides (2021).

[28] Assistant Secretary for Preparedness and Response (2021).

[29] Association of State and Territorial Health Officials (2012).

countermeasures. The PREP Act is clearly intended to protect covered entities from liability, but the law limits recovery for people injured by covered countermeasures. Therefore, despite the large-scale benefits of rapid development, distribution, and administration of life-saving countermeasures, the government should only issue PREP Act declarations after weighing the risks to individuals.

References

Administration for Strategic Preparedness & Response (n.d.) Public Readiness and Emergency Preparedness (PREP) Act. U.S. Department of Health and Human Services, Washington, DC. https://www.phe.gov/Preparedness/legal/prepact/Pages/default.aspx. Accessed 9 Oct 2021

Assistant Secretary for Preparedness and Response (2021) Expanding the COVID-19 vaccination workforce. https://www.phe.gov/emergency/events/COVID19/Documents/covid19-vaccination-wrkfrc-factsheet-508.pdf. Accessed 8 Oct 2021

Association of State and Territorial Health Officials (2012) Public Readiness & Emergency Preparedness Act–fact sheet, legal preparedness series: emergency use authorization toolkit 1. https://legacy.astho.org/uploadedFiles/Programs/Preparedness/Public_Health_Emergency_Law/Emergency_Authority_and_Immunity_Legal_Toolkit/07-EUA%20PREP%20Act%20FS%204-12%20final(1).pdf. Accessed 26 Oct 2022

Boufides CH (2021) Federal PREP Act liability protections for COVID-19 vaccination. The Network for Public Health Law. https://www.networkforphl.org/resources/federal-prep-act-liability-protections-for-covid-19-vaccination/. Accessed 28 Oct 2022

Hickey KJ (2021) The PREP Act and COVID-19: limiting liability for medical countermeasures, 3. Congressional Research Service, LSB10443. https://crsreports.congress.gov/product/pdf/LSB/LSB10443. Accessed 26 Oct 2022

Lazzarotti J (2021) PREP Act and COVID-19 vaccinations: health and human services dep't clears way to assist. Jackson Lewis. https://www.jacksonlewis.com/publication/prep-act-and-covid-19-vaccinations-health-and-human-services-department-clears-way-assist.   Accessed 26 Oct 2022

O'Shea J, White R (2021) PREP Act offers immunity to product manufacturers and premises owners from COVID-19 liability. JD Supra. https://www.jdsupra.com/legalnews/prep-act-offers-immunity-to-product-1827440/. Accessed 26 Oct 2022

Regulating Vaccine Misinformation Online **22**

Abstract

Anti-vaccine misinformation spreads online, and it can mislead people into not vaccinating. In a very real sense, anti-vaccine misinformation undermines informed consent by leading people to refuse vaccines for reasons that are untrue. This chapter examines what, if anything, the law can do to prevent anti-vaccine misinformation.

Misinformation is speech. Freedom of speech is one of the oldest, most fundamental rights in America, granted to all citizens in 1791 under the Bill of Rights. While the importance of freedom of speech is undisputed, heated debates on what the government can or cannot do to limit free speech and the boundaries of the First Amendment prevail. In the twenty-first century there have been over 30 Supreme Court cases directly focused on interpreting the right to free speech, with over 100 cases referencing the First Amendment's free speech clause in some way. In recent years, and especially since the explosion of the internet, the harms of unlimited freedom of speech have become a concern, particularly within the context of scientific misinformation and public health. Against the best scientific evidence, anti-vaccine activists claim that vaccines cause death or other harmful side effects. These activists share misleading articles and memes on social media platforms like Facebook and Twitter. This contributes to the observed increase in unvaccinated children, which undermines herd immunity and poses a direct threat to public health and safety, as demonstrated by the 2019 measles outbreaks, and perhaps more alarmingly, the recent refusal of COVID-19 vaccines. Reacting to this reality, the World Health Organization (WHO) added "vaccine hesitancy" to its list of the "10 Threats to Global Health in 2019", and vaccination has since continued to be recognized as a leading public health issue by medical centers around the United States (U.S.). Because high rates of vaccination benefit society, and anti-vaccine misinformation causes harm to the most vulnerable, governments may seek to act to limit it.

© The Author(s), under exclusive license to Springer Nature Switzerland AG 2023
Y. T. Yang, D. R. Reiss, *Vaccine Law and Policy*, Law for Professionals,
https://doi.org/10.1007/978-3-031-36989-6_22

That said, in a democracy we have real and well-supported concerns about allowing the government to determine what is and is not true. Any steps toward regulating misinformation must be done with the potential for abuse in mind.

22.1 Background: Misinformation and Social Media in the U.S.

Misinformation is not a novel challenge in societies; however, the internet has introduced new ways for misinformation to spread. It allows this information to proliferate and promulgate at such a fast and widespread pace that the harms of misinformation have become prominent in the modern era. Governments around the world have long expressed concerns about the potential harms of the internet, and especially social media, as it relates to misinformation. But citizens and courts are also often concerned about the risks of allowing governments to control information—after all, the government has its own interests. Furthermore, there is a long history of governments using their power to limit speech to silence critics, rather than for public good. In the U.S., the strong protections of freedom of speech limit the government's ability to prohibit misinformation, with a more-or-less narrow exception for certain types of commercial information. Therefore, the government has real limits on what it can do. The task, instead, has largely fallen on the shoulders of individual social media companies to implement policies regulating what information can be spread using their platform.

While companies have been tasked to regulate what information is shared on their sites, several laws and policies discourage this regulation. For example, the U.-S. recognized that interactive computer services have many benefits, so Congress enacted the Communications Decency Act to preserve the vibrant and competitive free market that presently exists on the Internet.[1] This law insulates interactive computer services, like social media platforms, from state tort liability. Under Section 230, a platform is not obligated to remove content that a court has determined to be defamatory. In subsection 230(c)(2), the policy further specifies that social media platforms may police content posted on their platforms, but that doing so does not leave them responsible for the remaining, unfiltered content (nor would they be responsible and liable for the removal).[2] Although this law shields social media platforms from massive self-censorship or being sued out of existence, it also protects platforms that facilitate, enable or support misinformation, assigning no responsibility for the subsequent consequences.

Since its implementation in 1996 the Communications Decency Act has been celebrated as a protection of free speech.[3] In recent times, however, politicians have attempted to repeal Section 230 on the claim that social media giants, such as Facebook and Twitter, should assume greater responsibility for the harm to society

[1] Communications Decency Act of 1996 (2022).
[2] Smith and Van Alstyne (2021).
[3] Section 230 of the Communications Decency Act (2022).

their platforms have enabled—and for perceived wrongs in censoring speech. Concerns over public safety beyond vaccine misinformation, such as social media's role in public catastrophes like the January 6th insurrection, prompted a closer look at Section 230 of the Communications Decency Act.[4] A bill was proposed in June of 2021 that would reform Section 230, effectively stripping companies of their protection against liability for the harmful effects of content posted on their platforms.[5] While the bill was never passed into law, the topic continues to be a fierce debate, and has prompted many social media companies to enforce stronger monitoring of content on their websites.

22.2   The Role of Government

Anti-vaccine content on social media platforms is often pecuniary in nature, seeking to promote and spread vaccine misinformation, like alternative remedies or anti-vaccine media, through advertisements. As such, the Federal Trade Commission and the Food and Drug Administration have the authority to address some of these deceptive claims. For example, they can warn or penalize promoters of homeopathic preparations that have not been tested for safety and efficacy. However, they cannot directly address anti-vaccine claims that are not tied to a product, which are common. Asking for donations for a non-profit likely does not make the activity commercial, even if the non-profit specializes in putting out antivaccine misinformation and pays its members to do so. Likewise, the Federal Communications Commission may regulate to prevent platforms from being utilized to amplify misinformation without banning the content outright. States can also leverage customer protection acts to impose fines on clear misrepresentations of scientific consensus—focusing on the speaker, not the platforms shielded by Section 230 of the Communications Decency Act (federal law is "the supreme law of the land," and would prevent states targeting social media companies, but there are no protections under federal law for the speakers themselves).

Another source of misinformation is from foreign manipulation. Researchers have found Russian-linked accounts attempting to sow discord in the U.S. by amplifying both sides of the vaccine debate via social media.[6] This issue demonstrates that the U.S. government needs to increase deterrence against foreign manipulation and false identities.

Another solution to these issues is to utilize the federal government's ability to authorize spending. Public health officials can provide resources to directly aid pediatricians and child health professionals who have a unique responsibility to confront vaccine misinformation. By virtue of their specialized knowledge and professional obligations, providers have a unique responsibility to use social

---

[4]Bambauer (2021).

[5]Bond (2021).

[6]Broniatowski et al. (2018), pp. 1378–1384.

204   22   Regulating Vaccine Misinformation Online

media platforms for education and proactively disseminate accurate information about vaccines. The government has very broad leeway to speak itself. This alternative acknowledges the powerful role that social media plays in society, but it requires improving support, research, and education on effective communication for these professionals in the face of anti-vaccine pushback. Similarly, governments could indirectly minimize the impact of misinformation through promoting health literacy training in public schools and health departments.

Ultimately platforms are the economic "least-cost avoiders"—that is, they are in the best place to identify and prevent harmful content from being propagated using their services. Furthermore, First Amendment protections do not prevent a private company from restricting speech if it violates a platform's Terms of Service. Governments can provide subsidies and tax breaks to platforms that incorporate consensus values reflecting social responsibility into these Terms of Service and enforce these terms. This may spur platforms to develop their own internal means of addressing the problem, catalyzing the formation of industry consensus and best practices. The option of using government funding or other economic incentives to tackle the issue indirectly helps avoid the risk of overhead government restrictions.

22.3   Self-Regulation from Social Media Companies

Prior to COVID-19, technology companies have not regulated content that users share on their platforms for misinformation because of the risks and backfires that they would create. In fact, the algorithm often rewarded and amplified misinformation, and provided additional misleading content to users who joined anti-vaccine groups or liked anti-vaccine pages. However, as the efforts to spread misinformation moved from sporadic and haphazard to organized and systematic, these companies have increasingly been pressured to act. In November 2016, Facebook banned misinformation from advertisements on their site. One study found that this ban led to a 75% decrease in sharing anti-vaccination misinformation on Facebook in comparison to Twitter, which had no change in its advertising policy during this time.[7] Other platforms have taken similar action: Pinterest banned all anti-vaccination content outright, while YouTube removed ad revenue and monetization from anti-vaccine channels and videos, eliminating financial incentives for those who profit from misinformation.

As with many preexisting social challenges, the harms of social media and misinformation escalated exponentially during the COVID-19 pandemic. Fear of vaccination, objection to government mandates, and conspiracy surrounding the legitimacy of the virus itself, prompted fierce content production through Facebook, Instagram, Twitter, YouTube, and TikTok. With this massive production of misinformation, social media companies finally chose to act.

---

[7] Chiou and Tucker (2018).

In February of 2021, Facebook expanded its policy on Coordinating Harm and Promoting Crime to prohibit the following: Content coordinating interference with the administration of the COVID-19 vaccine; Content calling to action, advocating, or promoting others not get the COVID-19 vaccine. Other major social media platforms followed suit, recognizing the severity of harm caused by their platforms, and made prominent misinformation policy changes in response to the fallout of COVID-19. Despite these recent actions, social media companies were criticized on the grounds that their efforts are not strong enough, or that they've arrived too late for the public to applaud.[8]

22.4   Challenges of Regulation

Social media platforms should continue to recognize and take responsibility for the role their websites play in modern society. Platforms should investigate how their sites are used to spread misinformation, the repercussions of that misinformation, and how they can limit the harm. Although platforms should invest in technology to find misinformation and identify it for users through algorithms and crowdsourcing, technology alone will not solve this problem. Artificial intelligence (AI) systems that automatically tag information as false has the potential to miss other misinformation. Furthermore, depending on the way it is done, it may label debunking efforts as misinformation as well.[9] Even complete removal of anti-vaccine content relies first on accurately detecting that content as false. Anti-vaccine activists creatively change their language to avoid detection. For example, in September 2022 they started referring to vaccines by using the emoticon for carrot. Furthermore, the removal of harmful content without first archiving it defeats the research efforts of health communicators who use this content to better understand concerns of the vaccine hesitant. Finally, algorithms would have to be continually updated—potentially at a significant cost—if they adapt to the tactics used by anti-vaccine activists, such as embedding anti-vaccine content into other media or changing group names to allude to, but not explicitly reflect, anti-vaccine sentiment.

22.5   Strategies to Combat Misinformation in the U.S. and Abroad

Social media misinformation is not unique to the U.S.; Nearly every major nation in the world has dealt with the consequences of deregulated speech on the internet in some fashion. As such, the U.S. can turn to examples abroad to analyze strategies adopted by other governments to deal with the regulation of internet speech.

---

[8] Wardle and Singerman (2021).
[9] Pennycook et al. (2020), pp. 4944–4957.

The European Union (EU) and the European Economic Area (EEA) recognized an early and dire need to respond to vaccine misinformation in order to avoid detrimental effects of low vaccination rates across European countries.[10] Following the first Global Vaccination Summit in 2019, led by the European Commission with support from the WHO, the EU spear fronted anti-misinformation efforts with a qualitative and quantitative study on vaccine hesitancy and vaccine misinformation in Europe. Their investigations into the landscape of misinformation included stakeholder consultations, social media analyses, case study reviews, and a country-by-country analysis. They used this information to understand how misinformation originates, why it is so influential on a large scale, and what types of misinformation exist to better understand the roots of the issue. This investigation led the EU to conclude three strategies are needed to tackle misinformation: (1) Monitoring misinformation on social media, (2) Pre-emptive interventions, and (3) Debunking. The EU health regulators also stress the importance of ongoing evaluation to ensure strategic efforts are in fact effective and adapting to the novel ways in which misinformation may emerge.

Some efforts in the U.S. also used evidence to guide anti-misinformation strategies. A recent study investigated the effect of flagging information on Twitter as generated by AI bots.[11] The results showed that flagging Tweets in this manner typically decreased respondents' positive attitudes towards the information, suggesting that flagging bot-generated content on social media websites could reduce the impact of misinformation on the internet. One Minnesota study, conducted in an effort to understand the types of people who might share misinformation, and what motivates them, found that individuals with a desire to "fit in" were more likely to share high-credibility sources than low-credibility sources, while individuals posting with a desire to "stand out" had no observed preference in terms of credibility.[12] Additional studies identified effective strategies in refutational messages.[13]

In addition to the studies outlined above and similar studies, the American Medical Association has called for greater action from technology companies.[14] Building on these efforts, additional sources have recognized the need for a collaborative and interdisciplinary plan.[15] The U.S. should take note of the power behind the widespread analysis conducted by the EU, and consider organizing its own collective study to develop a nationwide plan to combat medical misinformation on a large scale. The First Amendment is not, likely, a barrier to government funding or initiating studies, nor would it prevent government funding or undertaking debunking efforts; however, it may be a barrier to more direct government action.

---

[10]Rofagha et al. (2021).

[11]Lanius et al. (2021), p. 32.

[12]Ceylan (2020), pp. 863–867.

[13]Silberling (2021).

[14]YouTube (n.d.).

[15]Twitter (n.d.).

To some degree, government agencies do that by providing evidence-based information about vaccines, but in a world where some do not trust the government, it is a good idea for government to find ways to support other entities (such as nonprofit organizations and religious institutions) that are better trusted by these people.

22.6 Conclusion

While we value free speech, the pervasive availability and consumption of false health information can cause individual and social harm by nurturing false beliefs about medicine, disease, and prevention. Governments should consider if there are ways to address vaccine misinformation online without having to compromise free speech rights. The Supreme Court has recognized that commercial speech may constitutionally be restricted on compelling policy grounds if the restriction is narrowly tailored to that end and when the balance weighs in favor of the government interest.[16] Arguably, advertising so-called "vaccine alternatives" online may fall into that category. Owing to the constitutional limits on the government's powers to regulate private citizens' free speech in the public sphere, there may be relatively few regulatory tools capable of addressing aspects of the vaccine misinformation problem. However, the few identified can be used to neutralize some of the worst, most blatantly false and profit-driven pieces. Further, the government may have a role in supporting research into countering misinformation and funding or providing debunking efforts.

However, there is no "quick fix," or single policy or technological intervention strategy alone that works for all instances of vaccine misinformation. Whatever solutions are pursued, the concern for health must be balanced against free speech rights to prevent setting a dangerous precedent encouraging and expanding censorship.

Ultimately, the phenomenon of vaccine misinformation is likely a mixture of broader issues, such as concerns about vaccine safety and mistrust in the pharmaceutical industry and government agencies. Therefore, it would be helpful to have more research to better understand vaccine misinformation that influences options or confirms existing beliefs—and how that misinformation can be corrected effectively.

References

Bambauer DE (2021) What does the day after Section 230 reform look like? Brookings. https://www.brookings.edu/techstream/what-does-the-day-after-section-230-reform-look-like/. Accessed 29 June 2022

Bond S (2021) Democrats want to hold social media companies responsible for health misinformation. NPR. https://www.npr.org/2021/07/22/1019346177/democrats-want-to-hold-social-media-companies-responsible-for-health-misinformat. Accessed 29 June 2022

---

[16]Featherstone and Zhang (2020), pp. 692–702.

Broniatowski DA, Jamison AM, Qi S et al (2018) Weaponized health communication: Twitter bots and Russian trolls amplify the vaccine debate. Am J Public Health 108:1378–1384. https://doi.org/10.2105/AJPH.2018.304567

Ceylan G (2020) Antecedents of and remedies to the spread of false information in the social media era. Adv Consum Res 48:863–867. https://doi.org/10.1177/14604582211021470

Chiou L, Tucker C (2018) Fake news and advertising on social media: a study of the anti-vaccination movement. NBER working papers 25223, National Bureau of Economic Research. https://doi.org/10.3386/w25223

Communications Decency Act of 1996 (2022) The IT Law Wiki. Wikimedia. https://itlaw.fandom.com/wiki/Communications_Decency_Act_of_1996#cite_note-1. Accessed 28 June 2022

Cramer S (2019) Moving the needle. Royal Society for Public Health, London, United Kingdom. https://www.rsph.org.uk/static/uploaded/3b82db00-a7ef-494c-85451e78ce18a779.pdf. Accessed 28 June 2022

Featherstone JD, Zhang J (2020) Feeling angry: the effects of vaccine misinformation and refutational messages on negative emotions and vaccination attitude. J Health Commun 25:692–702. https://doi.org/10.1080/10810730.2020.1838671

Lanius C, Weber R, MacKenzie WI (2021) Use of bot and content flags to limit the spread of misinformation among social networks: a behavior and attitude survey. Soc Netw Anal Min 11:32. https://doi.org/10.1007/s13278-021-00739-x

Pennycook G et al (2020) The implied truth effect: attaching warnings to a subset of fake news headlines increases perceived accuracy of headlines without warnings. Manag Sci 66:4944–4957. https://doi.org/10.1287/mnsc.2019.3478

Rofagha B, Petrosova L, Jongh T (2021) Countering online vaccine misinformation in the EU/EEA. European Centre for Disease Prevention and Control. https://data.europa.eu/doi/10.2900/329304. Accessed 29 June 2022

Section 230 of the Communications Decency Act (2022) Electronic Frontier Foundation. https://www.eff.org/issues/cda230. Accessed 29 June 2022

Silberling A (2021) YouTube will no ban content with vaccine misinformation. TechCrunch. https://techcrunch.com/2021/09/29/youtube-will-now-ban-content-with-vaccine-misinformation/?guccounter=1. Accessed 29 June 2022

Smith MD, Van Alstyne M (2021) It's time to update Section 230. Harvard Business Review. https://hbr.org/2021/08/its-time-to-update-section-230. Accessed 29 June 2022

Twitter (n.d.) Introducing our crisis misinformation policy. https://blog.twitter.com/en_us/topics/company/2022/introducing-our-crisis-misinformation-policy. Accessed 29 June 2022

Wardle C, Singerman E (2021) Too little, too late: social media companies' failure to tackle vaccine misinformation poses a real threat. BMJ 372:n26. https://doi.org/10.1136/bmj.n26

YouTube (n.d.) Misinformation policies - YouTube help. https://support.google.com/youtube/answer/10834785?hl=en. Accessed 28 June 2022

Part VI
Policy

In the final part of the book, we take a step back to address broader policy issues related to the legal environment of vaccines. Chapters 23 and 24 share a focus on policy approaches to promote vaccination. Chapter 23 examines various incentives that could be used to increase vaccine uptake, such as financial incentives, social norms, and public health campaigns. This chapter also explores the potential drawbacks and limitations of each approach. Chapter 24 focuses on vaccine advocacy and politics, exploring the role of public health organizations, government agencies, and political leaders in promoting vaccination. This chapter discusses different policy approaches to increase vaccine uptake, including school and workplace mandates, as well as public education campaigns. Together, these chapters examine the possibilities and challenges of different policy options for promoting vaccination and reducing the spread of vaccine-preventable diseases.

Vaccine Incentives and Health Insurance Surcharges

23

Abstract

When COVID-19 spread across the globe, overwhelming healthcare systems and interrupting national productivity, many hoped that the discovery of a vaccine would provide necessary relief. When the Food and Drug Administration (FDA) granted emergency approval to the Pfizer-BioNTech COVID-19 Vaccine on December 11, 2020, a sense of celebration spread throughout the country. Many believed that this vaccine would provide the long-awaited return to normal that so many families had hoped for. Instead, however, the vaccine became a political talking point, dividing the nation between individuals lining up to take the shot and those who fell victim to misinformation, public skepticism, and opposition to vaccine mandates. More than 1 year later the United States (U.S.) is still dealing with low COVID-19 vaccination rates, struggling to reach herd immunity, and lowering the continued financial burden the pandemic imposes on healthcare systems.

Unvaccinated individuals are at a far higher risk of death and hospitalization from COVID-19, and hospitalizations of unvaccinated adults cost the U.-S. $13.8 billion from June to November 2021. The monetary cost of treating unvaccinated individuals for COVID-19 is borne not only by patients but also by society more broadly, including taxpayer-funded public programs and private insurance premiums paid by workers, businesses, and individual purchasers. Widespread vaccination promotes the health of employees and can assist businesses in assuring customers of their safety, reducing the harm of low staffing, and preventing lost productivity.

Vaccination has an important role in controlling the COVID-19 pandemic and preventing harms from it. With a significant portion of the U.S. population remaining unvaccinated or unboosted, incentives may be necessary for rapid vaccine uptake. Early on, employers began evaluating options to encourage employee uptake of vaccines with three goals in mind: to minimize transmissions, to lower absence due to illness, and to reduce COVID-19-related health care

© The Author(s), under exclusive license to Springer Nature Switzerland AG 2023
Y. T. Yang, D. R. Reiss, *Vaccine Law and Policy*, Law for Professionals,
https://doi.org/10.1007/978-3-031-36989-6_23

expenditures. Rather than mandating vaccination, offering incentives to vaccinate have become more and more popular for companies attempting to maintain a healthy and productive workplace. However, employers should be mindful of several key challenges and considerations of offering incentives to vaccinate. In this chapter, we evaluate the effectiveness and associated challenges with employer-offered vaccination incentives and highlight key strategies for employers moving forward.

23.1 Types of Incentives

Employer-based vaccination incentives can take many forms. One such option is to provide a reward for all individuals who choose to get vaccinated. Successful implementation of such reward incentives relies on three criteria (1) certainty of delivery (2) immediate delivery and (3) that recipients place value on the offered reward.[1] For example, a guaranteed cash payment is one of the most effective incentives studied, with some estimates showing increased uptake by 8%, likely because it meets all three criteria.[2] Furthermore, the incentive does not have to be very large, but should be valued by the recipients. Other incentives, such as movie tickets or t-shirt prizes, may not be of value to all recipients.[3] Meanwhile, incentives that enter participants for a chance to win a larger prize, a lottery incentive, appear not to be as effective because it lacks certainty and immediate delivery.

While evidence has shown that cash incentives can have some benefit on increasing vaccine uptake, another option is to impose higher premiums for unvaccinated employees under their group medical plans.[4] However, experts suggest that such incentives can actually have a negative effect and create waste and inefficiency in paying employees when most would gladly get vaccinated for free. Others argue that raising insurance premiums is a justifiable tool to promote COVID-19 vaccination because individuals who engage in riskier activities should pay higher premiums.[5] Essentially, this strategy places unvaccinated employees in a higher-risk, higher-premium insurance pool and thereby more equitably redistributes health care savings and costs. Similar surcharges are imposed on tobacco users, for example. Theoretically, higher premiums can incentivize people to behave more safely, improve overall health, and reduce health care costs.[6] Despite the potential benefits from this policy, employers assessing this option must ensure that they are in compliance with applicable federal and state laws and take into account additional policy considerations to avoid potential misfires.

---

[1] Hsu (2021).

[2] Dezhbakhsh (2021).

[3] Brewer et al. (2022).

[4] Hsu (2021).

[5] Dezhbakhsh (2021).

[6] Brewer et al. (2022).

23.2   Legal Considerations

23.2.1 HIPAA

The Department of Labor, Department of Health and Human Services (HHS), and the Department of the Treasury issued guidance affirming that employers can "incentivize employees by offering discounts on monthly insurance premiums for those who have been vaccinated" or "impose insurance 'surcharges' for those who choose not to be vaccinated."[7] However, these surcharges must comply with existing Health Insurance Portability and Accountability Act (HIPAA) wellness guidelines for activity-based wellness programs. Note that the issue here is not the privacy protections that HIPAA is most commonly associated with, but the specific regulation of wellness programs.

HIPAA prohibits employers from excluding employees from eligibility or coverage under a group health plan based on their health status.[8] HIPAA also prevents employers from charging their employees higher premiums based on health status. Under HIPAA, "health status" encompasses "any health status-related factor," which could include vaccination status. However, HIPAA also allows exceptions to offer employees financial incentives for participating in a "wellness program," if certain requirements are met under federal law.

Some believe it is possible that an insurance premium surcharge would meet the wellness program standards. However, insurers have never used vaccination status in setting premiums, so this novel approach may have unique implications. First, individuals may challenge surcharges for failure to make religious and other legally mandated accommodations. Second, employees may postpone being vaccinated if the policy is implemented mid-year. There is no requirement that employees meet the vaccination criteria by a given time during the year, making rapid vaccination uptake less likely under this scenario.

23.2.2 The Affordable Care Act

Any incentives offered through employers for vaccination must also be compliant with The Patient Protection and Affordable Care Act (ACA). The ACA allows for wellness programs to be participatory or health contingent, but these two categories are regulated differently. A participatory program has no limit on financial incentives but must be open to any employee, and the reward for participation may not be contingent on a health outcome. However, health-contingent programs are outcome-based, rewarding participants only if they achieve a health-specific goal. These programs must provide reasonable accommodation due to a medical condition.

---

[7] Ben-Shahar and Logue (2012).

[8] U.S. Dept. of Health and Human Services (2021).

HIPAA and the ACA limit the total financial incentives for such programs to be no more than 30% of the total cost of health coverage.

The ACA also imposes health care affordability requirements that limit the amount that an employer can charge for health insurance. Experts warn that any premium surcharge or discount must be included in the ACA health care coverage affordability determinations. A substantial surcharge for unvaccinated employees may risk violating these provisions of the ACA.

23.2.3 The Americans with Disabilities Act

The Americans With Disabilities Act (ADA) protects individuals from discrimination on the basis of disability.[9] Financial incentives—including penalties and surcharges—must not discriminate against workers who cannot get the vaccine due to a disability or other medical reasons. Wellness programs require reasonable accommodation for disabilities unless such accommodations are costly, compromise safety, decrease workplace efficiency, infringe on the rights of other employees, or require some employees to do more than their share of hazardous or burdensome work.

Employee participation must also be voluntary according to the Genetic Information Nondiscrimination Act (GINA); large incentives could violate the ADA or GINA by making wellness programs coercive rather than voluntary as financial incentives put excessive pressure on people with lower incomes. The Equal Employment Opportunity Commission (EEOC) enforces the ADA and limits general wellness incentives. To date, the EEOC has released only limited guidance on vaccine incentives, merely suggesting that employers keep incentives to small (or *de minimis*) gifts, such as "a water bottle or gift card of modest value." However, it has not defined the boundaries of what incentives are acceptable, even though many businesses have asked the EEOC to clarify the limits of vaccine incentives.

23.2.4 Additional Legal Considerations

State laws may also impose certain requirements on withholdings from employee paychecks. The Department of Labor takes the view that the Employee Retirement Income Security Act (ERISA)[10] preempts these laws—but if an employer's plan is not subject to ERISA, then the employer may need to consider whether these laws affect its ability to impose a new surcharge on employee contributions during the middle of a plan year.

Another concern is for monetary incentives or incentives paid via time off, which can be regulated by the Fair Labor Standards Act (FLSA). Monetary incentives can

---

[9] Williams (2012).

[10] A Guide to Disability Rights Laws: ERISA. U.S. Department of Labor (n.d.).

be deemed nondiscretionary bonuses. Therefore, under the FLSA they must be included in the employee's rate of pay for that period. The overtime pay rate calculation is impacted by including this additional pay, and failing to adjust for it would violate the law. These incentives not only add an additional expense (higher overtime pay rate), but also add administrative burdens for the employer to ensure they are compliant. The FLSA also requires compensation for employment-based costs if the expenses reduce the employee's wages. In this instance, incentivizing vaccination may take time or travel—leading to cost. Employers may choose to compensate employees for these costs, including time spent getting vaccinated or the logistical expenses of getting the vaccine. However, these costs must consider the potential limit that may be set by the EEOC.

Finally, Title II of the Civil Rights Act of 1964 may also apply.[11] Policies, including related surcharges, cannot discriminate against workers based on race, color, religion, sex, or national origin. Thus, an employer will need to evaluate any claim from an employee that the vaccination surcharge interferes with a sincere religious belief and a request for a religious accommodation. Similar to the challenges of imposing a vaccine mandate, evaluating claims of religious exemption further complicates the implementation of vaccine incentives and may draw into question the legitimacy of such claims. We discuss this issue in Chap. 16. When imposing an incentive system, employers may need to carefully draft a policy on religious exemptions, with clear guidelines on how to submit and receive approval for these exemptions.

23.3 Policy Considerations

Employers have good reasons to protect employees from the risk of COVID-19 and to mitigate the cost of COVID-19 hospitalizations. Premium surcharges would likely survive legal challenges if they follow the federal regulations, but it remains unclear whether surcharges actually encourage employees to get vaccinated quickly.

Critics of surcharge policies point to data from other health-contingent premium programs showing that they fail to change people's behavior.[12] For example, premium surcharges do not tend to increase cessation among tobacco smokers[13] nor decrease weight among overweight individuals.[14] Others disagree with this comparison. Behavior such as smoking cessation and weight loss requires long-term lifestyle changes, whereas getting vaccinated requires comparatively less discipline. However, it's been noted that incentives do not change the opinions and beliefs of the vaccine-hesitant and therefore do not make a lasting impact on

---

[11] Title II Of The Civil Rights Act (Public Accommodations) (2015).

[12] Baxter et al. (2014), pp. 347–363.

[13] Friedman et al. (2016), pp. 1176–1183.

[14] Alfred Lewis et al. (2015).

vaccine implementation moving forward.[15] Additionally, no empirical research provides strong evidence that tying vaccination status to premiums increases vaccination rates.

Some also argue that, unlike smoking and obesity, COVID-19 is an infectious disease, and therefore vaccination should be treated differently. Chronic illnesses such as obesity and lung cancer also do not overwhelm hospitals in waves like COVID-19 has. On the other hand, premium surcharges may also pose a risk that individuals who cannot afford the surcharge may discontinue coverage entirely, cutting off their access to family physicians and other primary care providers who can be trusted sources of information about the vaccine's benefits.

Employers who decide to impose a surcharge should also consider to whom the surcharge would apply. Many employees participating in employer-sponsored health plans pay for their spouses or other dependents to be covered under the plan. Employers will need to consider whether the surcharge will apply to everyone on the health plan or just their employees.

While increasing premiums may shift the financial burden placed on society by the hospitalization of the unvaccinated, this strategy does little to address herd immunity and attempts to decrease COVID-19 infections. Higher cost-sharing alone cannot overcome any of the structural barriers that hinder vaccination. This suggests that incentives must be paired with efforts to combat misinformation and increased research into why so many individuals remain vaccine-hesitant.

23.4 Implications for Employers

Employers are in a unique position to weigh the health and safety of their employees and customers against the financial burden of health care costs and the legal implications of imposing a surcharge. Some employers have moved beyond surcharges to mandate COVID-19 vaccinations as a condition of employment. Other employers have hesitated to impose a mandate for all employees, believing that a surcharge on health premiums for the unvaccinated appears less coercive, preserving the employees' freedom of choice. Under either approach, employers must prepare for employee resistance; consequently, they may face staffing challenges following employee resignation, difficulty in recruiting, or even residual resentment that surcharges are coercive or that mandates infringe upon their freedom.

Despite these challenges, there are examples that provide hope for employers seeking to adopt a surcharge or mandate policy. One employer, Delta Airlines, began charging $200 in additional monthly health insurance premiums for unvaccinated employees.[16] Delta reported that after announcing the premium surcharge, daily vaccination requests have "increased 5-fold." Although Delta's self-reported results

---

[15] Brewer et al. (2022).
[16] Duncan (2021).

are encouraging, especially considering that neither tobacco surcharges nor wellness programs aimed at other health-related behavior have been particularly successful at reversing bad habits, further investigation is warranted into how Delta's premium surcharge directly contributes to COVID-19 vaccine uptake and whether the experience is generalizable to other organizations.

23.5 Conclusion

Scientific experts state that COVID-19 vaccination rates must increase. The strategies chosen to accomplish higher vaccination rates must be careful not to infringe on the rights of citizens in doing so. Before imposing a surcharge on unvaccinated employees, employers should evaluate the legal and policy implications, as well as the interests of their employees and their businesses. Additionally, premium surcharges may be effective for some, but not all employers, and therefore companies should carefully consider the prevailing culture among their employees and assess the likelihood that a policy would be effective and noncoercive within their own context.

While some data has been promising for vaccine mandates and incentives, additional research is necessary to expand our understanding of the role of COVID vaccination incentives. It would be valuable to identify the types of vaccine policies that are likely to inflame skeptics' concerns versus those that would be welcomed—with hesitancy levels already high, increasing such hesitancy can have dire effects.

Employers considering a vaccine incentive program are likely on safer ground if they make the program voluntary, keep any incentives small in value, offer accommodations for medical exceptions and religious beliefs, and offer small monetary rewards, non-monetary or in-kind incentives to avoid violations, to preserve freedom of choice among the population.

References

A Guide to Disability Rights Laws: ERISA. U.S. Department of Labor (n.d.). https://www.dol.gov/general/topic/health-plans/erisa. Accessed 14 Mar 2022

Alfred Lewis JD et al (2015) Employers should disband employee weight control programs. Am J Manag Care 21(2):e91–e94

Baxter S et al (2014) The relationship between return on investment and quality of study methodology in workplace health promotion programs. Am J Health Promot 28:347–363. https://doi.org/10.4278/ajhp.130731-LIT-395

Ben-Shahar O, Logue KD (2012) Outsourcing regulation: how insurance reduces moral hazard. Mich Law Rev 111(2). University of Michigan Law & Econ Research Paper No. 12-004, University of Chicago Institute for Law & Economics Olin Research Paper No. 593. https://doi.org/10.2139/ssrn.2038105

Brewer NT et al (2022) Incentives for COVID-19 vaccination. Lancet Reg Health Am 8:100205. https://doi.org/10.1016/j.lana.2022.100205

Dezhbakhsh H (2021) Opinion: an incentive to encourage vaccination. The Atlanta Journal-Constitution. https://www.ajc.com/opinion/opinion-an-incentive-to-encourage-vaccination/3YNSPEIP45FSXDJPA6WMGYAASM/. Accessed 14 Mar 2022

Duncan I (2021) Delta Air Lines to require that employees be vaccinated or pay health insurance surcharge. The Washington Post. https://www.washingtonpost.com/transportation/2021/08/25/delta-employee-vaccines-covid/. Accessed 14 Mar 2022

Friedman AS et al (2016) Evidence suggests that the ACA's tobacco surcharges reduced insurance take-up and did not increase smoking cessation. Health Aff (Millwood) 35:1176–1183. https://doi.org/10.1377/hlthaff.2015.1540

Hsu A (2021) Companies are telling unvaccinated workers to pay more for health insurance. NPR. https://www.npr.org/2021/11/22/1056238770/covid-delta-unvaccinated-higher-health-insurance-premiums. Accessed 14 Mar 2022

Title II Of The Civil Rights Act (Public Accommodations) (2015) Department of Justice. https://www.justice.gov/crt/title-ii-civil-rights-act-public-accommodations. Accessed 14 Mar 2022

U.S. Dept. of Health and Human Services (2021) FAQs about Affordable Care Act implementation Part 50, Health Insurance Portability and Accountability Act and Coronavirus Aid, Relief, and Economic Security Act Implementation. Centers for Medicare and Medicaid Services, Washington, DC. https://www.hhs.gov/guidance/sites/default/files/hhs-guidance-documents/FAQs-Part-50.pdf. Accessed 1 Nov 2022

Williams CE (2012) FAQs on HIPAA portability and nondiscrimination requirements for employers and advisers. U.S. Dept. of Labor, Washington, DC. https://www.dol.gov/sites/dolgov/files/ebsa/about-ebsa/our-activities/resource-center/faqs/hipaa-consumer.pdf. Accessed 1 Nov 2022

Vaccine Advocacy, Politics, and Anti-vaccine Movements

24

Abstract

The influence of the anti-vaccine movement reaches beyond its actual members. Although there is widespread support for existing vaccine policies and medical experts refute many of the movement's claims about the dangers of vaccines (Lakshmanan and Sabo, J Appl Res Child, 10(1):11–12, 2019), the movement continues to influence perception of vaccines and vaccine mandates. The anti-vaccine narrative has increased vaccine hesitancy among people who are uncertain about vaccines, leading more people to seek exemptions, postpone vaccinations, or refuse to vaccinate themselves or their children (Benecke and DeYoung, Glob Pediatr Health 2019:6, 2019). Lower vaccine rates leave communities vulnerable to vaccine-preventable diseases. Pro-vaccine advocates are faced with the unique challenge of countering anti-vaccine messages and reaching those affected by them (Lakshmanan and Sabo, J Appl Res Child, 10(1): 11–12, 2019). This chapter addresses the origins and politization of anti-vaccine movements and discusses how immunization supporters can more effectively counter anti-vaccine advocacy.

24.1 History of Opposition and Fear of Vaccines

Fear of vaccines in the United States (U.S.) emerged in the eighteenth century after the creation of the first vaccine, the smallpox vaccine.[1] Suspicions surrounding scientific research led religious leaders to speak out against vaccines as "the devil's work."[2] In the nineteenth century, fear of vaccines was further politicized by distrust of government-imposed vaccine mandates.[3] Some scholars trace the politicization of

---

[1] Benecke and DeYoung (2019).
[2] Lakshmanan and Sabo (2019) and Benecke and DeYoung (2019).
[3] Benecke and DeYoung (2019).

© The Author(s), under exclusive license to Springer Nature Switzerland AG 2023
Y. T. Yang, D. R. Reiss, *Vaccine Law and Policy*, Law for Professionals,
https://doi.org/10.1007/978-3-031-36989-6_24

anti-vaccine advocacy to Britain, where laws mandated parents to vaccinate their children. Activists feared individual liberties were being "invaded" by government.

Rare adverse effects of vaccines also contributed to vaccine hesitancy. For example, after reports of 36 negative reactions to the pertussis vaccine in Britain, there was a decrease in pertussis vaccinations leading to a pertussis outbreak during the 1970s and 1980s. People became more afraid of potential adverse reactions to the vaccine than of the diseases vaccines were designed to prevent.[4] To the "anti-vaxxers," the benefits of vaccinations did not outweigh the risks.

The major rise in the anti-vaccination movement as it exists today was fueled by a 1998 report on 12 children published in *The Lancet.* The article alleged a connection between the measles, mumps, and rubella (MMR) vaccine and development of autism in young children. Fear of the effects of the vaccine caused a drastic drop in MMR vaccine rates. Although the study has been discredited and retracted, it influenced the way people view vaccines, and *The Lancet* article is still cited by the anti-vaccine movement to inspire fear and vaccine hesitancy. Simultaneously, concerns in the U.S. about an alleged link between a mercury-based preservative thimerosal and autism led to another crisis. Large studies have definitively shown that there is no link between either MMR or thimerosal in vaccines and autism, but that did not stop anti-vaccine activists from making claims without evidence on the issue.[5]

Most anti-vaccine rhetoric is rooted in fear of vaccines,[6] but some "anti-vaxxers" also suggest that vaccines are ineffective and unnecessary.[7] Furthermore, some "anti-vaxxers" suggest that the consequences of vaccine-preventable diseases are minor, and that the risks of vaccines outweigh the risk of the diseases they are designed to prevent.

24.2   The Rise of Politically Engaged Anti-vaccine Activists

There is a correlation between anti-vaccine views and anti-government views for those who believe vaccine mandates are a violation of civil liberties.[8] Messaging against vaccine mandates always emphasizes personal liberty, freedom of religion, and distrust of government.[9] These messages tend to resonate with politicians who value small government and personal freedom. For example, in the early 2000s right-leaning politicians dominated the Texas state legislature, giving the movement additional influence. The legislature drastically expanded exemptions to state-imposed school vaccination requirements in an effort to "keep government out of

---

[4]Benecke and DeYoung (2019).

[5]Gerber and Offit (2009), pp. 456–459.

[6]Lakshmanan and Sabo (2019).

[7]Matthews and Tan (2018).

[8]Lakshmanan and Sabo (2019).

[9]Lakshmanan and Sabo (2019).

people's lives."[10] Pro-vaccination policies were further politicized after the passage of the Affordable Care Act as critics drew parallels between big government and public health policy.

After a measles outbreak in 2016, California scaled back the state's vaccine exemption policies and specifically removed philosophical exemptions. When lawmakers in Texas considered similar actions to prevent an outbreak in their state, the anti-vaccine activists pushed back, going so far as to create a "vaccine choice" political action committee (PAC). While these organizations like to use the terms "choice" or "freedom", they oppose policies that would increase access to or availability to vaccines, decreasing choice for those who want vaccines. The only "choice" they seek to protect is the choice not to vaccinate, and where possible, they work to undermine vaccine usage generally.

Anti-vaccine activists, while a minority, had, and still have influence disproportionate to their size both in Texas and in the nation. The anti-vaccine advocates would not support candidates who supported pro-vaccine laws. Although the "anti-vaxxers" made up a small proportion of the political base, some politicians yielded to the movement's influence as they feared electoral consequences of opposing the anti-vaccine agenda. With low vaccination rates, Texas soon reported outbreaks of measles and pertussis—both of which are vaccine-preventable diseases. Despite the public health scares, the Texas legislature did not immediately take action to increase immunization rates in the state.

Like the anti-vaccine advocates in Texas, "anti-vaxxers" around the U.S. use fear-based narratives regarding the dangers of vaccines and the overreach of government to sway perceptions of pro-vaccine policies.[11] Although the "anti-vaxxers" make up a comparatively small group of the population, they sometimes successfully lobby to block pro-vaccine legislation and introduce anti-vaccine bills.[12] The anti-vaccine movement has been successful at leveraging vaccine exemptions and messaging platforms to gain support and influence, often with serious public health consequences.

Pre-pandemic, several factors helped anti-vaccine activists create a disproportionate impact on vaccine related issues. These factors include that they are often single-issue voters, strongly devoted to and passionate about their chosen issues, and such groups tend to have political success compared to more diffused majorities with various issues.[13] In addition, anti-vaccine activists in the U.S.—and several other places—tend to be wealthy and privileged, and this gives them political capital other activists may not have.[14]

That said, anti-vaccine activists are not without counters. In past decades, the rate of childhood vaccines in the U.S. has generally been above 90%, and in most states,

---

[10]Lakshmanan and Sabo (2019).

[11]Whelan (2016), pp. 462–465.

[12]Lakshmanan and Sabo (2019).

[13]Hillel et al. (2020), pp. 251–252.

[14]Yang et al. (2016), pp. 172–177.

vaccines are required for school—though most states have exemptions of varying degree. Until the pandemic, vaccines enjoyed overwhelming political support, and much of the efforts focused less on combatting anti-vaccine activism and more on providing access. Furthermore, in the past several years, online advocates, non-profits, and others have pushed back against anti-vaccine efforts.

24.3 The Pro-vaccine Apparatus

Because vaccines have large benefits and low risks, and substantially reduce social and individual costs, a large coalition of different actors has supported increasing vaccine uptake. Until the pandemic, the coalition included policymakers at the state and federal level—both elected representatives and administrators—from both sides of the political aisle. Medical associations like the American Medical Association, the American Academy of Pediatrics, the American Academy of Family Physicians, have also consistently supported increasing vaccine uptake. In addition, a number of non-profit organizations have acted to support vaccine access and uptake.

Other coalitions have also been successful in promoting vaccine uptake. The Immunization Action Coalition (IAC), created in 1994, has achieved a semi-official status as it works towards increasing immunization rates. One example of its status is the Centers for Disease Control and Prevention (CDC) refers people to use translations of the vaccine information statements (VIS) provided by the IAC rather than carrying its own official translations of the VIS. Furthermore, the IAC has translated the VISs into many different languages, providing an essential and comprehensive service. Another large organization is Vaccinate Your Family, a bi-partisan effort to increase access to vaccines. It was originally created as Every Child By Two, established by two first ladies, First Lady Betty Bumpers from Arizona and First Lady Rosalyn Carter.

In addition, several advocacy groups work to increase vaccination rates. The Association of Immunization Managers provides support, guidance, and help to immunization managers across states. Voices for Vaccines works on mobilizing and giving voice to pro-vaccine parents. In addition to these organizations, there are many coalitions and parents' groups—and other dedicated organizations—working to increase vaccination rates.

There are also many online advocates, loosely organized in Facebook and Twitter groups, or using list serves—that try to counter online misinformation. These activists have successfully put out responses to most pre-pandemic anti-vaccine myths. However, they mostly operate with no funding, voluntarily, and with the pandemic, found themselves swamped by the rise of misinformation. In response to this, several new groups developed during the pandemic to counter misinformation. For example, a group of Black doctors and community leaders successfully worked to push against vaccine hesitancy in black communities, with the rollout of COVID-19 vaccines. No such efforts are going to be 100% successful, but the effort substantially increased rates in that community. Much effort and thought goes into combatting anti-vaccine misinformation. But this serious problem has existed even before the pandemic. With the pandemic, and politicization of COVID-19 vaccines, this struggle has become worse.

24.4 The Anti-vaccine Movement

The anti-vaccine movement influences policy to undermine vaccine uptake, for example by making it easier to be exempt from vaccine mandates or by pushing against vaccine approval or funding.[15] "Anti-vaxxers" have also been successful beyond their size at spreading fear and distrust of vaccines, therefore encouraging people to seek out exemptions. More people seeking out exemptions leads to lower vaccination rates, perpetuating the spread of vaccine-preventable diseases.

While most people in the U.S. vaccinate their children on schedule (though adult uptake needed work even pre-pandemic), the threshold for an outbreak is very low. The risk of an outbreak occurs when there is 5–10% of non-vaccinated individuals, and anti-vaccine activists further increase this risk because they are not randomly spread: they cluster. This means that the anti-vaccine movement does not need to reach a majority of the population: when they reach beyond a trivial minority, they create a risk of disease—first and foremost for the children and adults left unvaccinated because of false anti-vaccine claims. Because "[v]accines protect not only the individuals who receive them but also those who cannot be vaccinated due to their age or other medical issues, such as a compromised immune system," anti-vaccine rhetoric can be harmful when it influences people to avoid vaccinations.[16] Clusters of under vaccinated populations fail to reach immunization rates necessary to achieve herd immunity, causing resurgence of vaccine-preventable diseases.[17] Although the outbreaks are caused by the unvaccinated, they also affect the most vulnerable who cannot be vaccinated.

The COVID-19 pandemic has led to politicization of COVID-19 vaccines, and a growth of anti-vaccine misinformation, which has, unfortunately, seeped into mainstream media. Anti-vaccine activists like Dr. Robert Malone, Dr. Peter McCullough, and attorney Aaron Siri have been on conservative mainstream media talk shows, spreading the message. One of the concerns is that this politicization would affect attitudes to other vaccines, leading to lower vaccination rates, pushback against school immunization mandates, and more disease outbreaks.

---

[15] Benecke and DeYoung (2019).

[16] Lasater et al. (2020).

[17] Whelan (2016).

24.4.1 Growth of Vaccine Exemptions and Vaccine-Preventable Diseases

Exemptions to vaccine mandates are intended to balance the public health goals with safety and civil liberty concerns.[18] Vaccine exemptions vary state to state, making it easier in some places to qualify for an exemption than in others.[19] The anti-vaccine movement has stimulated an increase in people seeking nonmedical exemptions, thereby lowering vaccination rates and leaving communities vulnerable to disease outbreaks. Some states, like California, have imposed more strict exemption policies in response.[20]

All 50 states have laws mandating vaccines for students.[21] Each state also recognizes medical exemptions for individuals who may be at risk for adverse medical effects from a vaccine.[22] Additionally, many states allow exemptions for people with religious beliefs that oppose vaccinations,[23] and some states grant exemptions for philosophical views against vaccines.

Because states regulate vaccine mandates, the availability of exemptions vary state-by-state. States that easily grant exemptions to vaccine mandates without requiring documentation or follow up tend to have lower vaccination rates, and therefore are at a greater risk for disease outbreaks as herd immunity is diminished. The politicization of vaccines has made exemptions into a politically motivated tool rather than a public health tool.[24] Some scholars observed that "narrowing or widening the scope of public school vaccine exemptions has become a policy flashpoint at state legislatures across the U.S."[25]

For example, Texas has loose vaccine exemption laws, meaning it is easy for parents to be granted exemptions for mandatory vaccinations for their children. Parents using exemptions to avoid vaccinating their children led to a decrease in vaccination rates. The decrease in vaccination has had serious public health implications. States with lower vaccination rates are experiencing cases of diseases like measles that were nearly eradicated due to previous high vaccination rates. According to experts, "some of this increase [may be attributed to the] rise of organized, coordinated, and vocal anti-vaccination campaigns."[26]

---

[18] Salmon (2003).

[19] Benecke and DeYoung (2019).

[20] Lakshmanan and Sabo (2019).

[21] Benecke and DeYoung (2019).

[22] Lakshmanan and Sabo (2019).

[23] Benecke and DeYoung (2019).

[24] Lakshmanan and Sabo (2019).

[25] *Id.*

[26] *Id.*

24.4.2 Growth of the Anti-vaccine Movement and the Role of Social Media

Fear-based messaging has been effective at influencing a significant minority of parents to skip certain vaccinations, delay vaccinating, or avoid vaccinating their children completely.[27] Public figures like celebrities and politicians play a role in spreading misinformation about the danger of vaccines, such as perpetuating the debunked claim from *The Lancet* that vaccines are linked to autism.

Social media has given anti-vaccine activists easily accessible platforms to spread misinformation. Anti-vaccination posts have become increasingly popular, and "[r]esearch suggests that it only takes 5–10 minutes on an anti-vaccine site to increase perceptions of vaccination risks and decrease perceptions of the risks of vaccine omission."[28] Online platforms run by anti-vaccination activists are ubiquitous. For example, the content of the first 100 search results found after searching "vaccination" and "immunization" on Google revealed 43% of websites were anti-vaccination.[29] The widespread and pervasive messaging of the anti-vaccination movement has changed a minority of parents' perceptions of vaccines, and consequently decreased vaccination rates among children, leaving them vulnerable to vaccine-preventable disease.

With COVID-19, misinformation has spread even more broadly, to a degree that in the U.S. vaccination rates in children remain low. While COVID-19 is less dangerous to children than to older people, it can still harm and kill children, and is much riskier than vaccinating.

24.5   Factors Influencing Anti-vaccine Advocacy

Anti-vaccine advocacy is enhanced by internet bots and malware that skew discussion about vaccination. The bots and malware spread ideas about elite groups forcing the vaccine on low-income people. These ideas encourage skepticism surrounding vaccine safety and efficacy. These scare tactics focus on a few specific factors that influence an emotional response from people who are unsure about vaccines: fear, distrust, and liberty interests.

"Anti-vaxxers" spread fear of adverse events caused by vaccines. A common story shared in the anti-vaccine community is known as "overnight autism," in which a parent takes their child to get the MMR vaccine and watches "[the child] digress cognitively almost immediately after."[30] Not only do large studies show that MMR does not increase rates of autism, this story is implausible: MMR is a live virus vaccine. Aside from allergic reactions that can be immediate, other reactions to

---

[27] Benecke and DeYoung (2019).

[28] *Id.*

[29] *Id.*

[30] *Id.*

the vaccine take some time, because the (weak) vaccine virus needs to replicate before the body responds. Reactions to MMR vaccine are typically delayed, not immediate.[31] Other sources report sudden deaths of children caused by vaccines, but most of these stories disregard medical expert reports refuting the claims or asserting the deaths were caused by non-vaccine related illness.[32]

The broad distrust of "Big Pharma" and skepticism about medicine and science also fuels the anti-vaccine ideology.[33] The anti-vaccine movement spreads skepticism that vaccines are a product of big pharmaceutical companies, and that health policy organizations and medical experts are motivated by profit, not by public health interests.[34]

The anti-vaccine movement also appeals to individuals who place a high value on liberty.[35] These individuals tend to be concerned with government-imposed vaccine mandates violating their civil liberties and personal autonomy. Additionally, individuals who value purity are more likely to disapprove of "contaminants" or "unnatural" ingredients they associate with vaccines.

Anti-vaccine advocates effectively appeal to the emotions through fear, distrust, and liberty interests.[36] Their narratives are concerning, especially for parents who fear that they may harm their child by vaccinating them.[37] The skepticism around the risks of vaccines is enough for some people to opt out of immunization.

24.6   Responding to the Anti-vaccine Movement

There are tools and strategies for the pro-vaccine movement to utilize in order to more effectively counter the emotionally-charged messaging of the anti-vaccine movement.

24.6.1 Pro Vaccine Advocacy

Pro-vaccine advocates should take into consideration the variables that influence vaccine hesitancy.[38] Targeting pro-vaccine messaging to address concerns of anti-vaccine advocates may be the most effective way to prevent the anti-vaccination movement from growing. Recently, pro-vaccine advocates have centered on one

---

[31] NHS (2020).

[32] Whelan (2016).

[33] Lasater et al. (2020).

[34] Lakshmanan and Sabo (2019).

[35] Benecke and DeYoung (2019).

[36] Lakshmanan and Sabo (2019).

[37] Whelan (2016).

[38] Benecke and DeYoung (2019).

message: "vaccines work and save lives."[39] But this message does not answer the concerns of those who worry about possible adverse effects or do not trust the source of the vaccine. Pro-vaccine advocates should develop and employ a dynamic message to listen and respond to the concerns of the uncertain.

Further, as documented in a report by Vaccinate Your Family, community-based organizations have an important role to play, and traditional advocates should work with those groups, offering support but letting local leaders take the lead.[40]

24.6.2 Broad Support for Vaccines and Immunization Requirements

The CDC estimates that vaccinating children prevented over 400 million illnesses and saved over $1 trillion in societal costs from 1994–2018.[41] When a high percentage of the population is vaccinated, this reduces the risk of vaccine-preventable outbreaks.[42] Many people recognize these undeniable successes. Indeed, there is broad support for requiring vaccines.

A 2015 Reuters/Ipsos poll reported that "78% of respondents. . . said all children should be vaccinated unless there is a direct health risk to them from vaccination."[43] A later Pew Research Center poll reported 88% of Americans "believe the benefits of vaccination outweigh the risks."[44] Other pre-COVID pandemic polls found bipartisan support, and no significant difference in support for mandatory vaccination among Republicans and Democrats.

Although there is support for immunization requirements, the anti-vaccination movement led to a plateau in immunization rates in the 2000s.[45] Additionally, the expedited development of the COVID-19 vaccine led to a new wave of hesitancy which in turn led to widespread use of vaccine mandates, which themselves added fuel to the fire. Vaccine mandates can be polarizing, but pro-vaccine advocates can leverage the support for vaccines to help educate people and counteract the messages of "anti-vaxxers."[46]

24.6.3 Progress of Pro-immunization Advocates

Some pro-immunization advocates have been successful in improving the laws to increase vaccination rates despite the efforts of the anti-vaccination movement. The

---

[39] Ball (2020).

[40] Supporting Community Based Organizations To Reignite a Culture of Immunization (2022).

[41] Whitney et al. (2014), pp. 352–355.

[42] Lakshmanan and Sabo (2019).

[43] *Id.*

[44] *Id.*

[45] Ball (2020).

[46] Lakshmanan and Sabo (2019).

source of their success comes from messaging that vaccines are safe, effective, affordable, and necessary. For example, in Texas, pro-vaccine advocates have made progress lobbying the legislature to pass "positive immunization legislation."[47] The Texas legislature successfully passed more than 20 pro-vaccine laws between 2007–2019, including a meningitis vaccine requirement, laws increasing access to vaccines, and information about vaccines. The 2023 Texas legislative session saw dozens of vaccine opposing bills filed by lawmakers; just two became law.

24.7 Recommendations for Actions

Some sources argued that the pro-vaccine community is not doing enough to counteract the anti-vaccine narrative during the COVID-19 pandemic.[48] Anti-vaccine narratives are more dynamic and emotionally charged than the pro-vaccine messages. "Anti-vaxxers" leverage this to appeal to people who are undecided or skeptical about vaccines. While pro-vaccine groups have worked hard for years to counter anti-vaccine messages, the groups that do this are often limited in funding (or, for online advocates, have no funding), human resources, and stretched thin. They have to address anti-vaccine messaging, issues of access, and keep up with the information that comes out (unlike anti-vaccine groups, who may make up claims or just create fear and doubt). Funding for pro-vaccine groups increased during the pandemic, but funding for anti-vaccine groups grew dramatically as well. This increase in anti-vaccine funding outstrips the funding for those seeking to counter.[49] While new voices came on the scene to counter misinformation, many new voices arose to misinform, and misinformation has become a lucrative business.[50]

Some scholars recommend that social media platforms should monitor and block certain types of content.[51] We address the legalities around regulating misinformation in Chap. 22. People who are uncertain about vaccines may trust a post they see on social media regardless of whether it is based in fact. Additionally, education may play a role in increasing trust between the medical community and skeptical parents. Pro-vaccine groups can organize people in their communities to help educate their neighbors.[52] State legislatures can also pass laws to increase access to information about vaccine safety and efficacy. Some skeptical individuals may need to be reassured about the safety of vaccines and the process by which they are approved.

---

[47] Id.

[48] Ball (2020).

[49] Smith (2021).

[50] Pandemic Profiteers: The Business of Anti-Vaxx (2020) (reporting on the profit and organization of a variety of anti-vaccine groups, complete with their income and salaries).

[51] Benecke and DeYoung (2019).

[52] Lakshmanan and Sabo (2019).

Transparency during vaccine clinical trials can show that efficacy and safety of vaccines helps boost confidence in vaccines.[53]

The successful pro-vaccine advocates recommend the following strategies that were effective at countering the anti-vaccine movement:

(1) Stick to a clear and focused message about the positive impacts of vaccines and the destructive power of anti-vaccine activism.
(2) Remain nonpartisan and stick to the science.
(3) Leverage state medical and nonprofit networks and work closely with like-minded partners to help create a unified and amplified front.
(4) Create a rapid response grassroots network.
(5) Stay vigilant at the local and state levels.
(6) Create an effective social media strategy.
(7) Craft stories to advocate effectively.
(8) Be politically present and visible.
(9) Raise public awareness.
(10) Obtain funding to build infrastructure and a national network.[54]

Ultimately, lawmakers should focus on the majority of the population that support vaccination policies. Pro-vaccine advocates should help increase confidence in vaccines and hold lawmakers accountable to base decisions on "factual and scientific information and not misinformation or false narratives."[55]

24.8   Conclusion

The anti-vaccine movement presents implications for public health policy. The movement has been effective at influencing lawmakers and gaining followers, but for pro-vaccine advocates, there is reason to be optimistic. Pro-vaccine advocates should consider the sources of fear and distrust of vaccines and craft more effective messaging to counteract the anti-vaccine influence. Additionally, pro-vaccine advocates should take advantage of the widespread support of vaccines to get already-supportive individuals more engaged with promoting vaccines to keep their communities safe.

---

[53] Ball (2020).
[54] *Id.*
[55] Lakshmanan and Sabo (2019).

References

Ball P (2020) Anti-vaccine movement could undermine efforts to end coronavirus pandemic, researchers warn. Nature. https://www.nature.com/articles/d41586-020-01423-4. Accessed 29 Oct 2022

Benecke O, DeYoung SE (2019) Anti-vaccine decision-making and measles resurgence in the United States. Glob Pediatr Health 6. https://doi.org/10.1177/2333794X19862949

Gerber JS, Offit PA (2009) Vaccines and autism: a tale of shifting hypotheses. Clin Infect Dis 48(456):457–459. https://doi.org/10.1086/596476

Hillel LY et al (2020) Stopping the resurgence of vaccine-preventable childhood diseases: policy, politics, and law. Univ Illinois Law Rev 2020:233, 251–252. https://ssrn.com/abstract=3524008. Accessed 29 Oct 2022

Lakshmanan R, Sabo J (2019) Lessons from the front line: advocating for vaccine policies at the Texas Capitol during turbulent times. J Appl Res Child 10: 11–12. https://digitalcommons.library.tmc.edu/childrenatrisk/vol10/iss2/6. Accessed 29 Oct 2022

Lasater SE et al (2020) Vaccine legislation in Texas and the rise of the state anti-vaccine movement: a survey of vaccine-related bills filed and passed in the Texas State Legislature from 2009 to 2019. Center for Health & Biosciences 3. https://www.bakerinstitute.org/sites/default/files/2021-12/import/chb-pub-tx-vaccine-112420.pdf. Accessed 29 Oct 2022

Matthews KRW, Tan MT (2018) Issue brief: medical freedom, privacy, and fear of discrimination: the 2017 Texas Legislative session anti-vaccine arguments. Rice University's Baker Institute for Public Policy. https://www.bakerinstitute.org/research/medical-freedom-privacy-and-fear-discrimination-2017-texas-legislative-session-anti-vaccine-argument. Accessed 29 Oct 2022

NHS (2020) MMR (measles, mumps and rubella) vaccine. https://www.nhs.uk/conditions/vaccinations/mmr-vaccine/. Accessed 1 Nov 2022

Pandemic Profiteers: The Business of Anti-Vaxx (2020) Cent. for countering digital hate. https://252f2edd-1c8b-49f5-9bb2cb57bb47e4ba.filesusr.com/ugd/f4d9b9_00b2ad56fe524d82b271a75e441cd06c.pdf. Accessed 1 Nov 2022

Salmon DA (2003) Unpublished commentary. Mandatory immunization laws and the role of medical, religious and philosophical exemptions. October 2003

Smith MR (2021) How a Kennedy built an anti-vaccine Juggernaut amid COVID-19. Associated Press. https://apnews.com/article/how-rfk-jr-built-anti-vaccine-juggernaut-amid-covid4997be1bcf591fe8b7f1f90d16c9321e. Accessed 29 Oct 2022

Supporting Community Based Organizations To Reignite a Culture of Immunization (2022) Vaccinate your family and Dia De La Mujer Latina. https://vaccinateyourfamily.org/wpcontent/uploads/2022/09/VYF_DML_CBO_Report.pdf. Accessed 29 Oct 2022

Whelan AM (2016) Lowering the age of consent: pushing back against the anti-vaccine movement. J Law Med Ethics 44:462–465. https://doi.org/10.1177/1073110516667942

Whitney CG et al (2014) Benefits from immunization during the vaccines for children program era--United States, 1994-2013. MMWR Morb Mortal Wkly Rep 63:352–355

Yang TY et al (2016) Sociodemographic predictors of vaccination exemptions on the basis of personal belief in California. Am J Public Health 106(1):172–177. https://doi.org/10.2105/AJPH.2015.302926

Printed in the USA
CPSIA information can be obtained
at www.ICGtesting.com
LVHW011125110923
757808LV00005B/64

9 783031 369889